Crisis in Utopia

Crisis in Utopia

The Ordeal of Tristan da Cunha

PETER A. MUNCH

Thomas Y. Crowell Company   New York
Established 1834

To the People of Tristan da Cunha

MANUFACTURED IN THE UNITED STATES OF AMERICA

L.C. Card 73-127611
ISBN 0-690-22075-8

1   2   3   4   5   6   7   8   9   10

Preface

In his introduction to *Cross-Cultural Understanding: Epistemology in Anthropology* (Harper & Row, 1964), the distinguished scholar and professor of philosophy and law F. S. C. Northrop, paraphrasing Clyde Kluckhohn, states that "philosophy is a universal category of cultures; and . . . any other factor, be it universal or provincial, of a particular culture is misunderstood unless it is interpreted in terms of that particular people's specific philosophy." This is also the view of a "comprehensive sociology" (to use Raymond Aron's translation of Max Weber's controversial *verstehende Soziologie*). Weber, the great German sociologist, states that all human action is meaningful and is fully comprehensible only in terms of the particular "complex of meanings" within which it is performed.

What the learned gentlemen are trying to say is simply that if one really wants to understand another person's actions, one must know, comprehend, and even accept his way of thinking—a requirement that so often, alas, remains unfulfilled in our everyday communications. The more removed the other person's way of thinking is from one's own the more important is this requirement. To anyone, therefore, who wants to understand a people of a different culture—whether he be a social scientist or a journalist or just a tourist—the most important task is to penetrate and comprehend the *thoughtways* of that particular people, for those constitute the social reality that alone lends meaning to the people's actions, customs, and moral convictions.

The present account of the people of Tristan da Cunha is a piece of "comprehensive sociology" in the sense that it attempts to understand the thoughtways of this remarkable people and to translate them into terms that would, it is hoped, be comprehensible, not only to fellow sociologists, but to most members of the modern industrial society. If it should occur to the reader that the account is "biased" in favor of the Tristan Islanders, especially in their confrontations with well-meaning authorities bent on leading them to progress and prosperity, it is not only because of a genuine attachment to a people who have given me so much in terms of friendship and warm human relations, but also because of a conviction that a true and *objective* understanding of their thoughts and actions could be obtained only through a respectful and sympathetic attitude. Had I not had this attitude, I should have returned home, like so many others, as ignorant about their way of life as when I first met them.

A totally balanced picture would, of course, include an equally sympathetic account of the thoughtways, the goals, and aims, of the British Administrator and other agencies and groups with whom the Tristan Islanders had contacts during their sojourn in England. This, however, was not the purpose of this study. In attempting to understand why the Tristan Islanders rejected modern industrial civilization the important and, in fact, the only relevant data are to be sought in the thoughtways of the Islanders themselves, in their values and norms as well as in their interpretations of other people's actions. This is the reality with which we have to deal.

The indebtedness of the author to a number of individuals and agencies is gratefully acknowledged. My first indebtedness is to Dr. Erling Christophersen, the leader of the Norwegian Scientific Expedition to Tristan da Cunha 1937–1938, presently Director of the Fridtjof Nansen Foundation at Polhøgda (near Oslo, Norway). He was the one who first introduced me to the unique community of Tristan da Cunha by accepting me as a member of the expedition, an act that changed the course of my life in a way that I never had occasion to regret, and out of which grew a lifelong friendship of rare quality.

In the second phase of the study after the volcanic eruption and the evacuation of the island, support and aid were received from many sources. The Medical Research Council, London, through Dr. Harold Lewis, gave full cooperation with exchange of data and offered valuable assistance vis-à-vis the British authorities by endorsing my one-man expedition to Tristan da Cunha in 1964–1965. The United Society for the Propagation of the Gospel opened up their archives and made valuable material available to me in photostatic copies. The Tristan da Cunha branch of the Colonial Office, London, gave me permission to land on Tristan and showed a keen interest in my work; special thanks are due to the former Administrators of Tristan da Cunha, Mr. P. J. F. Wheeler and Mr. P. A. Day, for valuable assistance during my recent visits to Calshot and Tristan.

During my stay at Calshot, England, in the summer of 1962, a close cooperation was established with my colleague and fellow anthropologist, Dr. J. B. Loudon, presently of Swansea University, Wales, who was then a member of the Medical Research Council team. Although our wish to go together to Tristan da Cunha for continued cooperative studies never was fulfilled, the extremely fruitful exchange of ideas has continued by letter. Much of what is presented in the following pages, particularly concerning the resettlement of the Tristan Islanders, stems from Dr. Loudon's keen observations and insight, for which I wish to express my deepest appreciation.

It was through Dr. Loudon that I first got in contact with Mr. Roland Svensson, a Swedish artist and writer with a warm and sensitive interest in island peoples. Not only have my conversations and correspondence with Mr. Svensson been inspiring; he also made available to me several interviews with Tristan Islanders recorded on tape, which are among my most valuable records.

Among the many other persons who contributed to the present account, special thanks are due to the Reverend Noel Brewster, of Fawley, and to the Reverend J. E. K. Flint, formerly of Tristan da Cunha—to the latter also for permission to quote from one of his letters. Likewise, Mrs. Doreen Gooch, wife of the resident Medical Officer of Tristan da Cunha during my stay on the island, gave permission to quote from one of her private newsletters, and with her several years of experience among the Tristan Islanders and her unique sensitivity to their way of thinking, she made substantial contributions to my understanding of life on the island and its significance to the Islanders. Mr. C. H. Gaggins, Director of the South Atlantic Islands Development Corporation, gave valuable information concerning the operations of the fishing company on Tristan, in particular about the *Pequena* Expedition of 1948. To Messrs Geoffrey Dominy and Bob Deacon, Master and Fishing Master of the *Frances Repetto,* I express my thanks for generous hospitality during a week's stay on board their ship.

Financial support, enabling the author to make several trips to

England and to the whaling centers of New England as well as a six-
month visit to Tristan da Cunha, was gratefully received from the National Science Foundation, the Social Science Research Council, the
American Philosophical Society, and Southern Illinois University.

My deepest thanks, however, go to the Tristan da Cunha Islanders
themselves. Without their cooperation and understanding, this story
could never have been written. And meeting these people, being allowed to share their life in work as well as leisure, in joy as well as
sorrow, has been a human experience of immeasurable value. While
they were in England, much was written about the Tristan Islanders.
The Islanders read it all, and I vividly recall the indignant snort of
disapproval with which they usually pronounced the judgment: "It's
all lies!" I can only hope that this will not be the sentence they will
pass on the story told here.

It is in this hope that I dedicate the present volume to the people of
Tristan da Cunha.

PETER A. MUNCH

Southern Illinois University
Carbondale, Illinois

Contents

Maps

Photographs

1

Utopia of the Sea

On a bright December day in 1937 the S.S. *Anatolia* of Bremen was nosing her way across the vast and desolate expanse of the South Atlantic Ocean. The wind was moderate, the sky was clear, and the endless sea reflected the sun in a myriad of glittering patterns. But a heavy ground swell came rolling in from the southwest, hitting the little freighter relentlessly on her port bow, causing her to pitch and roll and twist—a turbulent reminder to those aboard that not very far to the south billowed the tempestuous waters of the infamous Roaring Forties. Circling the ship like a watchful escort, although his intents were probably of a more material sort, was one of the most magnificent creatures of the southern seas. On his mighty wingspan he was gliding through the air in graceful arches, effortless, with hardly a movement of his enormous wings, swooping down into a trough of the rolling sea, making tiny ripples in the water with the tip of his pinion, then up into the wind with the bright sun shining on his snow-white flank. The great wandering albatross—I wondered as I watched his majestic maneuvers why anybody would give him such a prosaic name as "gony." But this is what the sailors call him, the Tristan Islanders too.

Passengers on board the little German freighter were thirteen young men—eleven Norwegians, an Englishman, and a South African—with different backgrounds, outlooks, and interests, but thrown together on this voyage for the sake of that insatiable human curiosity which properly goes under the label "adventure" but in its more pretentious form, as in this case, presents itself as "scientific inquiry." We were to make a thorough and, as we hoped, exhaustive study of every form of life on the island of Tristan da Cunha, from the peak of its towering mountain to the seashore and beyond into the adjacent waters, including the singular form of human society that we knew to exist in this most isolated inhabited place on earth. Never before had this tiny spot in the South Atlantic Ocean been the object of such an intense and versatile investigation by such an enthusiastic group of young scientists, or by anybody else for that matter. For most of us it was the first great adventure of our lives. Naturally, we all shared in the quickening excitement of regarding ourselves as trail-blazing pioneers in the field of knowledge. Yet, our enthusiasm was mingled with a peculiar, almost disappointing feeling that a scientific expedition of which you are a part somehow seems less awesome than the ones you read about in books.

We were not the only passengers on board the rolling freighter. Scanning the horizon for the first sign of land even more eagerly than any of us, were two Tristan Islanders returning home after several months' exile in a Cape Town nursing home. They had been sent abroad for medical treatment. One of them was William Rogers, a tall, rather dark-skinned man with black, sleek hair and a wispy mustache. He was nearly blind from a congenital eye disease, and this was the reason for his trip to Cape Town in vain hope for a cure. As is often the habit of blind people, he always had a half smile on his face when talking to someone, and he spoke in a slow, friendly singsong, with his soft, rather high-pitched voice. Blind William—as everybody called him, conveniently distinguishing him from all the other Williams and Willies and Bills on the island—was a happy man. Living as he did in a physical twilight, he always saw the bright side of things. It was as if the kindness of his own heart were projected to every person he met. Although his trip had been useless as far as his eyesight was concerned, he was bubbling over with happy chatter about how nice and friendly the doctors and nurses and indeed everybody had been to him in Cape Town. Now he was looking forward to getting home, where he could move around more freely, he knew every rock and stone about the Settlement. In his exuberant fondness for his island, he tried to dispel our worries about landing hazards on this weatherbeaten rock in the middle of a turbulent ocean and assured us that there was nothing to be concerned about: We would surely be able to land because "somewhere around the island there is always a lee," which sounded logical enough except for the fact that we had to land at the Settlement or else proceed with the ship to La Plata.

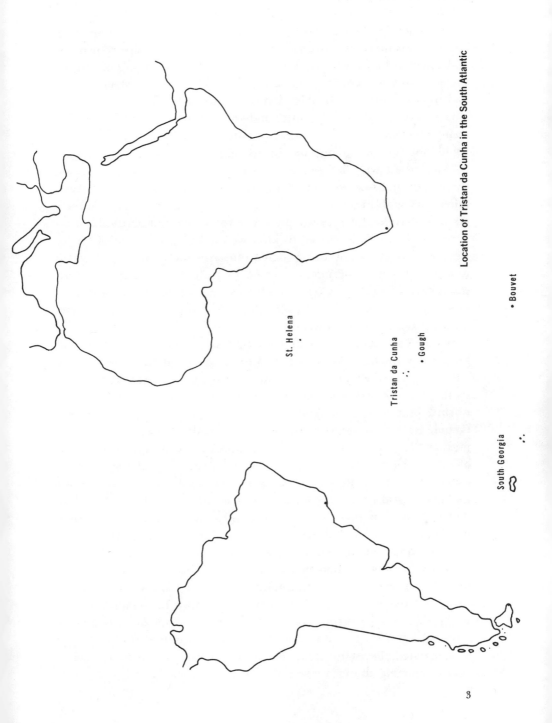

Location of Tristan da Cunha in the South Atlantic

St. Helena

Tristan da Cunha

Gough

Bouvet

South Georgia

3

The other Islander on board was Blind William's uncle, Tom Rogers, who was more of a cosmopolitan, having been to Cape Town several times in his youth. At one time he was even thinking of settling there for life, but changed his mind and, like so many Islanders who had tried life in the "Outside World," returned home.

Our two Islanders were polite and well-mannered, and their self-effacing modesty made their presence hardly noticeable. This, however, could not be said about our third fellow passenger, a boisterous, bearded priest who had previously served the Tristan community for three years and was now returning for a second tour of duty. He was a missionary with more than the usual zeal. He carried with him a regular menagerie of fowl, geese, pigeons, even a pig and a couple of canaries, with which he hoped to improve the living standard of his little parish in the sea. We considered ourselves lucky that the devoted minister of souls had not been able to realize his dream of bringing a pair of mules, as he had planned, for breeding purposes! Indeed, with the ship's German officers and Chinese crew, we comprised a rather motley crowd as it was.

We were six days out from Cape Town and could expect on the following day to come within sight of the goal of our long voyage. We had, of course, read everything about the island and felt that we knew it already. We had studied the topography of the ocean floor and learned that where the Mid-Atlantic Ridge is joined with the Rio Grande Rise from the west and the Walvis Ridge from the east, about midway between South Africa and South America, this gigantic system of submarine mountain ranges, rising from the Abyssal Plains about sixteen to eighteen thousand feet below the surface of the sea, thrusts its highest peaks into the Atlantic mist to form the island of Tristan da Cunha and its two satellites, Inaccessible and Nightingale. Tristan itself is, in fact, a single huge volcanic cone, about thirty miles wide at its base, some ten thousand feet below sea level. But it narrows to a mere seven miles in diameter where its towering mass emerges from the ocean to rise nearly seven thousand feet in the air. We had seen so many pictures of the island that it would almost be a familiar sight when the characteristic conical shape should appear through the morning haze. But we also knew that fifteen hundred miles of open sea separated the island from the nearest continent, which was not a very comforting thought when we realized that shortly we were to be put ashore on this isolated spot and see the *Anatolia* steam off, our last contact with civilization disappearing under the horizon.

The next day, however, came with a northerly wind—the worst possible, since the Settlement is situated on the north side of the island— and with a fog so dense that we could barely see from one end of the ship to the other. Sky and sea merged into one gray mass, and we seemed to be floating freely in an endless, bottomless, murky space. A ship on the ocean is always a separate world. But when fog settles down, there is nothing else: the ship is all the world, surrounded by a vast expanse of emptiness, a tiny Cosmos lost in Chaos.

Well aware of the treacherous currents that surround the island of Tristan da Cunha, and which have proven fatal to many a ship with a less cautious skipper, our captain maneuvered his vessel slowly toward the spot where his calculations had the island located. And good reason he had to boast the accuracy of his navigation, for soon we could discern a darkening spot in the fog dead ahead, an ominous shadow in the light-gray whiteness that surrounded us. Instantly our foghorn echoed forcefully back to us as if from a wall of solid rock, which indeed it was. The echo sounded frightfully close.

With less than forty square miles of land area, the island of Tristan da Cunha is a mere speck on the map. But to any human who ventures into its vicinity, it appears a gigantic ogreish mountain, wild, mysterious, and forbidding, rising out of the ocean where land is least expected, as if from an underworld where man was not destined to set his foot. A windswept, lonely rock in the middle of Nowhere—Utopia of the Sea.

This is how it must have appeared to the Portuguese admiral Tristão da Cunha and his crew, who first sighted the island in the year 1506, more than four hundred years ago—then as now, the steep and barren cinder slopes near the peak surrounded by a dense growth of queer looking tree ferns farther down, the island's precipitous flanks furrowed by deep ravines, where gnarled and wind-twisted conifers appeared to be clinging to the bare rocks, and—to the sailor most uninviting of all—the surf relentlessly battering against a solid shoreline only to be shattered into snow-white spray, with no inlet, bay, or cove to offer a sheltered port. No wonder that the island remained for centuries to come, as it had been for unknown aeons before, an undisturbed sanctuary for the wild of the sea and the sky, where the furry seal and the clumsy sea elephant ruled the narrow beaches, competing only with the hot-tempered rock-hopper penguin, while the slopes and precipices offered a home to the gigantic gony, the stately mollymawk, the sooty peeyoo, with its dismal shriek, and myriads of other seabirds.

Yet, somewhere within that wet blanket of fog that momentarily enshrouded us, a small community of human beings now dwelt, descendants of sailors and whalers who had settled on this lonely island only a little over a hundred years ago. And to judge from scant reports by missionaries and incidental visitors, a most remarkable community it was, without government or law enforcement, yet with no crime or violent conflict, where not even the common cold occurred, except after a rare visit by a ship. If the reports were true, it was the happiest and most harmonious community in the whole world—indeed, a Utopia of the Sea.

As we approached this lonely, forgotten settlement with youthful expectations, little did we know that twenty-four years later Tristan da Cunha would really become famous—and it was not the earth-shaking reports of a group of young, overenthusiastic scientists that did it. In October 1961, the name of Tristan da Cunha was flashed across the pages of the world press in dramatic headlines:

TRISTAN DA CUNHA BLASTED BY VOLCANO
TRISTAN FACES TOTAL DISASTER
LAVA FLOWS DOWN ON TRISTAN VILLAGE
260 ISLANDERS FLEE IN TERROR FROM BOILING VOLCANO
KRAKATOA THREAT TO CAPE TOWN

The spotlight of the news media soon shifted, however, from the smoking volcano in the South Atlantic to a more quiet but no less dramatic scene in England, where the evacuated and then abandoned Tristan Islanders fought a valiant battle against disease and reluctant authorities to preserve their identity and way of life, demanding to be returned to their lonely and humble island homes.

When the news came that Tristan da Cunha had been abandoned, and that the Islanders had been given permanent homes in a discontinued Royal Air Force settlement at Calshot, England, I dropped everything. I rushed to Calshot to see my friends—for that they were, although I had not seen them for twenty-four years.

What I found was amazing. From my previous contact with the

Tristan da Cunha

Inaccessible

Nightingale

The Tristan da Cunha Group of Islands

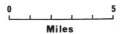

0   5

Miles

community I had never known the Tristan Islanders to agree on any-thing except to be free to disagree. For over a century, by their own choice, they had been living in a community where each man was at liberty to do as he pleased, where everybody was his own master and nobody's servant, where no one, not even "Chief" Willie Repetto, could tell the other fellow what to do. They had been a constant frus-tration to missionaries who tried to get any kind of community project started—it took seventy years and the pleading and thunder of four consecutive ministers to make them get together to build a church. But here, in Calshot, instead of every man trying to find his own inde-pendent place in this strange and noisy world, each going his own way as he had been wont to do all his life, this bunch of rugged individual-ists were in the process of changing into a solid, unified group, unani-mously bent on one thing only: to get back to their island of Tristan da Cunha, if necessary by their own organized effort in defiance of the British authorities. And it happened right before my own eyes.

Triumphant they were in the end, and soon the headlines read:

ATLANTIC ISLANDERS FLEE THE 20TH CENTURY;
THEY REJECT MODERN CIVILIZATION
EVEN THE TRISTAN CHILDREN WANT TO GO HOME

After two long years as captive refugees in a highly industrialized so-ciety, with all its affluence and conveniences, the Tristan Islanders did indeed return to their own simple life before the very eyes of an amazed, dismayed, and somewhat insulted Western World. One noted columnist described it as "the most eloquent and contemptuous rebuff that our smug and deviously contrived society could have received." Indeed, so it appeared. The action of these humble people had left a question mark attached to our Western civilization with all its great achievements in science, technology, economic affluence, and social welfare. It was as if our whole ethos and way of life had been put on trial, and had failed.

For me personally, all of this meant that my life was again com-pletely filled with Tristan da Cunha. I had many unanswered ques-tions, and I knew that the answers were nowhere to be found save in the hearts and minds of the Tristan Islanders themselves. Naturally, it all led to another trip to Tristan da Cunha, this time as a lone sociolo-gist, not so young any more, but still curious about the multifarious and sometimes mysterious Ways of Mankind.

To the thirteen young explorers who were approaching the enig-
matic island on that misty December morning in 1937, all this was, of
course, hidden in a very distant future. That anything of the sort
should ever happen to our island was far beyond our wildest imagination, for at that time Tristan da Cunha was believed to be an *extinct*
volcano, a safe dwelling place for man and beast, though windswept
and harsh.

Little by little the fog lifted, revealing at first only a white line of
surf beating against the narrow beach, from which the cliffs appeared
to rise vertically into the dark thickness of the fog, how far into the air
we could only imagine. As we rounded Big Point, the northernmost escarpment of the island, we figured that we were within earshot of the
village, and the captain blew three long blasts on the steam whistle to
attract the attention of the Islanders. Finally, after a long wait and repeated blasts, we spotted three boats making their way toward the
ship, dancing like tiny nutshells on the crest of each new wave and
dropping completely out of sight in the cradle of each following
trough.

At that moment the foggy curtain rose on the scene that we had
come such a long distance to see. There was the characteristic profile
of Hottentot Point: a low foreland stretching out toward the northwest, sloping gently from the foot of the almost vertical cliffs down toward the sea, until it ended abruptly in a ninety-foot drop onto the
beach, where the surf had nibbled for unknown ages. Scattered over
the grassy slope, almost merging with the landscape, about forty low
stone cottages were hugging the ground, their thatched roofs snugly
fitted between heavy gable ends, and prominent in their midst the
white-painted corrugated zinc roof of a long, low building, which we
were soon to learn was the village church. Sheep, cattle, and a few
donkeys were grazing around the village, and as we drew closer we
could see small flocks of geese waddling between the houses. Despite
the low ceiling of the mist still hanging over the mountainside, it was
a rather pleasant scene, laid out like a peaceful garden between the
gloomy mountain and the roaring sea.

Soon the ship dropped anchor, and the boats came alongside. At
this point I had a decided advantage over my colleagues in the expedition. They still had at best several days of preparations ahead of them
—establishing living quarters, unpacking their instruments, setting up
their field laboratories—before they could go out hunting for their

weeds and birds and fish and microbes or whatever else their special-
ties were. The object of *my* study came out to meet us.

Here they were, these rockbound mariners, whom we should soon
learn to know as the most cheerful, kind, and friendly people we had
ever met. We knew that their ancestral background was highly mixed.
The founder of the community was a Scotchman named William
Glass, a corporal in the Royal Artillery and member of a British garrison that was placed on the island in 1816. The garrison was removed
the following year, but William Glass decided to stay. His wife was a
Cape Creole of Dutch extraction. Throughout the nineteenth century,
sailors and other adventurers had arrived, often by shipwreck, from
England, Ireland, Holland, Italy, and Scandinavia and had settled
down, some of them for the rest of their lives. In the early days of the
community five women of mixed racial background had arrived from
Saint Helena in response to a distress call from five bachelors among
the settlers who had been looking with envy at William Glass's domestic bliss, evidence of which appeared with regularity every year or two.
Also, American whalers had been frequent visitors, and two or three of
them stayed and married Tristan girls.

The men in the boats coming out to meet us were as diverse in
looks as their backgrounds would indicate. Indeed, three or four generations of inbreeding had not at all created a uniform "Tristan type"
among them. Rather, they could aptly be described in the words of a
couplet from one of the songs so popular on Tristan, a local version of
"Ole Dan Tucker":

> Some wus white and some wus black,
> and some wus the color of chewed tobac.

In fact, most of them looked quite European—tanned, to be sure,
from a lifelong exposure to sun and sea and wind, but no darker than
would be found on the coast of England, Scotland, or Norway. There
were blue-eyed blonds among them as well as freckled redheads. Some
of them had the more swarthy Mediterranean complexions, while others were decidedly dark, two or three of them showing definite Negroid or Malayan traits.

Their attire was as diverse as their features, but there was no doubt
where most of it came from. Some were wearing ships' officers' jackets
adorned with shiny brass buttons decorated with anchors; many of

them had boatswains' caps, and one young man was the proud owner
of a mate's cap with brass trimmings on the front. Others were dressed
in sailors' jumpers with the characteristic flap on the back of the neck,
or in dungaree pants and jackets, such as is now more common among
sailors and whalers. Still others had old, worn-out suit coats and pants,
which seldom matched. But all had white socks of homespun wool,
their trouser legs tucked inside, and homemade moccasins roughly
fashioned from raw cowhide. It was obvious that the main supply of
clothing, at least for the men, was by barter with an occasional ship
passing by. Even now, the men had brought their "trade bags" along,
small canvas sacks filled with home-knit socks, decorative mats made
from penguin feathers, polished horns from steer or ram, and other
useless curios, for which they hoped to procure a piece of cast-off clothing from a sailor.

One man stood out from the rest. He wore a well-kept dark suit, a
white shirt, necktie, and shiny black shoes. We were soon to learn that
this was "Chief" Willie Repetto, whose "chieftainship" was the only
concession these freedom-loving Islanders had made so far toward the
establishment of governmental authority among themselves. The absence of any kind of government or representative authority had been
a source of confusion to visitors in the past. Reports from ships of
the Royal Navy, which had made official visits to the island from time
to time, contain frequent references to the difficulties encountered by
the officer in charge because there was no one on the island to whom
he could present himself or to whom he could, in proper fashion, de-
liver whatever stores and mail he might bring to the island. And we
had read numerous stories about the pandemonium raised by the Islanders whenever they came aboard a ship, presenting their various articles of trade and making a general nuisance of themselves because
there was no responsible leader of the group who could restrain their
activities and keep them from swarming all over the ship. Indeed, this
was one place on the planet Earth where it would make no sense for
either Martian or Earthling to step up to a fellow and demand: "Take
me to your leader." When asked who was in charge, the reply was always: "Nobody—there ain't no headman on the island," which was
both true and utterly confounding to the visitor.

This situation had been rectified only a few years before our visit
when a resolute missionary, who had declared himself His Majesty's

Commissioner of Tristan da Cunha, surrounded himself with a "Council" of Islanders and simply appointed a "Chief Man" to take his place in his absence. But so repulsive was the idea of a formal government to the Islanders—including, no doubt, the councilors themselves—that as soon as the missionary had left, his whole governmental system sank into oblivion from lack of use, and vanished. Only one function of the Chief Man was retained, presumably because the Islanders found it quite useful after all. He represented the Islanders in their rare contacts with the "Outside World."

So Willie Repetto, or "Chief" as he is called by everybody (the children call him "Uncle Chief"), became the permanent spokesman of the Islanders when dealing with visitors and other outsiders. And he performed his duty faithfully, although surely reluctantly, every time a ship stopped by. The fact that he always dressed up in his Sunday best when going out to a ship should not at all be taken as a sign of vanity or as an indication that he even liked his job. In this respect he was merely conforming to the protocol of the sea as one captain paying a formal visit to another on board his ship. Apart from his representative duties he had no more influence or authority among the Islanders than anybody else with a little gumption and personal poise, nor did he appear to want any such authority.

The boat that brought Chief out to the ship was a lifeboat, which had recently been presented to the Islanders from an American cruise ship and was carrying the name *Miss America* painted on each side of her bow. It was a big boat, twenty-four feet long, and much heavier than the homemade canvas boats that followed her at a proper distance. It took practically the whole male population of the island to launch or land her on the open beach, we learned, and for this reason she was used only for official visits to a ship.

Chief was, of course, the first one to climb aboard. He was a big man with a powerful frame and a deep, rumbling bass voice. He greeted all of us with a friendly smile and a husky handshake from his enormous fist and wished us "welcome to Trisst'n." There was a modest dignity in his manners, and we immediately felt the warmth of that natural, unobtrusive gentleness, which, from all accounts, has made an indelible impression on sensitive visitors from the early days of the community to the present.

Meanwhile, the rest of the men had climbed onto the deck. As soon as Chief had explained to them who we were, what we wanted, and that we needed their help to land our gear, they put aside their trade bags and went to work, while we were watching with some apprehension their frail-looking boats bouncing alongside the rolling ship.

The Tristan longboat is an open, double-ended craft, twenty-four to twenty-six, in more recent years up to thirty, feet in length. It is an obvious descendant of the whaleboat, or rather, perhaps, a cross between a whaleboat and a lifeboat, but adapted in various ways to the peculiar conditions of Tristan da Cunha, particularly to the necessity of launching and landing through the surf on an open beach with the whole Atlantic rolling in. For one thing, it is very light and quite flexible, made as it is of canvas stretched taut over a fairly slender framework of wood and then painted. It was quite obvious to us, however, as we leaned over the bulwark to examine these unusual craft, that wood, canvas, and paint were scarce items on this isolated island. One of the boats, especially, looked as if both frame and shell had been patched together from odd bits and pieces, which was indeed the case. We later learned that much of the wood in these boats was nothing but driftwood, and discarded mailbags sewn together sometimes had to serve as canvas. In these frail craft we and our hundred tons of supplies and equipment were now to be conveyed from the ship to the beckoning shore beyond. A glance at the beach, where the waves continued to pound and break into seething foam, convinced us that the most hazardous part of our voyage was still ahead, and we listened with mixed expectations to the thundering roar of the surf and the sharp sound of rushing pebbles as each dying wave receded.

But the boats came to life in the hands of the skillful Islanders and performed beautifully. Indeed, even the somewhat rough finish could not completely conceal the beauty of line in these homemade craft. Even though the paint might be old and dull and seldom in the preferred colors white, red, and black, a broad painted band, or "streak" (strake), under the gunnel, tapering toward stem and sternpost, gave accent to the slight sheer and furnished the boat with an elegance contrasting sharply with the clumsy burden of the *Miss America* and the ship's lifeboat, which was lowered over the side to assist in the offloading.

The real test, however, was going through the surf on the beach. This was also the part that the Islanders seemed to enjoy the most, probably because every landing on the beaches of Tristan da Cunha is a challenge even to their amazing skill in boatmanship. As we were riding the crest of a breaker dashing against the beach, with seething foam on both sides clear to the gunnel, I held on with a firm grip to the thwart and realized with amazement and considerable relief the importance of the extraordinary buoyancy lent to the craft by its light weight and characteristic shape. The contact with the beach was surprisingly soft, and as the boat came to a grinding halt on the loose skids dropped in its path by the beach crew, the oarsmen jumped over the side to hold it against the backwash, the receding waters gushing at their feet up to their knees and waists, while helping hands on the beach grabbed the bow rope and put their weight to it.

The landing operation looked easy enough; it always does when the Islanders handle the boat. But to anyone who has even the slightest acquaintance with the sea, it is clear that it requires the utmost of skill, coordination, and precision. Perhaps the most amazing thing about it is that hardly a word of command is heard either from the helmsman or from anybody else, only an occasional soft-spoken direction. Even in their mutual working relations these people are gentle. It is as though they had a mysterious surplus of security endowing them with dignity, poise, and generosity, yet a great deal of humility in all their conduct.

The village, like the people, appeared friendly and familiar. Perhaps it was because of the contrast it offered to the gloomy wildness that had struck us as we approached the island. Even here, at the village, the mountain rose abruptly from the gentle slope of the meadow, its sheer flank hiding the towering peak from our view. But it seemed as distant and unreal as the painted backdrop of a stage, and the thundering surf beneath the steep bank could only be heard as a rumble far away. The thatched stone huts were strewn over the grassy slope in picturesque disorder, but all facing the north, the sea and the sun, with small flower gardens behind low stone walls in front, where roses, chrysanthemums, geraniums, bleeding hearts, and daisies were blooming profusely. Here and there small groups of women in old-fashioned, ankle-length skirts and laced blouses were gathered at a brook to do their washing and exchange the latest gossip, which on this occasion surely was concerned with those new arrivals, while a primitive-looking cart on solid wooden wheels, pulled by a team of oxen, was wobbling along on well-trodden tracks between the houses. A tiny donkey

with an incredibly large load of firewood on its back came trotting
home with its very young driver half running alongside and holding
on to the load to prevent it from toppling.

An English artist who visited the island in the early days of the settlement could well feel at home in these surroundings. Mr. Augustus
Earle, who in 1824 spent some time in the then diminutive village,
found that "the houses, and all around them, had an air of comfort,
cleanliness, and plenty, truly English," and with some reservation with
regard to plenty, his words could still be applied to this little village
in the ocean. The whole picture had a genuine British atmosphere,
and the Union Jack flying from a flagstaff near the village did not
seem out of place at all. In fact, the houses reminded me strongly of
pictures I had seen of houses on the Shetland Islands—the same kind
of thatched roof sheltered between thick and heavy gable walls, with
no overhang and very short eaves, an obvious adaptation to a very
windy climate; and smoke rising from the top of the gables was evidence that the Tristan house even shared the unmistakably British
trait of having a fireplace in each gable end with a chimney leading
up through the wall itself.

It was obvious that we had come to a community poor in material
resources. Most of the houses could fairly be described as mere cottages
or shanties, low in structure, halfway dug into the sloping hillside, the
top of the up-hill back wall only a couple of feet above the ground,
and with a superstructure consisting of irregular chunks of rock,
roughly fitted. Inside, some of the houses had no ceiling or loft, leaving in full view the underside of the thatch resting on sagging purlins,
or "rafters," which were sometimes made up of old broken oars and
sundry odd pieces. Some of the rooms had no wainscotting or were
only partially paneled, the cold stone walls barely covered with "wall-
paper" consisting of old newspapes and magazines. And while most of
the houses had wooden floors, three or four of them had only a dirt
floor, at least in part of the dwelling.

Indeed, there was nothing in the subsistence level of the community
that would induce a feeling of security and comfort. We were soon to
learn that the diet of the Islanders fully matched their dwellings. It
was a rather monotonous fare of fish and potatoes with only a few
short periods of seasonal variation brought by the seabirds and their
eggs. No one could afford to eat beef or even mutton except on special

occasions, such as Christmas and weddings, when they liked to put on "big 'eaps" of their favorite dish, stuffed mutton. Bread was seldom seen, and flour for other purposes was always scarce, sometimes completely lacking.

The more amazing was the cheerfulness with which the Islanders accepted their hard lot and tried to make the best of it, and their stubborn conviction that Tristan was the best place on earth to live, at least for them. They had a standard formula with which they met all their privations, hardships, toil, and suffering: "We don't moind. We's use' to it."

These people even seemed to be "use' to" a little starvation now and then when the potato crop failed and weather prevented them from launching their boats for fishing. In fact, they appeared to think that *we* were the ones who were in need of compassion and help, our hundred tons of equipment and supplies notwithstanding, for we were not "use' to" life on Tristan. So they took it upon themselves as good hosts to look after us in every respect.

Their kindness to us knew no bounds, as we learned on the day of our arrival. Here we were, a bunch of complete strangers arriving absolutely unannounced with a baggage that probably exceeded that of any previous visitor both in bulk and in the novelty of its contents. After all, we did bring the first internal combustion engine and electrical generator, the first radio station, and the first X-ray equipment ever seen on the island, and some of the boxes were rather bulky and heavy, an awkward load to bring in through the surf in a canvas boat on an open beach. But the Islanders readily gave their assistance with their precious longboats, which were indeed put to a test they had never gone through before. All the men on the island were there, and for two full days they worked from dawn till dusk, in the boats and on the beach, lifting and heaving, soaked to the skin from salt spray and pouring rain. They did not even take time off to go home for meals; lunch was brought down to the beach by the women. No one had mentioned anything about a payment or reward for their work, and they did not appear to expect one. On the third day, when landing operations were finished and all our chattel was heaped up on the beach, they showed up once more without a request on our part, now with oxcarts and donkeys, and brought everything up from the beach to the site of our camp, again without asking for payment or expecting a reward. The tobacco and cigarettes we gave them were accepted as friendly gifts, and highly appreciated, since this was the first ship they had boarded in nine months, and they had been out of tobacco for three.

As Christmas came around, we were showered with gifts—new potatoes, fresh vegetables, firewood. On Christmas Day there was a constant stream of well-wishers, and they did not come empty-handed. In the course of the morning and early afternoon every child on the island must have been down to our house. They came one by one or in small groups, all neatly groomed in their very best Christmas outfits, and with beaming faces to match the rest of their appearance. Many of the boys wore suits and ties, and the little girls came in their characteristic white bonnets, or "kappies," which surely were a heritage from their Dutch-African ancestress, and in brand-new dresses with a wide, colorful ribbon around the waist tied in a large bowknot at the back. Shyly they presented their gifts—a bouquet of flowers from mother's garden or a tinful of berries picked by themselves—with the very best wishes for a merry Christmas almost whispered through a bashful smile. Sometimes in their flutter they got their occasions mixed up. One little boy wished us "many happy returns," rapidly corrected it to "happy New Year" but then gave up, presented his outstretched fistful of flowers, and ran away giggling. In the evening, toward dinner time, men and women came with dishes of hot food, samples of their Christmas dinners, and soon we had stuffed mutton, berry pudding, and potato cakes to last us for a week.

Throughout our four months' stay we were treated with the same generous kindness and readiness to help in any way possible. "We's only too pleased, sir," was the Islanders' constant answer whenever we asked for assistance, and they always made us feel that they really meant it, as if they were thankful for the opportunity to be of service. There was even an element of pride in showing the greatest kindness, particularly to us strangers. This was something that seemed to give them a sense of identity, like an intrinsic quality of being a "Trisst'n" —as one Islander, on a much later occasion, explained to a British reporter: "The worst thing you can do on Tristan is to be unkind to someone."

Was this the secret of the Tristan Islanders? Was it their cheerful generosity that gave them strength and endurance to survive in an adverse environment? Was this the source of their dignity and mysterious surplus of security? I believe perhaps it was. I could not help but think, however, how utterly out of place, how vulnerable, they would be in a competitive society where the motto is not live and let live but push or be pushed, trample or be trampled, kill or be killed.

2 In Search of a Better World

Tristan da Cunha was uninhabited by man when first discovered in 1506, and it was to remain that way for more than three hundred years to come. Not that the island was entirely forgotten. During the following centuries, two or three expeditions went out from the Dutch colony at the Cape in South Africa, reportedly to find out if the island could be made useful as a naval base in case of war. The most famous of them is the one sent out about 1650 in the *Nachtglass* by van Riebeeck, then Governor of the Dutch East India Company's station at the Cape. The expedition returned with negative reports, probably because of the total absence of a sheltered harbor, and again the island lay undisturbed for more than a hundred years. In 1760, the famous British naval officer Captain Gamaliel Nightingale paid a visit. It is his name that is attached to one of the smaller islands in the group.

Explorers and seafarers had a predilection in those days for putting their names on the map by discovering new islands and naming them after themselves. In this way many an explorer's name that would otherwise have been forgotten, has gone down in history, such as Juan Fernández, Diego Alvarez, Captain Gough, and Tristão da Cunha himself. Captain d'Etchevery, of the French ship *Étoile du Matin*, must have been of a more modest bent, for instead of his name he recorded a failure. In 1778 he anchored off Tristan da Cunha and effected a landing both on Nightingale and on Tristan itself. An attempt to land on the third island was unsuccessful, and he named it Inaccessible.

Soon, however, the island of Tristan da Cunha became a familiar landmark to sailors of all nations. Situated in the West Wind Belt of the Southern Hemisphere, called "the Westerlies" by sailors, its location could well be described in the days of the sailing ships as "in the

direct route from Europe and the United States to India, China, and
New Holland." Indeed, as Far Eastern trades and colonization projects
developed and sailship traffic increased accordingly, Tristan da Cunha
was located right by what was to become one of the most heavily traf-
ficked eastward sailing lanes. Besides, even if the island had little attraction for government officials who were sent out to explore and ran
a fair risk of being stationed there if they came home with favorable
reports, the abundance of sea elephant, fur seal, and whale could not
fail to attract the attention of the adventurous hunter in search of
riches. In fact, the first man known to have stayed on Tristan da
Cunha for some time was a seal hunter named John Patten, master of
the sealing schooner *Industry*, of Philadelphia. He landed on Tristan
with some of his crew in August 1790 and stayed through the southern
summer until April 1791. Evidently his seal hunt was a successful one,
and he reported favorably on the possibility and prospects of a continued exploitation of this practically virgin hunting ground. To this
kind of people, unspoiled by the luxuries of refined living, the island
could even appear quite attractive in itself. A Frenchman who visited
Tristan da Cunha in 1793 actually described it as *très-habitable*.

Even more enthusiastic in his appraisal of the island was Jonathan
Lambert, an adventurer from Salem, Massachusetts, who had roamed
much on the sea—some say he was a fugitive from justice after a
stormy career of piracy. He had apparently touched at Tristan da
Cunha once or twice before he decided to settle permanently on the island. He conceived the idea of taking advantage of the island's location by making it a fitting station for sailing ships, a place where they
could call for fresh supplies of meat, vegetables, and water. And he set
out to realize his plan. He embarked at Rio de Janeiro with two companions in the sealing vessel *Baltic* of Boston, was taken to Tristan,
and landed there in December 1810. He had brought with him a
goodly supply of various kinds of vegetables, which he hoped to raise,
sugar cane, coffee, tobacco, along with some pigs, geese, and other
poultry. In a document he drew up a few weeks after his arrival and
published in newspapers in Cape Town and Boston, he pompously declared himself the "sole proprietor" of Tristan da Cunha, "grounding
my right and claim on the rational and sure principle of absolute oc-
cupancy."

Lambert's dream of felicity and prosperity in sovereign independence never came true. On the 17th of May, 1812, he and two other Americans who had recently joined the party took off to go fishing. They never returned. It is assumed that they perished at sea, although rumors were soon afoot that Lambert had been seen in South America and had entered the service of the republican revolutionaries.

The sole survivor of Lambert's original party was now an Italian of Irish extraction named Tomasso Corri, or, as he was usually called, Thomas Currie, a native of Livorno. He had met Lambert in Rio and, "being in a state of extreme poverty and wretchedness," had agreed to join him in his Tristan adventure "for a certain trifling sum." After Lambert's disappearance, according to some reports, he was the lone inhabitant of Tristan da Cunha for a while and, of course, appropriated whatever there was to claim—domestic animals, cleared and cultivated land, houses, and movables. His solitary state did not last long, however. In November 1814, when Captain Peter Gordon, master of the *Bengal Merchant,* visited the island, Currie was found in the company of another pair of Americans, John Tankard and John Talsen, who had decided to join him. The three of them seem to have made a tolerable living with their elephant oil and sealskin business, albeit on a smaller scale than Lambert had dreamed of. Captain Gordon reported that Currie had about twenty casks of "seal oil," which he "was desirous of disposing of for necessaries," besides an assortment of vegetables to supply ships, and that he "always expressed himself contented with his situation in every respect except one, which was the want of a female companion." He had asked Captain Gordon "to request of His Majesty's Government that by the next opportunity a passage might be granted to any female settler who would be found willing to partake of his fortune, also that a few ewes and rams with a few plants and seeds might be supplied him."

Both Lambert and Currie, although different in character and style of operation, were typical children of their time and the kind of persons who would appeal to the romantic imagination of the era. Both were adventurous men of enterprise, each in his own way quite colorful. But with all the pomp and circumstance surrounding Lambert and his doings, the name that still lives in the folk tradition of the island itself is that of the more unpretentious Thomas Currie. To young and old alike, "Old Thomas" is a well-known figure on Tristan even today. But few have heard of Jonathan Lambert.

On official maps of Tristan da Cunha, on the shoreline east of the Settlement, at the far end of the former landing place Big Beach, which is now covered by lava from the recent eruption, a mysterious place name appears: Tommy's Eyeloose. The surveyor who first recorded the name in 1938 was apparently attempting to preserve a peculiarity of Tristan speech. The name is indeed pronounced "Tommy's Ileous," and few outsiders would suspect, on first hearing the name, that it is really a contraction of "Tommy's Oil House." Even before the latest disturbance of the coastline, there was no trace of a structure. But the older people on Tristan still know that this is where Thomas Currie had a shack in which he stored his oil casks.

Not much is known with certainty about Old Thomas. Augustus Earle, the English artist who spent some time on Tristan in 1824, heard his story from William Glass, who had met him personally while serving as a member of the British occupation force that arrived in 1816. Earle describes him as "a morose, mysterious person, . . . who always had plenty of money at command . . . and, tempted by the easy access his money gave him to the military canteen [of the British occupation party], he was constantly seen in a state of intoxication." He is also supposed to have told Glass that he had "plenty of money" buried somewhere, and that he would someday show the place to that man in the British garrison who pleased him most, "thus insuring constant good treatment from the men, each hoping to be the favoured heir."

Another member of the British occupation party, Midshipman W. B. Greene, who kept a diary during his stay on the island, mentions nothing about Old Thomas's predilection for liquor and describes him as a man full of cunning and foresight:

It was also plain to us that he had salt provisions (which he had attained from ships), carefully concealed in different parts of the woods, as he was frequently seen to return from his walk with a fine piece of salt beef. As this happened during the time of our want, he was frequently watched by the men in the hopes of finding out his burying ground, but Italian cunning proved an over-match to English simplicity. And as our pride would not allow us to question him, his secret remained undiscovered.

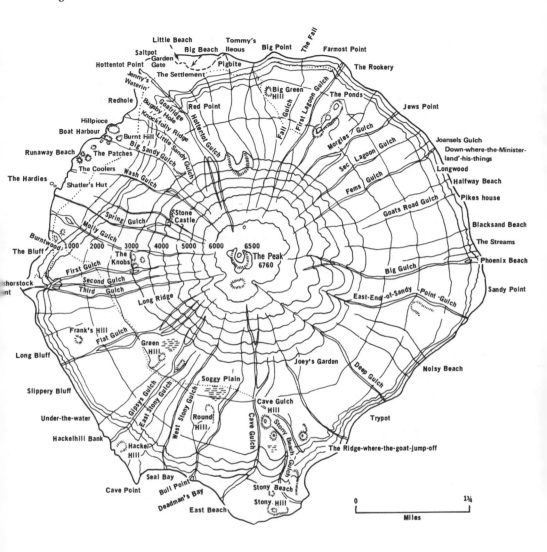

Relief Map of Tristan da Cunha

Shatler's Hut, from Charlie Taylor's Hut.

Tommy's Ileous, from Tommy's Oil House.

Joansels Gulch, from Jones's Gulch.

East Stony Gulch is actually to the west of West Stony Gulch because on the island "east" means "in a clockwise direction," and "west" means "in an anti-clockwise direction."

Of course, treasures of money had more appeal to a romantic imagination than salt beef, and the Tristan Islanders still tell tales of the
enormous treasures Old Thomas had hidden in a kettle somewhere
near the settlement, "between the two waterfalls." Tradition has it that
he would occasionally disappear into the woods and would always return with handfuls of gold and silver coins, pearls, and diamonds. But
he never revealed his hiding place to anybody, and all that was ever
found after his death—so the story goes—was an old teakettle with a
wooden bottom. No one, of course, really believes the story, and so
"Old Thomas's kettle" has become a joking expression on Tristan
with many applications. You can swear by it (not very convincingly, to
be sure), or you may make a teasing remark about somebody "going to
look for Old Thomas's kettle." You can even express utter disbelief by
simply exclaiming: "Old Thomas's kettle!"

Despite earlier reports to the contrary, the usefulness of Tristan da
Cunha as a naval base was proven during the Anglo-American war of
1812–1815. American privateers cruising against British commerce off
the Cape of Good Hope used to retreat to Tristan for refitting. Evidently, they procured provisions from Thomas Currie and could, in
fact, have been the source of his legendary riches, although he after-
ward reported to the British, of course, that he had been "constantly
robbed by the Americans, whether vessels of war or merchantmen." By
this traffic, honest or not, the Americans were able to keep the seas
and to inflict heavy losses on the British. The *Penguin*, a British brig-
of-war, was dispatched from the Cape to check on the traffic but at
Tristan encountered the American corvette *Hornet* and was captured,
then sunk. A recollection of the encounter is contained in two place
names still in use on Tristan: the wooden stock from one of the anchors of the *Penguin* was washed ashore on the western point of the island, which is still known as Anchorstock Point; and the name of
Deadman's Bay, on the south side of the island, may have its origin
from the fact that, some two years later, a half putrefied body was
found there alongside a wrecked boat and the main boom of the
sunken brig.

Finally, after the war was over, news reached London about the role
of Tristan da Cunha in the operations of the American privateers. To
prevent a repetition of the situation in the future, the Governor of the
newly established Cape Colony, Lord Charles Somerset, proposed to

the Secretary of State, Lord Bathurst, that the island be formally annexed and furnished with a small British garrison. No action was taken, however, until Napoleon had been banished to Saint Helena. It was feared that the French might use Tristan da Cunha as a base for any rescue operation that might be attempted, and in September 1815 Lord Bathurst directed Lord Somerset to place a garrison on the island. But almost a year passed before the order was carried out.

On the 2nd of August 1816 Captain Festing, of H.M.S. *Falmouth,* sailed from Saint Helena with orders to proceed to Tristan da Cunha, take possession of the island, and leave a small detachment there until it could be relieved by a regular garrison from the Cape. The *Falmouth* arrived at Tristan on August 14, and Captain Festing immediately went on shore and took formal possession in the name of King George III. He found Thomas Currie in company with a boy, Bastiano Commilla, a native of Minorca, who had come from an English ship and had agreed to serve Currie for two years as an "apprentice." It was reported that the two "were both overjoyed in placing themselves under the protection of the British flag," although the Spanish boy took the first opportunity to leave the island. What had happened to Talsen and Tankard was not ascertained.

Three months later, in November 1816, the detachment from the *Falmouth* was duly relieved by a garrison from the Cape Colony, which consisted of about forty men under the command of Captain Josias Cloete, of the Twenty-first Regiment of Light Dragoons. Among them were several "Hottentots," a general appellative used at that time for aboriginal South-Africans, regardless of tribe. Some of the British soldiers had their families along, and the party was well supplied with horses, cattle, sheep, pigs, and poultry, besides a variety of seeds and seedlings. Lord Somerset had issued detailed instructions to Captain Cloete, who was charged with the duties not only to continue the occupation of the island but also to cultivate the ground for growing vegetables and grain and, on the whole, to make his garrison as self-supporting as possible. It was quite evident that this was going to be a permanent British colony.

The party established themselves in what was named "Somerset Camp," on the northwestern foreland, where Lambert and Currie had settled before, and where the village of Tristan da Cunha has re-

mained ever since. The Islanders usually refer to it simply as "the Settlement." The rank and file Hottentots camped on the other side of a
ravine, which cuts through the plain from the foot of the cliff to the
sea, and which is still known on Tristan as "Hottentot Gulch." In accordance with his instructions, Captain Cloete immediately set to work
constructing fortifications and clearing ground for a vegetable garden.
He even adopted Lambert's idea of making Tristan a refitting station
for sailing vessels, and he appears to have been full of confidence
about the future prosperity of the new colony.

But if Lambert's independent kingdom had been of brief duration,
this official colonization project was even more short-lived. The garrison had been on the island for only three months when Lord Bathurst
in London changed his mind and ordered the withdrawal of the garrison and the evacuation of the island. The decision was made on the
advice of Sir George Cockburn of the Admiralty, who apparently saw
no danger to Napoleon's security resulting from a possible French base
thirteen hundred miles from Saint Helena. In May 1817, after only six
months' residence on the island, Captain Cloete and most of his party
were removed in H.M.S. *Conqueror*. Only a few artillery men, with
Lieutenant Aitchison in charge, were left behind for the time being
because they could not be accommodated on board the ship. They
were to be released shortly. But their final removal was attended by
disaster.

H.M.S. *Julia*, brig-of-war, was dispatched from the Cape to pick up
Lieutenant Aitchison and his party and arrived at Tristan in late September 1817. She was riding at anchor just off the Settlement when
suddenly during the night, as a fair demonstration of landing hazards
at this unprotected island, a heavy swell came in from the north,
parted the ship from her anchor, and drove her on to a reef, where she
was wrecked, with the loss of fifty-five men. As a reminder of impending danger to any mariner attempting to ride at anchor after nightfall,
the rock where the *Julia* struck is still marked on the charts as Julia
Reef. It is now under several feet of lava.

The twenty-nine survivors from the *Julia* were taken to Saint Helena
by H.M.S. *Griffin*, which happened to arrive at Tristan a couple of
days after the wreck—the ship had been sent out to remove stores left
by the garrison. But Lieutenant Aitchison and his party had to wait

another month and a half before news of the wreck reached the Cape and H.M.S. *Eurydice* could be dispatched for their rescue. They were finally removed on the 19th of November, 1817, after having spent nine days short of a year on the island.

In the meantime, an important decision had been made, and one may wonder how much the present community of Tristan da Cunha owes to the wreck of the *Julia*. For it was probably *after* that disastrous event that Corporal William Glass decided to remain on the island. Had Aitchison's party been removed by the *Julia* in October as planned, Glass and his two companions might have gone with them without any further thought of creating a perfect community.

Glass was a different sort of person from Lambert or Currie or most of the early settlers of Tristan da Cunha. In the first place he was not a sailor or mariner of any sort but a regular landlubber. And all contemporary descriptions give him an air of serenity that definitely puts him out of the class of the ordinary adventurer. In his very young days he had been a gentleman's servant "in a family of some note" at Alnwick in northern England, not far from his native town of Kelso in Roxburgh, Scotland. But having been crossed in love—so the story goes—he enlisted in the Royal Artillery and was only nineteen when, in 1806, he was sent to the Cape of Good Hope, which at that time was still a Dutch colony but under British occupation. Here he was employed by an officer as a personal attendant. He eventually advanced to the rank of corporal and in 1816 was selected to be a member of the British garrison on Tristan da Cunha, where he was put in charge of a party of native South-African artillery drivers.

By all accounts William Glass was a deeply religious person and, although he had grown up in Presbyterian surroundings, a devout member of the Church of England. He was held in very high esteem by his superior officers, and throughout his life, evidence of his gentle character was given by all who met him, including numerous castaways who had the good fortune to fall into his hands on Tristan and experience his generous hospitality. He appears to have exercised a remarkable influence upon those around him, and in the tradition of Tristan da Cunha he has assumed the image of a distant and venerable patriarch, who is always referred to, even by his own descendants, with a respectful "Corporal Glass."

While still at the Cape, Glass married a very young girl named Maria Magdalena Leenders. If we can believe the available records, she was not even fourteen when she married Glass in July 1814, and before she was sixteen, she accompanied her husband to Tristan da Cunha with their little son, William, Jr., just over a year old. Before the garrison left, the Glasses also had a daughter Mary, and the family continued to grow at that rate until there were sixteen children, eight sons and eight daughters, all duly entered, in the somewhat strained but legible hand of one unaccustomed to the use of a pen, in the Glass Family Bible, which is now, with several other Tristan documents of this early period, in the British Museum.

There have been speculations that Maria Glass was a Cape colored, and that this was the main motivation for Corporal Glass to remain on Tristan rather than return to a world where such a "mixed" marriage would be an embarrassment. There is no evidence, however, to support this contention. By people who met her, Mrs. Glass was described as a "Cape Creole," which means simply that she was born at the Cape of European parents. From her maiden name we may conclude that her parents were Dutch.

Whether Thomas Currie's death had something to do with Corporal Glass's decision to remain on Tristan, we do not know. Currie, to be sure, did have some sort of a claim to the island, at least to part of the pastures and to the piece of cultivated land cleared by Lambert and himself, maybe also to the hunting grounds near the Settlement, and it is reported that Captain Cloete respected these claims. But Currie died suddenly on the 27th of September, 1817, only a few days before the wreck of the *Julia*. As there was no heir or companion to uphold his claims, whatever they were, and as the British authorities were about to abandon the island, there seemed to be nothing to prevent anybody from repossessing the whole thing, including some thirty acres of land already cleared and cultivated. In the absence of an heir, however, the personal property of the departed appears to have been regarded as government property.

At any rate, Glass went into partnership with two civilian members of the colony, who had been employed as stonemasons in the fortification works, and the three of them decided to purchase jointly what probably were all the wordly possessions of the late Thomas Currie:

"viz, 30 Pigs, 24 Fowls, 2 Blankets, 3 lbs. of nails, 2 razors, 4 pr. of stockings, some old casks, an old chest of drawers, . . . [tools of various descriptions], 3 old Boilers, Some odd volumes of Book, amounting in the whole to Sixteen Pounds, one shilling, and ten pence, sterling . . . ."

A certificate of sale was issued on the 6th of November, 1817, by Lieutenant Aitchison, who duly signed a receipt for "an order upon the Commissioner of His Majesty's Navy, at Simon's Town, Cape of Good Hope." On the same day the three men received as a gift from the government stores a long list of items, including two cows, a bull, etc., and Glass was even put in charge of a variety of stores that could not be embarked on board the *Eurydice*, including six troop horses and some more cattle.

The following day Lieutenant Aitchison signed a formal permission for William Glass to remain on Tristan da Cunha "until the pleasure of his Excellency Lord Charles Somerset, Governour and Commander-in-Chief at the Cape of Good Hope, is known." On the same day, in the presence of Aitchison and a man from the Royal Navy, Glass and his two companions signed another rather remarkable document, which has aptly been described as the Constitution of Tristan da Cunha:

We, the Undersigned, having entered into Co-Partnership on the Island of Tristan da Cunha, have voluntarily entered into the following agreement—Viz

1st That the stock and stores of every description in possession of the Firm shall be considered as belonging equally to each—

2nd That whatever profit may arise from the concern shall be equally divided—

3rd All Purchases to be paid for equally by each—

4th That in order to ensure the harmony of the Firm, No member shall assume any superiority whatever, but all to be considered as equal in every respect, each performing his proportion of labour, if not prevented by sickness—

5th In case any of the members wish to leave the Island, a valuation of the property to be made by persons fixed upon, whose valuation is to be considered as final—

6th William Glass is not to incur any additional expence on account
of his wife and children—

                                        [signed] Samuel Burnell
                                                 Wm. Glass

                                                    his
                                         John X Nankevel
                                                   mark

                                                   ⎧ R. S. Aitchison
                                    Witnesses ⎨ Lt. R.Ri.Ay.Commdt.
                                                   ⎪ Charles Madan
                                                   ⎩ Royal Navy

Somerset Camp
Tristan da Cunha
7th November 1817.

On the face of it this document sets up a partnership in business,
with equal sharing of capital as well as of expenditures and profits.
But it does not state anything about the nature of the business the
"firm" intended to operate. It looks as if such material concerns were
entirely subordinate to much more far-reaching intentions. Clearly, despite the difference in style, this document was conceived and composed in the same spirit of liberty and independence that inspired
Lambert's pompous declaration some seven years earlier. While Lambert, however, was mainly concerned about his own individual liberty
as a sovereign possessor of Tristan da Cunha and its equality among
sovereign nations, Glass and his companions did in fact establish a corporate fraternity based on communal ownership, and with particular
emphasis given to the principle of *equality* among the members. One
recognizes in this brief document the first tender germs of such lofty
ideas as later crystallized and took form in the powerful political
movements of socialism, communism, and anarchism. It was, in fact,
an attempt to realize the ideal human community, based on perfect
freedom and solidarity, without any form of government control—
another evidence of the early dissemination of these ideas into the
grass roots of our Western civilization.

Soon after the solemn signing of this document, the *Eurydice* departed with the remainder of the British garrison, and the little party

of three men, a very young mother, and two small children stayed behind to start a new and, as they hoped, a better life under the gentle
leadership and example of William Glass, which soon earned him the
unofficial title, or nickname, "Governor." As "the pleasure of his Excellency," the Governor of the Cape, concerning permission to stay,
was never made known, and as no ship ever came to pick up the Government stores left on the island, Glass remained undisturbed on Tristan for the rest of his life and eventually raised for himself not only a
large family but also a handsome herd of cattle and sheep.

The precious document was carefully put away in a drawer in the
"Governor's" house, and as a new generation of Tristan Islanders grew
up, its very existence was apparently forgotten. William Glass died of
cancer in 1853, at the age of sixty-seven. The document must have
been taken from the island, along with the Glass Family Bible and
other papers, by his widow, who left Tristan in 1856 with all but two
of her remaining family to join several of her whaler sons in New London, Connecticut. It was there that the "Constitution" of Tristan da
Cunha was rediscovered in 1932 in the custody of an aging granddaughter of William Glass. It was then deposited in the British Museum, like a relic of a bygone age.

But on Tristan the spirit of that document never died. Certainly,
there were modifications in the style of life as time and circumstances
required, necessary adjustments to situations as they arose. But the
spirit of freedom, equality, and idealistic anarchy, although frequently
put to a test, remained a living force and a governing principle in the
community's whole system of values to the present day, firm enough
to withstand pressures and assaults from inside and outside the community.

3   Shipwrecks and New Settlers

Had the founders of the utopian community on Tristan da Cunha been sailors, they might have known better than to set their ship adrift without a skipper or even a helmsman. Whether it was because of an idealistic faith in the natural goodwill of man or because of negligence, Corporal Glass and his men had even failed to make provisions for a selective recruitment to their little Island Paradise. As it turned out, the fraternity was open to anyone who cared to join; in fact, anybody could come and go as he pleased. There were rules all right, and duties to perform for the common good, but by principle no one to enforce them. The advantage of joining appeared to be mostly to the newcomer, who could expect to become a partner to all the assets of the community just for the price of a little work that no one would supervise.

Small wonder, then, that there were many who wanted to try the new easy life of freedom and equality. And we may presume that, although there undoubtedly were idealists among them who fully shared Corporal Glass's dream of peace and harmony, not all of them came with the best of intentions or in the most congenial frame of mind.

Some of them came, in fact, more by fate and accident than by design—at least, so it appeared. The waters around Tristan are indeed dangerous seaways, with treacherous currents, unexpected swells, and sudden shifts in wind. Not all of the shipwrecks, however, that occurred at Tristan up through the nineteenth century were entirely unavoidable. Some, no doubt, were due to carelessness and poor seamanship; others may have been induced by a pull of the island that was not only physical. So it happened that the Tristan Islanders from the very outset played the frequently recurring role of hosts to shipwrecked crews, sometimes finding themselves greatly outnumbered by their guests. This, of course, could not fail to have an impact upon the little community and its mode of life, especially since nearly every shipwreck yielded one or more converts to the peaceful, egalitarian life.

The very first shipwreck that occurred after the establishment of the community was one of those in which fate may have received more than a helping hand from the crew. The *Sarah,* a small English sloop, with but five men on board, had sailed from London on a sealing expedition to the southern seas. The five men, no doubt, were experienced seal hunters, but on this voyage they had bad luck. After cruising all over the South Pacific without obtaining a single skin, they set course for Tristan da Cunha. Approaching the island after having circled almost the entire globe, with so little success, they apparently decided to make this the end of their voyage. They ran their ship ashore, saving themselves and a few belongings in a boat.

The captain and the mate left almost immediately in another sealer, but the others remained and were even joined by two men from the ship that rescued the captain and the mate. The five newcomers were warmly received by the settlers, who welcomed this unexpected addition to their company, especially since their own number had just been reduced to two men and a woman.

Three years had passed since the founding of the community, and the settlers had accumulated a small stock of sealskins and elephant oil, which they sent to Cape Town in a small ship that happened to call. Samuel Burnell went as their agent. A receipt from a Mr. William Hollett of Cape Town, dated June 10, 1820, shows that Burnell had sold him 119 sealskins for 250 rix-dollars less 5 percent discount, making "237 rix-dollars and 4 bits." He also sold 2 tons and 80 gallons of oil at £15 per ton, amounting to £33-11-10. He even paid a couple of old debts, including one that William Glass had contracted before he had gone out to Tristan with the garrison almost four years earlier. But Burnell never returned to Tristan with the money. According to the Reverend William F. Taylor, who served as a minister on Tristan in the 1850's and probably heard the story from William Glass, Burnell "met with bad companions, spent all the money he got in drink, and then, being ashamed to return to the island, made his way back to England." Somehow, the documents of his transactions in Cape Town found their way back to Tristan and are now among the Tristan papers in the British Museum.

The wreck of the *Sarah* took place in December 1820. Six months later there was another increase in the number of settlers when three man-of-war's men decided to retire from the British Navy and join the utopian community on Tristan da Cunha. They arrived in June 1821. One of them was Alexander Cotton, whom we shall soon meet as one of the prominent figures in the community.

There were now ten men on the island, eight of them newcomers, a situation that could become critical for any utopian fraternity of this kind, especially for one in which authority is banned in principle. And the problem of keeping the peace, serious enough in this situation, was soon to become acute. Only a month after the arrival of Cotton and his two shipmates, another shipwreck occurred, which soon led to events that threatened to shatter the utopian dream of a harmonious anarchical community with freedom for all. That was the wreck of the *Blenden Hall,* the most famous of all the shipwrecks that took place at Tristan da Cunha up through the whole of the nineteenth century.

The *Blenden Hall,* a large East-Indiaman, had sailed from England on the 9th of May, 1821, bound for Bombay with 52—some reports say 80 or more persons on board. As the ship entered "the lonely expanse of the South Atlantic," her commander, Captain Alexander Greig, steered for a sight of Tristan da Cunha to get his bearings because "thick weather" had made him uncertain of his position. But as the ship approached the islands, a heavy fog set in, and the wind died down to a dangerous calm that left her absolutely unmaneuverable in the strong current. Helpless in the dense fog, with her sails hanging limp, the great ship drifted to her doom. She struck on the west side of Inaccessible, at a place still known as Blenden Hall, and was rapidly broken up in the heavy swell. Two of the crew were drowned attempting to swim ashore. The rest managed to save themselves but hardly any of the ship's stores except what was washed ashore from the wreck.

For more than three months the shipwrecked lived on sea birds and their eggs. A party of men climbed over to the northeast side of the small but rocky island and could see the large cone of Tristan in the distance. They knew that a colony of British had settled there, but they had no means of getting across or of making their situation known to the settlers since the ship's boats were lost or wrecked when the ship struck. To make things worse, serious conflicts developed between the passengers and the crew, and two newly fledged "ladies" among the passengers, both of humble birth and recently married above their station, are reported to have quarreled constantly, continuing a fierce and vulgar battle of epithets that even the sailors would be hard put to match.

At long last, the more sober-minded among the crew managed to patch up the only remaining boat well enough for an attempt to reach Tristan. Six men took off in it but were apparently driven off by contrary winds. They never reached Tristan, nor did they return to Inaccessible, and they were assumed lost. Finally, the ship's carpenter and the boatswain succeeded in framing a new boat out of parts of the wreck, and in this frail craft the two of them with a few more of the crew made their way across to Tristan, where—according to a contemporary account intended for the press and signed by the captain and seventeen officers and passengers—they "had the good fortune to meet with a man named William Glass." The account goes on to report in a dramatic, flowery language how Glass and his men immediately proceeded to Inaccessible with food and refreshments and eventually, after several crossings "in a dangerous, and uncertain Sea, in small boats three times backwards and forwards," brought all of the unhappy sufferers to Tristan, where they put them up and took care of them in the most hospitable manner.

Trouble was the reward that Corporal Glass and his party reaped for their gallantry and kindness. It is reported that the shipwrecked, who greatly outnumbered their hosts, "made fearful inroads upon what slender stock of provisions the little settlement contained." But more critical to the welfare of the community were the disturbances of the peace caused by the continued quarrels and conflicts among the rescued. These conflicts seemed to have their roots, at least in part, in the deep social cleft that existed at the time between yeomanry and gentry, and in the growing resentment of these social inequalities on the part of the "common" people. It appears that some of the passengers insisted on certain privileges, material as well as social, even in this rather unusual situation, and as this was resented by the sailors, class solidarity divided the castaways into two sharply opposed camps. It was the fermenting Western World transferred in miniature to a tiny island in the ocean.

Glass and his men, in spite of their commitment to the principle of equality within their own ranks, apparently recognized a social distinction in relation to their guests. Arrangements were made for the officers and passengers to pay Glass half a crown per day each for board and lodging, while the crew, possibly by order of Captain Greig, were expected to work for their keep. We may perhaps also assume that the gentry among the castaways had somewhat better accommodations. All of this was deeply resented by the rescued sailors, whose discipline had broken down badly already on Inaccessible, and some of them refused to work. On one or two occasions, there were serious threats of violent insurrection amounting to mutiny, and to set an example, the captain had one sailor flogged. It was surely a relief to all parties concerned when finally, in January 1822, the shipwrecked obtained passage to the Cape in two ships passing by. They had remained on Tristan for almost three months.

It is obvious that the conditions prevailing during the presence of the rebellious sailors from the *Blenden Hall* were a serious threat to the solidarity and unanimity without which no truly anarchical community could exist. Only a month after the arrival of the castaways it was found necessary to try to restore peace by tightening the organization and strengthening the control of the community. A new document was drawn up to replace the original agreement of 1817 between Glass and his two companions from the British garrison. The new agreement was signed on the 10th of December, 1821, by all the male members of the community in the presence of Quartermaster Ben Gormby, one of the passengers in the *Blenden Hall*. One must assume that Mr. Gormby also helped compose the document, which was in essence a greatly expanded version of the original "Constitution," with some very important revisions.

According to the new agreement, "the whole of the Land, Stock, &c. &c." was declared to be "the sole and joint property" of the two remaining original settlers, Glass and Nankevil, and all newcomers were to "make an allowance (which will be duly settled and agreed upon by all hands hereafter) for the use wear and tear" of farm utensils, boats, oil casks, etc. Although the produce of the land as well as the profits from the sale of oil and skins were still to be equally divided "as long as the People continue to Work at the same," the provision about

ownership obviously put a powerful control in the hands of the original settlers. Particularly interesting is the following paragraph:

7th No person subscribing to these articles are to continue reminding
     particular persons of their Duty in point of Work, or otherwise, as
     in such Case nothing but *Disunion* will be the consequence; Wm.
     Glass being at the head of the firm, will allot to each individual
     every evening, his work for the following Day, not by way of task
     but merely for the purpose of causing all to do their best for the
     general good, which will be the means of insureing peace, and good
     will among the people, as well as benefitting the Establishment, in
     which all are concerned.

Also, Nankevil, Glass's remaining original companion, was ex-
empted from any kind of boat work "in consequence of disability, as
well as his presence being at all times required in the more immediate
concerns of the Firm." Finally, "the whole charge of and management
of the Boats" was given to Thomas Fotheringham, with John Turnbull as his assistant, a duty which explicitly included the "arrangement
of the Crews for the different Boats." Fotheringham and Turnbull
were two Americans who arrived with the wreck of the *Sarah*.

The new document reveals the rather tragic story of the Tristan
community during the first four years of its existence, especially after
the wreck of the *Sarah* and the arrival of the first newcomers. It appears to have been a period of increasing disruption and disunion,
until it came to the point where the choice seemed to be between complete chaos on the one hand and submission to a central authority on
the other. In either case the result would be all but a total abandonment of the high ideals of equality and freedom from control upon
which the community had originally been founded.

The settlers, rather than giving in to chaos, chose to submit to authority, and in this we might possibly see the hand and counsel of the
army officer who helped set up the revised agreement and who certainly would have been sensitive to the importance of discipline and
control in time of crisis. In the process, the settlers jeopardized the
principle of equality by confirming and consolidating an elite that appeared to be taking shape around William Glass, consisting of Nankevil, Fotheringham, and Turnbull. Nevertheless, the eglitarian com-

mitments of most of the settlers were not entirely abandoned, and the authority that was established was greatly tempered by these commitments. Although the agreement does recognize Corporal Glass as "being at the head of the firm," it does so almost with an apology, "not by way of task but merely . . . for the general good" and as a "means of insureing peace." Power for its own sake continues to be clearly rejected.

So the little Utopia of Tristan da Cunha survived its first serious crisis, if not without scars. Gone was the community of ownership and most of the much-cherished freedom from formal control. But the settlement was still a working whole, with equal distribution of the fruits of the toil. And prosperity appeared to be in store for the future.

Before the castaways from the *Blenden Hall* were taken away from Tristan, another couple had joined the ranks of the pioneers. One of the sailors of the *Blenden Hall,* Stephen White, had fallen in love with the servant maid Peggy, and the two agreed to get married and to cast their lot with the other settlers. William Glass performed the marriage ceremony in this first wedding on Tristan da Cunha, which brought the population to a temporary "peak" of eighteen—the eleven men, including White, who signed the new "constitution," besides two women and the Glass children, now numbering five.

With more men available to work the beaches, the settlers had soon collected another handsome store of sealskins and sea elephant oil. Reports of these riches had been brought to the Cape by the people of the *Blenden Hall* and induced the master of a small schooner, the *Jane,* to go to Tristan in the hope of procuring a cargo. A cargo he got, and this time Glass himself, cautious after the previous experience with Burnell, went along as an agent for the community. But the purpose of his trip was more than the sale of oil and sealskins. With abundant prosperity apparently ahead, the settlers decided they did not want to rely on occasional ships to take their products to market. They wanted a schooner of their own, and since the *Jane* looked as good as any, Glass was to make a bargain for her with the owners. He was successful in his mission, and on May 26, 1822, Henry Nourse & Co., of Cape Town, sold the schooner *Jane,* of 71 $\frac{4}{49}$ Tons Burthen pr. Register, to Wm. Glass & Co., of Tristan da Cunha, for £700, payable with interest in twelve months from the date of sale. The first cargo of 35 casks of oil and 150 sealskins, valued at $233.75, was accepted as the first payment. Future payments were to comprise various items salvaged from the wreck of the *Blenden Hall,* including a log of mahogany and some copper, besides all the oil and sealskins that could be produced until the schooner was fully paid for.

Proudly, Corporal Glass returned to Tristan on board his very own ship, bringing with him two additional settlers, John Murray and his wife. Indeed, with three married couples now on the island, the settlement was beginning to look like a real village. According to plans, there would be another cargo ready for the schooner on arrival, and a crew had already been picked, with Thomas Fotheringham as captain —he apparently had some experience in navigation. Surely, Glass and his men foresaw no difficulties in paying their debt in full within the year.

Just as everything seemed to be going well, however, misfortunes struck, one after the other. On his arrival at Tristan, Glass found no cargo ready because most of the men had shipped on board the *King George,* an English sealer who had made the shores of Tristan and the neighboring islands her regular hunting grounds. And the schooner proved to be a liability because, in the absence of a harbor, she had to be fully manned at all times. William Glass himself tells the story in a letter to Henry Nourse, an undated draft of which was found among his papers:

Sir,

I am sorry to inform you that on our arrival here we found most of the people we left on shore had gone on Board the *King George* of London, induced to do so by the high wages given by Captn. Bryan, who had lost several of his own men by the upsetting of a Whale Boat. In consequence of which instead of finding as we had every reason to expect we should a Cargo ready for us, we have been obliged to look after & get one ourselves, and which from the Ship's being here, and having very bad weather we have been longer in getting than we would otherwise have been. Indeed the Weather has been so very bad we could not lie long at Anchor, and have several [times] broken the Cable and Grapling &c. The Schooner has also sprung a Leak, which makes it necessary she should be hoved down and overhauled. Mr. Fotheringham will however give you every information you require. Owing to the *King George* being here we find the Elephants very scarce, and from the

Sea running so very high it is seldom we can work the Beaches, but next voyage we hope to be more successful.

Having lost one of our Boats it will be necessary for us to have two Whale Boats for the better working the Beaches. When at Inaccessible we should have got off the Mahogany, had the weather permitted, but the Sea ran so high on that part of the Island it was impossible to Land or to get anything belonging to the *Blenden Hall,* but when the Schooner comes next it will be Summer time, when we shall be able to get all off. We have however got [18] Ton of Oil, and what old copper we could pick up and two Bags of Potatoes for your own use which we beg you will accept.

> I am Sir
> Yr obt. Hmble Servt
> [signed] Wm. Glass

With this rather sad message, a ton of copper salvaged from the *Blenden Hall,* and a small cargo of oil, Fotheringham brought the *Jane* back to Cape Town and then returned to Tristan for another load. Summertime and favorable weather had indeed arrived. But the settlers soon discovered that the most serious obstacle between them and prosperity was the ever-increasing number of sealers from England visiting the shores of their island. Not only did they continue to persuade settlers to leave the community. The fur seal is an easy prey, and as seems to have happened frequently both in the Arctic and in the Antarctic, when the hunter walks in among a large herd of these helpless creatures on the beach with his club, he often gets into a frenzy of wanton killing. William Glass seems to have observed this kind of behavior among the seal hunters on Tristan and thought it was directed against the settlers, as we see from another letter to Henry Nourse & Co.:

> Tristan de Acunha Feby 5th 1823

Sir,

I was in hopes we should have had a much better cargo this time then we have, but you will not be much surprised when you know that independent of the *King George* and his Shallop, there has been the *Sovereign* & *Saucy Jack,* which when not content with killing what they could get off but killed and left to spoil vast quantities merely to prevent our taking them. The mates and crew likewise burnt all the Bedsteads &c. they could find on Inaccessible &

the *King George the Fourth* Cutter, and *Dart* Schooner, the latter took all the Blocks, Ropes and everything she could carry away that we had put into Huts for safety.

The Willful waste they made of both Elephants and Seals has of course for the Season injured us very much. There is however 20 Ton of Oil, 155 Skins, and one log of Mahogany on board, the latter I hope will fetch something very handsome. I have likewise sent all the Sheeps Wool, Mr. Fotheringham can give you every other particular.

> I am Sir
> Yr. obt. Servt
> [signed] Wm. Glass

Carrying this letter, the 13th of February, 1823, the *Jane* sailed once more from Tristan da Cunha on what turned out to be her last voyage. On this trip also Nankevil went along to settle some unfinished business concerning the cattle left on Tristan by the British garrison. The schooner reached Cape Town safely enough, but sank while at anchor in Table Bay. All the men on board got ashore, but none ever returned to Tristan.

This was the end of the Tristan community's commerce with Henry Nourse & Co. All that was brought in by the *Jane* on her three voyages for the Tristan Islanders was retained by her former owners in payment for the ship, including £117 earned "for attending the *Appolo* with the schooner *Jane* the time she was on the rocks." Although there is no document to show that the account was ever closed, the former owners probably got their money's worth. The Tristan Islanders, however, were back where they had started six years before.

The seal and oil business was never taken up again in any systematic way. Through constant and wasteful hunting by English and American sealers, the sea elephant and the fur seal, once so abundant on the shores of Tristan, became more and more scarce and eventually disappeared altogether. Today, the only reminder of this once so promising trade is a number of place names around the beaches of Tristan—Elephant Bay, Bull Point, Seal Bay, Trypot, the Coolers, and, of course, Tommy's Ileous.

Thus ended the first turbulent era of the Tristan community, with many trials and almost as many errors, with hopes and dreams rising to a crest only to be crushed and die, like the mighty waves breaking against its shores. Of the three founders of the community, only Glass now remained. Soon the Murrays also grew tired of their new home on the lonely island and found their way back to civilization. With most of the others shipping out in seal catchers, there were only four men and two women left on the island.

About this time, a noted visitor came to Tristan. The English artist, Augustus Earle, who later went as a draftsman in the *Beagle* on her famous voyage around the world with the young Charles Darwin on board, had sailed from Rio de Janeiro in the sloop *Duke of Gloucester,* Captain Amm, bound for the Cape of Good Hope. After a stormy voyage of thirty-seven days with heavy sea and fog, the ship finally reached Tristan da Cunha on the 26th of March, 1824, and while she was taking on provisions and water besides a cargo of potatoes for the Cape market, Mr. Earle went ashore to look around and make a few sketches. The settlers had assured Captain Amm "he might anchor with perfect safety, as long as there was no north in the wind; but that the moment it touched that point, he must get under weigh, and be off as soon as possible." Mr. Earle notes in his diary:

27th—The crew were all engaged in stowing away their fresh freight, while I passed the time in scrambling round the rocks, and making sketches.

28th—So strong a north wind was blowing, that it was impossible to get off in a boat; the sloop remained in the offing.

29th—As the wind had moderated, I prepared to set off. I had purchased some stock, which was already placed in the boat, and they were preparing to launch her, to take me on board, when the sloop tacked, and stood out to sea! I concluded she was only making a long stretch, and waited on the beach some hours; but she stood quite off to sea, and I never beheld her more!

After having been tossed around on a stormy ocean for so long, one can well imagine that Captain Amm was fed up to the gills playing tag with the weather. Perhaps he was over-cautious, perhaps he had felt a whiff of "north in the wind" and was heeding the Islanders' warning. Whatever the reason, the *Duke of Gloucester* did not return to Tristan da Cunha again for about two years. Her marooned passenger remained on the island for eight months before another ship was sighted.

Mr. Earle later published an account of his adventures on Tristan and included a rather vivid description of the strange quartet he met on this lonely island. And a strange one it was indeed.

There was William Glass, the gentleman's servant with the indelible stamp of his profession, who became a corporal in the Royal Artillery but never would have made a good sergeant—gentle, well-mannered, considerate. "I experienced from him," says Earle, "attention and hospitality such as are rarely found in higher situations in life." His associates still referred to him as "the Governor," and although in this context it was probably more a nickname than a title, it was not merely a holdover from the time when Glass headed a "firm" of seal hunters. All accounts confirm that William Glass continued to have a remarkable influence over his companions. The house where he lived with his young wife and children—there were now six of them—was a social and religious center of the little settlement, commonly called "Government House." Here, each Sunday, Glass would conduct a short service, reading a passage from the Bible. And every night, the little group of settlers would gather in Glass's sitting room "round a large and cheerful blaze," each telling his story of adventure or singing an old sailor's song. It was in this peaceful circle that Earle heard the life stories of these men.

The one whom he described as "next in rank" was Alexander Cotton, one of the British Navy Jacks who had settled on Tristan shortly before the wreck of the *Blenden Hall*. He commonly went by his nom de guerre, John Taylor. It was not unusual in those days for a man to enlist in the armed forces under an assumed name, which sometimes (but not necessarily) meant that he had a reason to conceal his identity. Whether this applied to Alexander Cotton or not, his story was one of glorious naval service. He had seen much active duty during the war against France and had taken part in some rough battles. Of course, he had learned to worship Lord Nelson, of whom he remained a devout admirer all his life. In short, he was "a thorough man-o'-war's man," as another source describes him. Later on, Cotton was stationed at the Cape and served in a schooner, which was acting as a tender to the commander of the naval station in Simonstown. In this capacity he had visited Tristan a couple of times during the British occupation, and he and a shipmate had sometimes served on shore. The two of them even paid Glass a visit once after the garrison had left. And so delighted were they with this little independent and egalitarian community that they decided to join it and settle down on Tristan.

The pair went home to England, were paid off, and, after spending all their money in a last fling on shore, proceeded to make a bargain with the Admiralty for a passage to Tristan. Since Earle got the story directly from "Taylor" himself, let us listen to his version:

. . . Accordingly these two men marched off to the Admiralty, to consult "the Lords" on the subject. When they arrived there, they requested to be introduced; and as the Board was then sitting, they were formally ushered into their presence. They immediately informed their Lordships that they had each served upwards of twenty years in the navy, and were entitled, by length of service, and by their wounds, to a pension; that they would willingly wave that right, and had come to them to beg a passage to the island of Tristan d'Acunha.

The unusual nature of the request did not fail to arouse the curiosity of their lordships, particularly of Sir George Cockburn, who had been the one to recommend the evacuation of the island a few years earlier:

Taylor used to describe this interview with the Lords of the Admiralty with a great deal of humour, and the mirth they excited, and the numerous questions put to them by Sir George Cockburn, who, to Taylor's infinite delight, addressed him by the title of *shipmate;* for he had served under him some years before. They told their Lordships all the particulars of Glass's establishment, the wish they had to retire from the world, and the comfortable prospect that island offered them of independence; and that at a time of peace, when it was almost impossible for the most prudent and industrious to gain their bread. So humble, so just a request, was instantly granted; and all the gentlemen composing the Board cordially wished them success, and assured them that the first man-of-war bound round the Cape should land them, and all their worldly goods, on this island.

In June 1821, the two adventurous jacktars were landed on Tristan da Cunha from the brig-of-war *Satellite,* bound for India. As it happened, they were also joined by a sailor who jumped the ship.

Cotton does not appear to have been part of the clique that formed

around William Glass. Maybe his boisterous pride in being a genuine
navy tar kept him somewhat aloof from the landlubbers and money-
grabbing seal catchers as it later did from the whalers. But when Fotheringham and most of the others left, Cotton quite naturally acquired
some prominence among the settlers. No one, of course, could challenge Glass's leadership during his lifetime. But in this practically sea-
borne community, Cotton had the distinct advantage over Glass, the
landlubber artillery man, of being an experienced sailor. So he simply
assumed the responsibility of coxswain in the whaleboat, "and, as is
usual amongst all gangs of men engaged either in fishing, sealing, or
any boating work of that description, those who are at the helm assume a superiority over their comrades."

At the time of Earle's visit, Cotton was sharing his dwelling with "a
dapper little fellow," whom Cotton, in benign contempt, used to describe as "half sailor, half waterman, and half fisherman." His name
was Richard Riley. He was the cook in the *Sarah*, the sealing sloop
that was run ashore and wrecked on Tristan in December 1820. But
his humble job on board the sealer in no way reflected his varied experience and boisterous career.

Riley—or Old Dick, as he was called—seems to have been the jester
of the little group that gathered in Glass's house in the evenings. He
used to delight the party with his old sea songs, and Earle relates how
he sometimes would pride himself on being a "man-of-war's man."
This claim always brought about the deepest indignation on the part
of Cotton, who would shower the little fisherman with such epithets of
contempt that he was silenced in every attempt he made at a nautical
yarn. Old Dick, however, had a comeback. He would resort to stories
of his service as a dragoon in the army of Buenos Aires, ". . . but here
Glass always came athwart his hawse; and the contempt he had for his
dragoonship was equally as strong as that of Taylor for his seamanship. However, Dick described an army such as Glass could form no
idea of, the half-naked, wild warriors of South America. . . ."

Born and raised in the East End of London, Riley had worked for a
time as an apprentice in a Billingsgate fishing smack but was pressed
by the navy and did, in fact, serve three years in a ten-gun brig. Dis-
charged at the end of the Napoleonic war, he went sealing in the
southern seas. He ran away in Buenos Aires but was seized by the authorities of the rebellious La Plata Union, who were then at war with

Portugal, and made to serve in their primitive army under General Artigas. It was here that Old Dick had his experience as a horseman. He finally managed to escape and made his way back to England. He soon, however, started out on another sealing trip, this time in the small sloop the *Sarah*. It was this trip that ended on Tristan da Cunha.

The fourth male member of the little party remaining on Tristan seems to have been of a more quiet, unassuming, and even unadventurous sort. He was Stephen White, the crewman from the *Blenden Hall* who stayed behind with his Peggy. Reports that he was one of the ringleaders in the near-mutinous conduct of the sailors from that ship contrast sharply with Earle's impression of him as "an excellent specimen of a young English sailor." Stephen and Peggy White remained on Tristan for almost six years but then moved away with their children.

It was indeed a reduced Utopia that Mr. Earle found on Tristan da Cunha—but exactly for that reason, peaceful and quiet. All thought of prosperity through business and trade seems to have been abandoned. The settlers were content to live off the land, farming and fishing for their own consumption: "Money is unknown at Tristan d'Acunha: Glass had none . . . . Here our food is of the coarsest description: bread we never see; milk and potatoes are our standing dishes; fish we have when we chance to catch them; and flesh when we can bring down a goat."

The peace of mind was serene. Having shed the undesirable elements, the Tristan community had come closer to realizing William Glass's utopian dream than ever before.

Soon, however, there were new arrivals. In 1825, almost a year after Earle's departure, another shipwreck, that of the English brig *Nassau,* brought a new settler, a Dane named Peder Pedersen. The same year an Englishman, George Pert (or Peart), made his escape from an emigrant ship bound for New Zealand, reportedly to save himself from being put on trial at the end of the voyage for an offense committed on board. Both Pedersen and Pert remained for several years; but eventually Pedersen died from an injury received while hunting in the mountain, and Pert left.

A more permanent addition to the community, and the first one after Glass whose name is still found on the island, was Thomas

Swain. He was another "thorough man-o'-war's man" and might have bid fair to outshine Cotton in that respect if it were not for the fact that he was a deserter, for Swain had actually served under Lord Nelson. Island tradition even identifies him with that very sailor who is said to have caught the admiral in his arms as he fell mortally wounded on the deck of the *Victory*—a story that was warmly supported, and maybe even invented, by Swain himself.

As a matter of fact, Thomas Swain never served in the *Victory*. Born at Hastings in 1774, at the early age of thirteen he began life aboard the *Fox* cutter, which served as a tender to Nelson while he was Captain of the *Agamemnon* and later when he sailed as commodore in the *Captain*. After that Swain did indeed serve for a short time directly under Nelson in the *Theseus*. After eighteen years in the service he ran away in Lisbon but was taken prisoner by the French and compelled to serve with them against his native country. It was possibly at this time that he adopted his nom de guerre, Francis Marquet. He continued for three years in the French service, was then recaptured by the English, and spent nine years as a French prisoner in England, not daring for his life to reveal his true identity. Released at the end of the war, he went in a merchant ship to the Cape, where he was engaged in more peaceful pursuits. At one time he was gathering seabirds' eggs along the coast, and it was in this occupation that he was found by Captain Amm, master of the *Duke of Gloucester,* and persuaded to start a new life on Tristan da Cunha.

Swain joined the little colony on Tristan in 1826 at the age of fifty-two. As a fair indication that he was indeed serious in his intention to start a new life, he joined the four other bachelors of the community —Riley, Cotton, Pedersen, and Pert—in a scheme to provide themselves with wives. The five of them made a bargain with Captain Amm, who by this time had become a regular visitor, shuttling back and forth between Tristan, Cape Town, and Saint Helena on various kinds of business, of which this was probably the strangest. The agreement was that the good captain should go in search of five marriageable women who would be willing to return with him to Tristan da Cunha in pursuit of husbands. Tradition has it that his promised fee for the transaction was twenty bushels of potatoes per head.

There are conflicting reports as to how well Captain Amm conducted his part of the bargain. One can imagine that it was not an easy task to find five volunteers for such an unusual enterprise, and he probably could not be too fastidious in his choice; besides, it may have been of small concern to him as long as he found the required number —after all, *he* was not going to live with the women. At any rate, he proceeded to Saint Helena and apparently lost no time making his mission known, and he seems to have filled his quota with less difficulty than one might expect. The governor of Saint Helena showed some concern about the whole matter and had his aide-de-camp, Captain Dan Taaffe, make it clear in a note to Captain Amm that since his passengers were "unmarried women and some of them having children the Government do not deem it advisable to allow them to go unless they are regularly engaged as Servants, and have some fixed and certain maintainance for themselves and their children . . . ."

Captain Amm, apparently, was able to reassure the Governor, for he did return to Tristan on April 12, 1827, with five prospective wives for his lonesome clients. Two of the women brought along at least four children between them.

We know very little about these women and their backgrounds. Although some of them stayed on Tristan for the rest of their lives and lived to a ripe old age, the sources are remarkably silent about them. The only reliable information by one who actually met some of them comes from the first resident clergyman on the island, the Reverend William F. Taylor, who was full of moral indignation about the whole deal and therefore, we must assume, somewhat biased in their disfavor. From his census of 1851 (now in the archives of the Society for the Propagation of the Gospel), we know at least the names of some of them: Sarah and Maria Williams were sisters, and one of Sarah's daughters was named Mary. Another woman went by the name of Sarah Basset Knip and had a daughter, Fanny. The women were young, probably in their twenties, except Sarah Williams, who must have been in her early thirties. As far as their backgrounds are concerned, one of the women, Sarah Knip, apparently was White—according to a note in Mr. Taylor's census, she had "English parents." Sarah Williams, according to the same source, had an "English father," but it is uncertain whether this also applies to her sister Maria. Most of the women, notably the three Williams women, who are the ones who have descendants on Tristan today, were apparently of mixed racial origin.

Despite his bias, Mr. Taylor admits that "to the credit of one or two of the women, they proved better than could have been hoped for; but none were such as would be wished. All were very ignorant, and some were viciously enough disposed." We may perhaps assume that Captain Amm had not exactly carried a cargo of angels to Tristan on that trip. There is no positive evidence, however, that there was any dissatisfaction on the part of the grooms. Each bachelor took one of the women as a partner for life and apparently lived happily ever after.

This, of course, meant a tremendous boost in the population of Tristan da Cunha within a few years. We just happen to have an informal "census" of the island from William Glass's hand, dated January 20, 1832, in which he appears to have included at least two yet unborn children. According to his list there were then six couples on the island—Glass, Riley, Cotton, Pedersen, Pert, and Swain—with twenty-two children between them (ten of the children belonged to the Glass family). In addition, there were two bachelors who had arrived too late to get in on the bargain with Captain Amm, making a total population of thirty-six—indeed, a substantial increase from the twelve or thirteen persons living on the island eight years earlier, when Mr. Earle was there.

The first eight years of the Tristan community saw four shipwrecks. But after the wreck of the *Nassau* in 1825, eleven years passed before there was another. The schooner *Emily*, of Stonington, Connecticut, sailed from New York on September 9, 1835, on a sealing voyage to the South Atlantic and the Indian Ocean. Among the crew was a young Dutchman, Pieter Willem Groen, about twenty-six or twenty-seven years old. A native of Katwijk aan Zee, on the North Sea coast of Holland, he was quite a young lad when he first went to sea. Now he had shipped out in the Stonington schooner to go on this sealing trip, which turned out to be the last of his sailing career.

The schooner reached Tristan da Cunha on November 30, after almost three months at sea, but proceeded directly to Gough Island, and from there to Marion, Prince Edward, and Crozet Islands. After spending the winter at "fish Bay," on the west coast of "Affrica" (presumably Walvis Bay), she returned to Tristan August 30, 1836. After another short trip to Gough Island to land a party of men with a boat and provisions for six months, she anchored in "Emily's Harbour" (Seal Bay?) "to take oil and skins." The latter phrase in the contemporary report may have a more literal meaning than usual, for island tradition says that the sealers intended to *steal* the oil and skins that the Islanders had stored in caves on the unpopulated south side of Tristan. It would not have been the first time that this had happened, and the fact that they anchored on that side of the island instead of going to the northwest side, where they could contact and negotiate with the settlers, may indicate that the rumor was correct.

However this may be, during the early morning hours of October 5, 1836, a heavy south-southeaster set in, and the schooner started to drag her anchor. A second anchor was dropped, but to no avail: "at 6 A.M. she dragged on to a reef, and at 10 A.M. she bilged, the surf being so bad we did not save anything except part of our clothing, a very little provision, and 36 seal skins." A few days later they made their way across the island to the Settlement, where they were "kindly received and entertained by Mr. Glass and his worthy family."

Out of this shipwreck came no less than three new settlers, and as Tristan now had its own marriageable girls, the men soon married. One of them, an American named William Daley, became a son-in-law of Governor Glass.

Pieter Groen was among the new settlers also. As he was now becoming a British subject, he immediately changed his name to Peter William Green, and his choice for a marriage partner was Mary Williams, the daughter of Sarah Williams, Thomas Swain's wife. This marriage, as well as his inclination, for he always remained a sailor at heart, brought him into a particularly close relationship with the two navy tars, Thomas Swain and Alexander Cotton, whose wives were sisters. This relationship, as we shall see, grew stronger as time went on.

Such were the beginnings of the Tristan community, and those were its founders—Glass, the gentle landsman, who always remained the soft-spoken but influential leader of the party, mild-mannered and idealistic, finding himself in the company of sailors, rough, mostly illiterate, and supremely independent, with boisterous careers behind them, which only seemed to emphasize their roughness and independence, and sharing their lives with women who, regardless of their personal qualities, must themselves have been somewhat rootless outcasts of the society that produced them.

4   Sailors and Whalers

There is no evidence that the little band of sailors, Cotton, Swain, and Green, ever formed a downright opposition to William Glass's leadership in the community. As long as Glass was living, everything seemed to run smoothly enough. Whatever cleavage that might be developing, however, between the fiercely independent sea dogs and the mild-mannered artillery corporal was certainly widened and deepened by the growing impact of American whaling upon the relatively peaceful community.

The first American whaling ship called at Tristan da Cunha in 1828. She came from New Bedford, Massachusetts, and her master was a Captain Moses Samson. Apparently, as he approached the island in the South Atlantic, Captain Samson did not know that it was inhabited and was delighted to see a boat put off to him loaded with potatoes, butter, and eggs, which he gladly bartered from the Islanders for whatever his ship's stores could spare. American whaling was then just developing, but it grew rapidly during the following decades to become the most important industry of the New England coast. These whaling operations were carried on from fairly large sailing vessels, mostly from three-masters of the bark class, more rarely from full-rigged ships. They required a substantial crew for manning the whale-boats, and they often kept the sea for two or three years, cruising all over the Pacific and the South Atlantic, before returning to their home ports. They were therefore in need of refitting while at sea, and nothing could be better for the purpose than an island situated right in the middle of a rich whaling field. So, as Captain Samson carried home his message about the settlement on Tristan da Cunha, the island attracted the attention of other whalers and soon became, along with

Saint Helena, one of the most important supply stations for the New England whaling fleet.

The number of American whalers calling at Tristan for supplies increased very rapidly during the 1830's and reached a peak during the 1840's. There must have been literally hundreds of them each year. It is reported that sometimes as many as sixty or seventy ships could be seen at one time whaling off the island. Many of the whalers, such as Captain Samson himself, made Tristan a regular stop. Returning year after year, they often came on shore while the ship was being loaded, and some of them became steady friends of the Islanders. For a short period Tristan da Cunha became practically an outpost of the whaling communities of New Bedford and New London.

Most of what we know about the impact of American whaling on Tristan da Cunha during this early period comes from the Reverend William F. Taylor, who served the congregation for six years, 1851 to 1857. The day he arrived, he started to keep a "Shipping Intelligence" record, listing all the ships that called at the island. By that time the whaling traffic had already passed its peak—"the trade is now much reduced; very few ships, in comparison, call here"—but his list is of great interest as it still gives an impression of the extent of the Islanders' contacts with the whalers. The list covers only the period from February 10, 1851, to November 9, 1852. During these twenty-one months, however, about seventy ships were observed near the island, most of them whalers, and about forty-five calls were made for provisions and water. Some of the ships stayed at anchor off the Settlement for two or three days, sometimes up to a week.

As far as Mr. Taylor was concerned, this traffic was a mixed blessing. In his account of his visit to Tristan da Cunha, after having aired his moral indignation over the fivefold nuptial adventure of 1827, he continued:

Just after this, too, the island began to be much frequented by whale-ships. This led to still further evil. Drunkenness, and other vices, began to prevail more among them, and consequently the highest duties of life could not fail to be so much the more neglected. The children that sprang from their union were badly cared for, and grew up mostly very ignorant. And ignorance is ever the fruitful mother of vice; . . . altogether, things were changing sadly for the worse.

But the whaling traffic meant trade, and trade meant ample supplies for the Islanders—it also meant Christmas flour for Mr. Taylor himself, bartered from the *Wave,* a New Bedford whaler bark. Indeed, one could even arrange for special orders to be brought out on the next trip, either from Saint Helena or from one of the New England ports, for the whalers were always willing to do little errands for their friends on Tristan. Last but not least, the whaling traffic greatly widened the horizon of the Tristan people and gave the young men an opportunity to seek their fortune elsewhere if they so wished, as well as for the girls to select a husband from a wider range of suitors than the island itself could offer.

The first Tristan girl to do so was Governor Glass's oldest daughter, Mary. She was only sixteen when she married Samuel Johnson, a whaler who came ashore from his ship and fell so deeply in love with the Tristan belle that he decided to break with his past and start a new life with her. Since his ship was homeward bound, he apparently had no difficulty getting permission to leave, and so he settled down and built himself a house on Tristan. This was in 1833.

Three years later another very young daughter of Glass's, Elizabeth, was married to William Daley, one of the men who came with the wreck of the *Emily.* He, too, was an American, although he was not a whaler. And only a few months after that, still another Glass girl was married to another man from an American whale-ship. Jane was only fifteen when she became the wife of a man named Rogers—Jock they called him—who likewise settled down, at least for awhile, and became the progenitor of the present Rogers clan on Tristan. Island tradition gives him the special distinction of being a "Segaba man," which is one of those mysterious folklore items that have been faithfully preserved, although the meaning has been completely forgotten. No one on Tristan today could explain what kind of a sinister character a "Segaba man" was. But it is fairly safe to guess that Jock Rogers came from Sag Harbor on Long Island, New York, which was another prominent whaling port in those days. And that was a distinction of sorts, since most of the whalers touching in at Tristan came from New Bedford or New London.

Despite his aversion to American whalers, Mr. Taylor described Samuel Johnson, Mary's husband, as "a generally well-conducted man,

although he does not seem to have always agreed with his neighbours." Mary's sister Jane was not so lucky. Her man stayed for two
years and then went away on another whale-ship to fill a vacant spot.
He promised to go only for one trip and then return, but he never
did. After that, Jane and her little son Joshua lived all by themselves
out in the woods across Hottentot Gulch from the Settlement. The
place is still referred to by the Islanders as "out Jenny's." A slight depression in the ground even now shows where her cottage stood, and it
is a favorite spot for the little girls of Tristan to go and "play house."
A little brook flows by, where Jane used to fetch water and do her
washing. It is still called "Jenny's Waterin' "; and on the beach below,
where Jane often went fishing, a large flat rock running halfway out
into the surf is still known as "Jenny's Rock." But to most people on
Tristan today, Jenny herself is only a vague figure in a distant, half
forgotten tale.

The man whose vacant spot was so generously filled by Rogers was
Charles Taylor, a stonemason who was brought ashore to die, it was
feared, for he was very sick; but he recovered and married Annie, another daughter of Governor Glass's. He became a valuable member of
the community as a house-builder, and two or three houses built by
him are still standing, easily distinguishable by their superior masonry.
One might wonder what a stonemason was doing in a whaler; however, a stonemason's skills were sometimes in demand to build storage
huts and shelters on desolate islands. Besides, the promise of big
money associated with whaling—a promise, to be sure, not always
fulfilled—might incite anybody to sign on, especially if he were not
averse to some adventure; and the whaling captains were obviously
not too concerned if some of their crew had never seen a sail or a spar
as long as they had muscles to pull an oar in the whaleboat or swing a
flensing knife on the "cutting-in stage."

As whaling men were coming and going, often spending a couple of
days on shore, it was inevitable that Glass should also acquire a few il-
legitimate grandchildren. There seem to have been two or three of
these urchins, one carrying the pretentious name of Thomas Jefferson
Griffiths. Another was named Joseph Fuller. Surprisingly, however, all
of them were later claimed by their respective fathers and taken to
America.

With all these alliances, licit and illicit, of Governor Glass's daughters with whalers, the one who made a better catch than any of her sisters was Selina. She got married to a whaler *captain*.

This was a case of a captain jumping his own ship. As the story goes, Captain Andrew Hagan had had a long streak of bad luck and had returned home with a very small catch. The owners of his ship were displeased, of course, and before he left on the next voyage, they told him in no uncertain terms that he had better come home with a full ship this time or they "didn't want to see his face again." He cruised the South Atlantic with no better luck than before, and when he came to Tristan, he was "clean," that is, he had nothing. Heeding the owners' warning in a more literal sense than probably intended, he left the ship, went ashore during the night, and hid away in the bush. Island tradition usually adds a little color to the story by telling that Jenny, staying in her house out there by the brook, heard him whistle a tune as he went by. Finally, the mate, tired of waiting, took the ship home. The story is sometimes rounded off by saying that the ship came back the following year, but then the mate was captain.

Captain Hagan settled down on Tristan in 1849, married Selina Glass, and had his brother-in-law, Charlie Taylor, build him a magnificent house, which is now occupied by his grandson, David Hagan.

Thus five of William Glass's eight daughters were married to Americans, four of them whalers. The remaining three left for New England and eventually became part of the whaling circle there. One of his eight sons died in infancy. Of the seven who grew up, at least six went whaling. The two oldest boys, William and James, returned for visits fairly regularly and continued for some time to regard Tristan as their home, although they spent most of their days at sea or in port at New London. James even came back to marry his Tristan sweetheart, Mary Riley, but then took off again and did not return for two years. The four other boys made their homes in New London and had their two youngest sisters sent over in whale-ships while they were still little girls. In the meantime, Samuel Johnson had grown tired of living on Tristan, and already before the arrival of Captain Hagan, he had moved back to America with his family.

This almost unanimous drifting of the Glasses to American whaling and whalers definitely set them apart from the rest of the settlers, who seem to have kept rather aloof from these intruders in their little independent and familiar, if not always peaceful, island Utopia. We are reminded of the traditional attitudes of the typical jack-tar of the days of the windjammers, who would give slight and condescending contempt to the landlubber but had nothing but scorn for the whaler. And with the Glasses associating so closely with this "scum of the earth," it was only to be expected that some of this attitude should be directed against them as well. If the sailor settlers of Tristan did indeed harbor such feelings towards the whalers, the contempt was undoubtedly mutual. Possibly the cleavage went even deeper than that. Ironically, in this utopian community pledged to communality and equality, there may have been an inkling of a "color bar" between the all-White Glass clan with its adjuncts of American whalers and the presumably more dark-hued families of Cotton, Swain, and Green.

Anyway, it is a rather striking fact that, even with the extensive contact and trade with American whalers that was going on during these years, probably only two or three of the eleven sons born to Cotton, Swain, and Green ever went whaling. Those who went, moreover, did not ship out in American whale-ships but settled down in South Africa, where they were engaged mostly in shore-based whaling operations for a few years, and then returned to Tristan. And not one of the eighteen daughters of these bluejacket Islanders ever married a whaler from outside of Tristan. On the contrary, the ties of kinship and friendship that already existed, particularly between the Cotton, Swain, and Green families through their Saint Helena mothers, were strongly reinforced by extensive intermarriage in the second generation. Three of Peter Green's four sons eventually married daughters of Alexander Cotton, and when a fourth daughter of Cotton's was married to Thomas Swain's eldest son, her cousin, an intricate network of important kinship relations was established.

The Glasses were almost completely excluded from these kinship relations. It is obvious that their strong ties to the New England whalers had removed them from any close bonds with the Cotton and Green families especially. None of the nineteen children of Alexander Cotton and Peter Green found a mate among William Glass's fifteen sons and daughters. And the cleavage seems to have continued into the following generations, for in the whole history of the Tristan community, there was never a marriage between a Cotton and a Glass, and the first marriage between a Glass and an agnatic descendant of Peter Green's took place in 1939.

So it appears that, from an early date, the little community on Tristan da Cunha was divided into two factions, and if there were no outbreaks of open conflict between them during the lifetime of Governor Glass, there must have been some tension, which probably was in the background of certain fundamental changes in the economic and social structure of the community that took place during this period.

Exactly how these changes came about is not quite certain. Very soon after the founding of the community, as we have seen, it had become clear that the original agreement between Glass and his two companions contained provisions that were extremely difficult to carry through, trying as they did to combine a communal enterprise with absolute equality and freedom from control. This, obviously, would require a unity of minds which, if it ever existed, vanished with the arrival of new settlers with a lust for independence. An attempt was then made to save communality by sacrificing equality and freedom, giving William Glass not only the authority of a taskmaster but also exclusive property rights (along with Nankevil, who soon left), and putting the two Americans, Fotheringham and Turnbull, in charge of the boats.

It appears that William Glass took steps to secure his privileged position as the sole proprietor of all land, stock, etc., and even tried to transfer that privilege to his children. In 1824, while Augustus Earle was staying with him on the island, he drew up a last will (witnessed by Earle) bequeathing the whole of his property "of every description" to his wife and children "to the exclusion of all other claimants." Eight years later—again in the presence of outsiders, Moses Samson, the whaling captain, and Benjamin Parkhurst, a teacher who spent a couple of years on the island as a guest of the Glasses—the will was revised to give one-third of the property to the oldest son, William, who was also to act as the head of the family in case his mother should die or remarry. It looks as if Governor Glass intended to put essential controls of the community in the hands of his oldest son, thereby securing his position as a successor. Obviously, his earlier experiences had taught him that if the community were to continue as a communal enterprise, there had to be someone in charge.

Although Cotton had put his mark to the revised agreement of 1821, its execution may have gone against the grain of Glass's British sailor companions with their proverbial independence. What had attracted them to the island in the first place was not so much its communal organization as the prospect it offered of equality and freedom, and one can imagine that it was not easy for an old sea dog to receive orders from a mere landlubber. Even after the departure of the men from the *Blenden Hall,* Glass may have had difficulties making his "subjects" do the work he assigned to them. Earle indicates that grumblings did occur, and it may be an understatement when he tells that Cotton and his companions, "though a little addicted to the characteristic growling of old sailors, . . . jog on pretty smoothly, their quarrels seldom going further than swearing a little at each other." As far as we know, it never came to a downright revolt against Glass and his mild form of authority. Perhaps the early settlers had already developed the technique of "passive resistance," which the Islanders have used in later years with such remarkable success against any person trying to usurp power among them: they simply ignore him.

Obviously, Glass was ignored. Whatever his intentions were for the future of the community, they were set at naught by the fact that, at the time of the Governor's death in 1853, his monopoly of ownership was no longer recognized by the other settlers, nor was there any authority on the island who could enforce the execution of his will against the consent of the others.

However it came about, when the Reverend Mr. Taylor arrived in 1851, he found a community of economically independent households, each man cultivating his own plots of land and raising his own flocks of sheep and cattle. Glass still had the most, "none of the others having a large flock as yet." But the trend had been reversed. The communal enterprise had been abandoned, and individual freedom and equality had been restored, strongly upheld, we must assume, by the group of fiercely independent sailors, particularly Cotton, Swain, and Green.

It is very likely that these developments, along with the slight tension between the American "whalers" and the British "sailors" of the island, were an important factor in the decision of practically the whole Glass family to quit the island and its utopian dream. The Glasses, as we have seen, had already been gravitating strongly to the whaling centers in New England, and when the old man died in November 1853, there was actually not much to keep them on Tristan any longer. Little more than two years later, on the 17th of January, 1856. William Glass's widow and the greater part of the remaining clan—

twenty-five souls in all, including Jane Rogers and Charlie Taylor with their families—sailed from Tristan in two whale-ships bound for New London. For some time to come, the name Glass was obliterated from the island of Tristan da Cunha.

Another factor in this decision may have been the influence of Mr. Taylor. With all his concern for the moral welfare of his parishioners, Taylor did recognize the economic importance of the whaling traffic for the Tristan Islanders, and with this traffic on the decline, he held a rather pessimistic view of the future of the community. After the Glasses left, there was even talk of total evacuation, and when Mr. Taylor's term of service expired, he persuaded three or four of the remaining families to leave the island and settle with him in his new parish at Riversdale in South Africa. So, just over a year after the departure of the widow Glass and her family, another thirty-five persons left Tristan. Among them were William Daley and his wife and family of eleven children, whose departure thus removed another large part of the Glass clan from the island.

There were now only four families left on Tristan: Cotton, Swain, Green, and Hagan—a band of sailors with their "Saint Helena Colored" wives and children holding strong British loyalties, and an American whaler with his Caucasian family. So the little Utopia emerged from another crisis, again sharply reduced in number, and again not without undergoing certain changes that appeared to remove it even further from William Glass's original dream of communal cooperation but in the end were a vindication of the undying spirit of freedom, equality, and anarchical independence.

In this community, now entering its second generation, there was little need and even less tolerance for a boss or a taskmaster. Here each man was minding his own business and expecting everybody else to do the same. No one was ever appointed or elected by the Islanders to replace Glass as "being at the head of the firm." In fact, the strongest opponents of any form of authority or privilege, Cotton and Green, now became the prominent figures in the little community. Cotton, being the older, appears to have been the most important person in this band of independent anarchists and regularly acted as the spokesman of the Islanders in their dealings with visiting ships. According to one report, ironically, he was even "placed in charge" of the community by a visiting naval officer, an act that probably had no effect on the inner structure of the community because it was ignored by all, including Cotton himself.

After Cotton's death, which occurred within a decade of the great exodus of the 1850's, Peter Green emerged as the "grand old man" of Tristan da Cunha. Not only was he now the oldest man on the island and the only real old-timer of the bunch; in this community, with so many remarkable personalities among its settlers, his was the most remarkable of them all. From all contemporary accounts, he was a commanding character, a buoyant and irresistible wit, "a hale and hearty-looking gentleman," boisterous, straightforward, "a veritable fund of good humor." He was the kind of man who attracts attention in a crowd. With his flowing blond hair and beard, which early turned white, he looked like a patriarch. One visitor describes him as "a most intelligent man," and no doubt he was. Having gone to sea at an early age, and having lived on Tristan since he was twenty-eight, he probably had little or no formal education. Yet he was well read, had some knowledge of *belles lettres,* and appeared to be familiar with Darwin and his theory of evolution, which was a rather new idea at that time. He once wrote to a friend in England that since he had "brought himself to anchor" on Tristan, he had read nearly all of Walter Scott's novels, and for many years he carried on a regular correspondence with the otherwise little-known English poet George Newman. Although his mother tongue was Dutch, he had a more than adequate command of the English language and is said even to have known some French.

Quite naturally, Peter Green usually acted as the spokesman of the community when dealing with outsiders. The esteem he enjoyed, the respect he commanded among his fellow Islanders must have been obvious the moment the island boats approached a ship. Captain Tipstaff, of the famous *Cutty Sark,* who called at the island in 1876, describes with great enthusiasm the "grand sight" of an island boat approaching in heavy sea, "with old Peter Green standing up at the helm with the spray dashing over him." So the visitor, whether he was the skipper of a sealing sloop or the Duke of Edinburgh on official visit, would naturally turn to him. At one point he was even considered for the official position of Magistrate of Tristan da Cunha. This resulted from an incident that took place on Tristan during the American Civil War.

The Confederate ship *Shenandoah,* purchased in England in 1864, had been commissioned to destroy Union shipping on the high seas, particularly the New England whaling fleet operating at that time mainly in the Bering Strait. On the way to her target via the Cape of Good Hope and Melbourne, Australia, the *Shenandoah* captured and destroyed several ships in the Atlantic, and passing by Tristan da Cunha, she landed some forty prisoners without providing for their keep. When the Islanders protested, claiming that the island was a British possession under the jurisdiction of the Cape of Good Hope, Captain Waddell asked them to present a document to prove it. As the Islanders were unable to produce such a document, he proceeded on his way, leaving the prisoners behind.

The prisoners remained on the island only a few days and were then picked up by the Union gunboat *Iroquois.* But the incident eventually came to the attention of the British authorities in London, apparently through a report from Captain Noel Digby, Commander of H.M.S. *Sappho,* who had visited the island in January 1875. How lightly the Islanders considered the whole affair is indicated by the fact that they had previously let two opportunities slip by without reporting the incident. H.M.S. *Galatea,* with the Duke of Edinburgh on board, visited the island in 1867, and H.M.S. *Challenger* made a call in 1873. But in none of the reports from these visits is the *Shenandoah* affair included. Apparently, the Islanders just happened to mention it to Captain Digby, who reports:

It appears desirable that there should be some recognized authority on the island, or that it should be occasionally visited by a man-of-war, as it seems that, during the American war, the Confederate cruiser "Shenandoah" made use of it for landing prisoners from her prizes, which the islanders were powerless to resist.

Although the American Civil War was over by then, the situation was studied, and to everybody's surprise, it was found that Tristan da Cunha had never formally been put under the jurisdiction of the Cape or any other established authority. Neither was it an independent colony, either directly under the Crown or otherwise. In fact, it was not even certain whether the island and its community had any status whatsoever within the British Empire, although no one doubted that it was indeed a British possession, a fact that was sealed and confirmed by the official visit in 1867 by His Royal Highness the Duke of Edinburgh in H.M.S. *Galatea*. It was on this occasion that the settlement was officially named Edinburgh in honor of the noble Duke.

This, then, became a matter to be dealt with personally by the Earl of Carnarvon, who was then Secretary of State for the Colonies. The case was brought to his attention by Captain Digby's report, which was submitted to him by the Admiralty in February 1875. On behalf of Lord Carnarvon, a reply was sent to the Admiralty June 15, 1875, in which his Lordship, since the islands "do not appear at present to form a portion of the Cape Colony," and since the Government of the Cape "appears unwilling to undertake the supervision of the affairs of the islands," recommended "the appointment of some person or persons in the islands to be a magistrate or magistrates" and requested that the officer in command of one of Her Majesty's ships "likely to be in the neighborhood of those islands" should touch in and make the appointments:

When authority has been established, the chief magistrate should write a letter now and then to the Secretary of State for the Colonies reporting as to the welfare of the community, and seeking advice on any matters on which the inhabitants may desire to have his Lordship's guidance.

Lord Carnarvon trusts that the Lords Commissioners of the Admiralty will cooperate with him in the manner proposed with a view to the establishment of some provision for the maintenance of order among these people.

As a result of Lord Carnarvon's deep concern "for the maintenance of order among these people," H.M.S. *Diamond,* under the command of Captain G. Stanley Bosanquet, was sent to Tristan and arrived there in October 1875. Captain Bosanquet, however, found no reason to establish a formal government on the island, at least not for the time being:

. . . On becoming acquainted with the settlers, I was unable to see any need for establishing rules for their future guidance . . . .

They have certain rules of their own, and the present senior male member of the community, Peter Green, is made their referee if necessary. This position has been conceded to him, not alone from his superiority in years, but also from having greater force of character, being a European, than the rest of the community, who are half-castes, and of more plastic materials . . . .

Apart from his prejudiced mistrust in people of mixed race and his conviction of European superiority, which in those days was taken for granted as en unquestionable matter of fact, Captain Bosanquet's report was sympathetic to the Islanders' desire to be left alone. Nevertheless, in accordance with instructions, he offered detailed suggestions for the future administration of the community, including provisions for handling criminals. Lord Carnarvon, who apparently could not imagine that an orderly community could exist without an established authority, proceeded to recommend that officers in charge of visiting warships should be given magisterial powers:

In any grave case, such as the graver forms of felony, it is proposed to confer jurisdiction on the Courts of the Cape of Good Hope, under the 23rd and 24th of Victoria, cap. 121, section 2; and in any such case . . . Lord Carnarvon hopes that the Lords Commissioners of the Admiralty would consent to the prisoner and witnesses being conveyed to the Cape of Good Hope in the first of Her Majesty's ships touching at Tristan d'Acunha en route for the Cape.

The draft of an order in Council for carrying out the proposed arrangements was submitted to the law officers of the Crown.

In the meantime Tristan da Cunha was visited by Captain Lindsay Brine, Commander of H.M.S. *Wolverene,* who was directed to stop at the island on his way to Australia. He arrived at Tristan in late October 1876 and made a conscientious study of the situation. He came up with a report that strongly recommended leaving the Islanders in peace:

I found upon inquiry among the men and women at the village that there were no complaints and no quarrels; that all were on good terms with each other, and that there was no recollection of any crimes or misdemeanours having been committed.

This satisfactory state of manners among a society so peculiarly situated is probably due in some degree to the existence of certain unwritten customs and rules . . . .

Any cases of dispute are usually referred for the decision of Peter Green, but practically the community act as a simple republic, and are bound by the customs enforced by common consent . . . .

The actual social condition of the community seems to be so satisfactory that it is very questionable whether any change made by authority would benefit them. There was a rumour prevalent among the men that magistrates were going to be sent to rule over them, with powers of fine and imprisonment, and this created a feeling of uneasiness. It is certain, with their present republican customs and habits of freedom, that the introduction of any system of positive authority would meet with great dissatisfaction. It is also doubtful if the establishment of a local magistrate with powers of enforcing certain regulations would be advisable, for there is no one at Tristan d'Acunha fit for such a position or capable of exercising judicial power

Evidently, this put an end to all plans for the establishment of a formal government on Tristan da Cunha, at least for the time being. Peter Green was never formally appointed a magistrate of the island but continued undisturbed to act as a "referee" when occasion demanded. For the most part he would be the arbiter and negotiator on behalf of the community when a barter of stores was to be agreed upon. In the absence of a clergyman, he performed marriage ceremonies and emergency baptisms when required. He also took it upon himself, in accordance with Lord Carnarvon's suggestion, to write to the British authorities "now and then" on island affairs, regularly addressing himself, the old salt, to the Admiralty rather than to the Colonial Office. In these communications, some of which were published in the official Blue Books concerning Tristan da Cunha, he showed himself to be a man with a gifted pen, capable of sarcasm and wit, with a somewhat philosophical bent and an utterly unconventional style, which later made Sir Douglas Gane remark that "it is seldom that our Blue Books are lit with such a patch of sunshine."

Performing all these functions on behalf of the community, Peter Green continued to be regarded by outsiders, including the British authorities, as an unofficial Governor of Tristan da Cunha, in this respect a successor to William Glass. He received citations and acknowledgements from the British government, the king of Italy, and the President of the United States for services rendered in saving lives from shipwrecks. When official registration books for births, deaths, and marriages were placed on the island in 1880, they were naturally put in the hands of Peter Green, and when it was thought that the island should fly the British colors, a Union Jack was presented to Peter Green, who erected a flagstaff at the gable end of his house.

Among the Islanders, however, Peter Green was only *primus inter pares*. Actually, the respect he enjoyed among his fellow settlers probably depended more than anything else on the fact that he did not appear to want a position of authority. Green himself pointed this out repeatedly to visitors, especially to commanders of British warships, who simply assumed that there would be a "headman" and were anxious to report that they had been in contact with the "proper authorities" of Tristan. Said Captain East, of H.M.S. *Comus,* visiting the island in February 1880: "Peter Green is looked up to as their chief, but he does not consider himself in any way above the others." And five years later, Captain Brooke, of H.M.S. *Opal,* " [found] from the people that there was no regularly deputed governor of the island" but apparently deemed it proper to pay a visit to the house of "Mr. Green, the oldest inhabitant." The anarchical ideal prevailed fully, a fact that was reflected in Peter Green's warning to the Admiralty that packages and stores should not be addressed to "the inhabitants of Tristan da Cunha" because there was no one to take charge of them: "Suppose I was to direct a box to the inhabitants of England, what would become of that box? They may as well direct it to Jericho or the Philistines, for we have good, bad, and boobies."

Even in Peter Green's day it was by no means a foregone conclusion that one and the same man should always represent the community to outsiders, to the exclusion of all others. Obviously, Peter Green did not go out to every ship that touched at the island. And even when he went, confusion might still arise as to who was the leader of the group, as shown by the reports from the visit of the Norwegian research ship *Antarctic* in 1893. Captain Kristensen, the master of the ship, describes "Mr. Green" as the chief of the island, while Mr. H. J. Bull, the leader of the expedition, in a separate account, refers to "kaptein Higgins" as the leader and representative of the community. Obviously, Mr. Bull is referring to Captain Hagan.

Whether Andrew Hagan, the American whaler, had any ambitions to step into the shoes of his father-in-law, William Glass, and become the head of the community, we do not know with certainty. But with his practical sense of business carried over from his whaling days, he clearly had ideas about carving out for himself a position of prosperity, even if it meant direct competition with the other settlers. Since the departure of William Daley with Mr. Taylor in 1857, Hagan was the only one remaining of the whole Glass clan and the sole heir to William Glass's property, including herds of cattle and sheep, which were considerable by Tristan standards. By prudent management, his herds continued to increase, and he soon was the owner of nearly half the cattle on the island. This in itself was apparently felt to be a threat to the egalitarian ideals of the community, and the fact that it came from a whaler probably made it even more detestable to most of the Islanders. But it soon also became a real threat to the economic welfare of the community.

Trading with passing ships, supplying them with fresh meat and vegetables, was the one remaining activity in which the community still performed as a collective unit. Since the community as such no longer owned any cattle or raised any vegetables, however, a system of taking turns in providing the necessary supplies had developed. The system, which seemed to work well, is described by Captain Brine, of H.M.S. *Wolverene,* in his report from his visit in October 1876:

It is arranged that all provisions or produce of any kind supplied to a ship for the general use of the crew and passengers are to be deemed the property of the community, and the proceeds of the sale in clothing, stores, or money are taken to Peter Green's house, and there equally divided among the families.

To prevent this system acting unfairly, each family takes its turn in providing the supplies demanded. Thus the cattle and vegetables sent to this ship formed part of the stock of Jeremiah Green, the next ship will be supplied from the stock of Cornelius Cotton, and so on.

But to allow for some measure of individual profit, it is agreed that private sales may take place, provided that these do not affect the quantities required by the masters of vessels for the ship's use. Sheep, potatoes, seal skins, penguin and wild cat skins, and articles of like nature, can be sold by their owners, and the money or stores received in exchange are retained by them for their own use.

In other words, the community had retained a monopoly for cooperative trade with any ship's storeroom, while private barter with individual crew members and passengers was allowed. In accordance with the anarchical ideals of the community, of course, there was no formal agreement to uphold this arrangement, nor was there any authority in existence to enforce it if necessary. It was just a custom that had developed, had proven itself workable, and was enforced by common consent.

Now it appears that Andrew Hagan attempted to go his own way, ignore the agreement, and break the monopoly. He may even have had visions of restoring the supremacy that once belonged to the Glass clan, and since he could not restore the monopoly of ownership that William Glass once enjoyed, the only way to do it was by sheer economic power, establishing himself as a "cattle king" on the island. He could then go into private business with visiting ships, offering beef for the ship's stores from his own surplus of cattle, to the prejudice of the communal barter. This, of course, was not only a threat to the economy of the community; it also put in jeopardy the common consent, which was the foundation upon which the whole anarchical order of the community rested. What made the situation even more dangerous was the fact that Andrew Hagan did not stand alone. He apparently had support from two other members of the Glass family who had returned from exile. One dissenter is a threat to an anarchical order; a group of them might easily turn it into chaos.

Peter Green reacted strongly to the whole affair, although he obviously had neither the authority nor the power to do anything about it. In a long letter to the Admiralty, dated December 29, 1884, and written in protest to a pamphlet published by by the Reverend E. H. Dodgson, a missionary who had just completed a tour of duty on Tristan, he takes the opportunity to air his feelings about Hagan, being careful not to mention his name:

Mr. Dodgson says we have a strange dislike to killing cattle and sheep for our own eating. Now, I will give you the reason for it. A certain man has by this mean action [of accumulating stock by not killing for his own eating] come in the possession of nearly half of the cattle on the island, likewise the pasture; he found the pasture [already cleared]; the pasture was the labour of the English pioneers. There was only a small portion of the land cleared when I was wrecked; I had to clear my share. Now this man came after all the land was ready for cattle; now he can kill, sell, and have plenty left.

With reference to a suggestion by Mr. Dodgson that Tristan da Cunha ought to be evacuated and the people removed to a better place, Peter Green continues:

If Mr. Dodgson can get some of our people away from Tristan, I hope he will include the three whaling boys. One is an American, the other two are natives of Tristan, but they have spent the best part of their lives in whale ships. They have brought a very small stock of knowledge back to Tristan, and that is of a very vulgar kind. If you can guess or calculate you will know the cattleman.

Besides the "cattleman" Andrew Hagan, the "whaling boys" obviously include Thomas Glass and Joshua Rogers, a son and a grandson of William Glass, who had left with the rest of the Glass family in 1856 but returned some ten years later and each married a daughter of Thomas Swain. Twenty years after their return, to Peter Green they were still the "whaling boys," and we must assume that the three of them—Andrew Hagan, Joshua Rogers, and Thomas Glass, with their families—again formed a separate coterie, a restored Glass set, in slight opposition to the Cotton-Green set (although the "color bar," if it ever existed, had been broken), with the Swains now split between the two factions and taking an intermediate position.

But there were others besides Andrew Hagan and the Glasses who grumbled at Peter Green, not so much because they had a design on a leading position in the community as because they resented *anybody* taking such a position. The recognition given to Peter Green by the British and other governments did not exactly enhance his standing among his confreres. The core values of this utopian community had by this time crystallized into a system of norms for social conduct that strongly discouraged a man from putting himself forward in any way or manner, and there seems to have been some grumbling among these independent mariners about the fact that one man was singled out for honors and rewards that were not rightfully his alone.

Even some of the Cottons seem to have been disgruntled with Peter

Green's dominant position. Cornelius Cotton, the most prominent son of Alexander Cotton, had taken up that abominable occupation of whaling, one of the few Cottons or Greens to do so, and had even brought home from Saint Helena a wife who appears to have been a character in her own right. She started to teach the children of the island, gathering them at her house on Sundays, and from what we can glean from the scant reports, she seems to have done it in competition rather than in cooperation with Peter Green's efforts in the same direction. She also read prayers for those who wanted to come to her house on Sundays, which of course tended to draw attention away from Peter Green's house as a community center.

What may have strained the once so close relationship between the Cottons and the Greens more than anything else, however, was what happened in connection with the wreck of the *Mabel Clark,* an American bark that foundered on the west side of the island in May 1878.

The three-masted bark *Mabel Clark* was on her maiden voyage, en route from Liverpool to Hong Kong with a cargo of coal, when high winds and currents drove her off her course. In the darkness of a moonless night, unaware of her nearness to the islands of Tristan da Cunha, she struck a rock off the shore near Molly Gulch. The sea was very high and breaking over the listing ship firmly grounded on the reef, making it impossible to lower a lifeboat. Dawn revealed the rugged shore of the towering island only a few hundred yards away. The sailors could see cattle grazing peacefully and unaffectedly in the sloping pastures under the steep cliffs beyond. But no people were in sight.

As in the case of the *Blenden Hall* fifty-seven years earlier, two young seamen volunteered to swim a line ashore through the foaming breakers. They did not make it, and their dead bodies were hauled back to the ship by the line tied round their waists.

It was still early morning when William Green's eleven-year-old boy, Alfred, started out from the Settlement to round up his father's bullocks. As he came over the rise by Big Sandy Gulch, he saw the bark on the rock, the sails in tatters, and the people clinging to the listing deck. He ran back to the houses with the news. Men, women, and children—the whole village—rushed to the scene, bringing with them a long rope, hot tea, and brandy. The bark was now sinking as her hull was battered to pieces against the rock by the heavy sea. The deck was awash, and the sailors clambered onto the rigging while the captain's wife and ten-year-old daughter were lashed to the mast. Two Is-landers, Cornelius Cotton and William Green, flung themselves into the surf and swam toward the wreck. A sailor leapt from the ratlines, plunged into the sea, and with the help of the two Islanders scrambled to safety. The captain jumped from the poop; William Green swam out again and dragged him ashore. Then the mate, with an injured arm, dived into the sea and was rescued by Cornelius Cotton. Again and again these two Islanders, with incredible strength and endurance, swam out and rescued whoever dared brave the raging surf. The last one to do so was the sailmaker; but as he was dragged onto the beach he died from exhaustion. Another hapless sailor had lashed himself to a hatch in the hope that he would be washed ashore; he was taken by the current and washed up dead near the Hardies.

After this, no one else dared risk his life by jumping from the ship, and further rescue attempts had to be given up for the time being in the hope that the following day would bring calmer sea. Those al-ready rescued, including the captain, were brought to the village and given food and dry clothes. Those still remaining on board, including the captain's wife and daughter, had to spend another chilly night on the pitching deck or in the swaying shrouds, wet and hungry, not knowing whether they would ever get safely ashore. The story is still told on Tristan, and the Islanders continue to show furious indigna-tion over the captain leaving his ship before his crew and enjoying his meal and warm bed in Peter Green's house while his wife and child re-mained lashed to the mast out there on the rock.

The following day, with calmer sea, a whaleboat was launched from Little Beach and brought as close to the wreck as was considered safe; and with the aid of a jolly boat and a line, the remainder of the crew and passengers were eventually brought safely ashore.

Reports of the disaster and gallant rescue traveled swiftly for a time with no radio, and five months later, in October 1878, the U.S.S. *Essex* was dispatched from Buenos Aires to Tristan da Cunha to pick up the crew. Most of them, however, had by that time already departed, get-ting passages a few at a time in passing ships. The captain and his family were taken by the British ship *Cambrian Monarch* and brought to Singapore, from where they eventually got a passage back to New York.

It was the American consul in Singapore who, on the basis of the captain's report, brought the matter to the attention of the United States Government, which in turn led to the dispatch of the *Essex.* And since the United States Government wanted to "reward these people for their gallantry, heroism, and humanity," the consul was authorized to send twenty-five dollars each "and the thanks of the Government" to five named Islanders "who were chiefly conspicuous for their good conduct on the occasion." The list included Peter Green and his son William but not Cornelius Cotton.

The reward never reached Tristan in this form for lack of communication with the island. Eventually, however, in February 1880, H.M.S. *Comus* brought to Tristan, as a gift from the President of the United States, a gold watch and chain for Peter Green, "the acknowledged Chief of the Colony," besides a binocular glass and forty pounds in gold to be distributed among the Islanders. The awards were presented by Captain East, Commander of the *Comus,* in the presence of the assembled Islanders at Peter Green's house. Here, Captain East heard the story of the dramatic rescue from eyewitnesses, and in his report to the Admiralty, he recommended that William Green be given a medal for saving lives. In November 1880 a citation and a medal from the Shipwrecked Mariners Society were presented to William Green by Captain Dawson, Commander of H.M.S. *Miranda.*

In all this, Cornelius Cotton was ignored. It did not soothe the ruffled feelings of the Islanders much that William Green declared he would never wear his medal since Cornelius Cotton had not received one. The Islanders knew that Peter Green had been the main source of the information, particularly to Captain East, which led to the awarding of a medal, so he had to take the blame for the omission of Cornelius Cotton's name in the reports.

The incident was never forgotten and had obviously tarnished the picture of Peter Green in the eyes of many of the Cottons and some of the other Islanders, too. George Cotton, a son of Cornelius, whom I met as an old man in Simonstown in 1937 (he had left Tristan in his youth and remembered Peter Green well), told me with a snort: "Old Green didn't save a soul!" and he "drank like a fish." He was the one who told me the story of Peter Green wanting to walk on the water. They were rowing home from a ship, and Peter Green was raving drunk. He then decided he would walk home on the water, for "when Saint Peter could do it" (as he put it), he, Peter Green, should be able to do it, too. So he stepped over the side and nearly drowned, for he could not swim. If the story is true, it was probably regarded as a grand joke at the time it happened. But George Cotton told it with disgust as an example of Peter Green's stupidity and conceit. In this community, it seems, any man who attempts to stick his head above the crowd is quickly cut down to size.

Then came the lifeboat disaster of 1885 with the loss of fifteen able-bodied men, which we shall hear more about later. Another great exodus followed, in which some sixty persons, about half the population, pulled up stakes and left the island. For several years these events overshadowed the ongoing rivalry between the Glasses and the Greens. Besides, most of the actors in the drama left the scene. Within one year, Peter Green had lost all his sons: three were in the lost lifeboat, and one had died shortly before. A son-in-law, three grandsons, and three brothers-in-law also were in the lost boat. Three of his four daughters had left before the disaster (two of them were living in Cape Town), and now most of his remaining grandchildren went away, some with their widowed mothers, others on their own. In the end, out of some thirty grandchildren of Peter Green's born on Tristan, only four remained.

But among the lost men were also three of Andrew Hagan's sons besides Thomas Glass and two of the Cotton boys, Cornelius and Thomas. The ensuing emigration included all of the Cottons, and all four of Thomas Glass's sons (this was the second time that the Glass clan quit the island). And Joshua Rogers, the second supporter of Andrew Hagan's bid for power, had gone mad, with violent fits of convulsion. He died a few years later after a fall from a cliff during one of his fits.

News of the lifeboat disaster brought the eyes of the world upon the little community and its struggle for survival on a rock in the South Atlantic, and for several years to come, Tristan da Cunha remained in the spotlight of the world press. It became clearly evident that the British authorities and the rest of the world looked upon Peter Green as the chieftain of the island. It was during this time that he received some of his citations and rewards, and to top it all, Queen Victoria presented him with a huge portrait of Her Royal Self, personally autographed, in a crowned, gilded frame with the inscription: "Presented to

Mr. Peter Green, of Tristan d'Acunha, by Queen Victoria, August 1896."

Andrew Hagan was completely ignored, both by the Islanders and by the world, and in June 1898 he committed suicide. He was discovered lying on the beach with both his wrists cut by a razor, which was found neatly folded in his pocket. He was eighty-two years old.

Four years later, at the age of ninety-four, Peter Green died.

5   *Anarchy and Freedom*

By the time of Peter Green's death, the principles of freedom and anarchy were firmly established in the Tristan community. And they were to remain one of the strongest elements in the heritage of the Islanders—not in the sense of license and disunion but as a social order based on the voluntary consensus of free men and women. In such a community, not only is authority, control, or any kind of formal and informal government considered unnecessary and undesirable; it is felt to be a menace and a threat to the established order and an infringement of recognized individual rights. It is obvious that here we can not expect to find a strong communal organization or even a well-defined leadership. The reward of high esteem goes to the one who minds his own business, and minds it well, but leaves everybody else to do as he pleases. Such a person may, in fact, become a leader by example if not by action; that is, his views and opinions might carry a little more weight than those of others, provided he does not attempt to impose his views on anybody.

William Glass had been such a man. With his strong but kind and mild-mannered personality, he obviously had great influence among his contemporaries on the island, the effect of which may perhaps still be seen in the Islanders' deep religious devotion to the established church. But during his lifetime, with the tension that appeared to exist between sailors and whalers, and Glass and his family being strongly identified with the latter, the consensus necessary for a strong leadership under freedom was lacking. We have seen the result. The communal organization fell apart, and the community developed into what some anthropologists, following Ruth Benedict's suggestion, will call an "atomistic" community, which "recognizes only individual allegiances and ties" but "lacks the social forms necessary for group action."

Peter Green's influence was perhaps even greater than Glass's. He, too, was a strong personality, almost to his own detriment, for he seems to have been anything but mild mannered. During his time, however, the problem of consensus had been solved by the departure of most of the dissenters, and those who remained were few enough to be ignored. Besides, Peter Green was himself the epitome and most vociferous spokesman of the principles which now had become the dominant tradition on Tristan, the spirit of anarchical independence.

After Peter Green's death there was no one on the island quite able to fill his place. The British authorities, who at this time concerned themselves a good deal with Tristan da Cunha and its people, were looking in vain for a substitute. Lieutenant Watts-Jones, Commander of H.M.S. *Thrush,* who visited Tristan in January 1903, reported: "There is no form of government, and the men were curiously averse to any individual being considered to have more influence than the rest."

And a year later, Mr. Hammon Tooke, special Commissioner of the Cape Government, elaborated in the same vein:

In the days of Peter Green the Government might have been described as patriarchal, but since his death there is no recognized head of the settlement. Here we have in the present century, in a civilized community, society reduced to its most elementary form, when the parent bears rule only over his own family as *pater familias,* the family being the social unit.

This leads to rather an extraordinary state of things. There is no real head or recognized authority—each doing as seemeth right in his own eyes. Even [Old Sam] Swain, although from his being the oldest man and an excellent character, he appears to command the respect of his fellow islanders, can command nothing else, nor can the most intelligent and energetic man there—Repetto—impose his will on anyone but his wife and children.

In fact, the community exactly fits Herbert Spencer's definition of a simple society which "forms a single working whole unsubjected to any other, and of which the parts cooperate with or without (in this case *without*) a regulating centre."

It appears, however, that some of the aura of prestige or "charisma" that surrounded Peter Green's person still lingered over his house, "the house with the flagstaff," for it continued to be regarded as a village center even after the old man's death. This may have put ideas of grandeur into the head of his daughter, Tilda Hagan, who was living in the house with her three adolescent children. Ironically, this daughter of Peter Green's had married a son of his arch enemy, Captain Hagan, and since she was the last of Peter Green's children remaining in the house, she stayed on according to Tristan custom, her husband moving in to become a new member of the old household. The lifeboat disaster of 1885 left Tilda a widow, and when Peter Green's old wife died a few years later, Tilda Hagan became the queen of the household consisting of her father, herself, and her three children.

The trouble was that she also, as one of the Islanders expressed it, "thought she was the Queen of the Land." Apparently she was more a Hagan than a Green, and as the old patriach Peter Green faded away in a severe case of increasing senility during the last few years of his life, she gradually took over the affairs of the island and added a few ideas of her own as to how it should be run. On one occasion she attempted to stop the construction of a house on a site just below hers as it would "ruin her view of the ocean." Of course, like any other autocrat or would-be ruler on Tristan, she was ignored by the others, and two years after Peter Green's death, she and her family left for South Africa.

During the following several years, there was no one who stood out clearly as a leader in the community. The one who came closest to it was Andrea Repetto, an Italian sailor who arrived at Tristan by the wreck of the three-masted bark *Italia* in 1892. He had married Frances Green, a granddaughter of Peter Green, and when Tilda Hagan left with her children, the Repettos moved into Peter Green's house on Tilda's invitation, not because they had a design on a prominent position in the community but simply because Frances was the nearest kin to Peter Green in need of a house.

Andrea Repetto was described by contemporary visitors as the most intelligent man on the island during his time. More importantly, he was just the kind of person who tended to have influence among these principled anarchists: quiet, kind, unobtrusive, even modest in all his conduct, but firm and confident in his opinions. Besides, he could read and write. Naturally, he became the one to whom the British authorities would turn when dealing with the Islanders, and the official registers of births, marriages, and deaths, which by this time had become an important symbol of prestige and status on the island, were put in his hands.

Repetto, however, was even more explicit than Peter Green had been in explaining to the authorities that he was *not* the governor or headman of the island. On March 10, 1905, in one of the few communications we have from his hand, he wrote to the Colonial Office in his clumsy English, which contrasted sharply with the buoyant language of Peter Green:

If that is possible to publish before our mail departure to address the gift send to the Island to me instead to the Governor whom we have here no sort of governor and no kind of head man.

Many letters where address to me and tell me to distribute the content of the parcel but the parcel is address to the Governor so I cannot say if I receive it or not, however I am no able to thank the good people which take interest to send a gift to the Islanders.

As it appears, Repetto did not feel that he could assume authority to accept, open, or even acknowledge letters or parcels addressed to the "Governor" of the island. Besides, it was not certain that they would ever get into his hands. Such mail seems to have been regarded as fair game for anyone who could put his hand to it, and as Peter Green had explained before, the community had both "good, bad, and boobies." The Earl of Crawford, who visited Tristan in his yacht *Valhalla* in January 1906, reported to the Colonial Office: "I enquired from Repetto if he was their Headman or Chief Magistrate—or who was—but they all resented the idea that one should be any greater than another, and Repetto himself is only their mouth-piece, according to him, as no other man could *write* to you."

So it turned out that Repetto, and his family after him, came to stand in the eyes of the Islanders as the incarnation of the tradition of egalitarian anarchy and personal independence, a direct continuation of the tradition handed down from Alexander Cotton and Peter Green.

Apart from the slight difficulty with mail addressed to the "Governor," the system (or absence of one) seemed to work perfectly well. The reports are unanimous in attesting the absence of crimes, misdemeanors, or any kind of disturbances in this community. Lieutenant Watts-Jones admitted that "there are occasional squabbles, but I could not hear of their ever having come to blows; in fact, a man who had been away from the island said they did not know how to fight." In 1938 I was told that there had not been a fistfight on the island within the memory of the oldest people. Even if I would have had reason to doubt the truth of this, which I did not, the statement is interesting because it was made with pride. This was not a virtue by default. It was a cherished part of their self-image. Mr. Hammond Tooke, in his detailed and insightful report of 1904, gave the Islanders this testimony:

Living in honesty, sobriety, and harmony, free apparently from all crime, vice, dissention, or double-dealing, they seem to have unconsciously carried out the purpose entertained by the original settler in 1811, Mr. Jonathan Lambert, by keeping themselves "beyond the reach of chicanery and ordinary misfortune;" but they must also have lost the instincts of suspicion and circumspection, which ultimately, in less favoured countries, are necessary in order to carry on successfully the struggle for existence. Of course, we cannot lose sight of the fact that the present position of the islanders is one of "unstable equilibrium" and that the advent of one evil-minded man might easily convert the Arcadia into a scene of strife and misery.

Four years later this is just what happened when the state of harmonious anarchy was once again challenged by returning members of the Glass-Hagan set, causing another crisis in this island Utopia.

It may not be entirely fair to say that Bob Glass was an evil-minded man, although I know a few older people living on Tristan today who would use stronger words than that about him. I still remember well the first time I saw him. He was in the leading boat that came out to meet us on that foggy, drizzling December morning in 1937 when we first arrived at Tristan. With sixty-five years on his shoulders, he was too old, or perhaps too honorable, to pull an oar. He was seated with Chief in the stern of the boat, just in front of the helmsman, looking rather unimpressive, I thought, with his wispy gray moustache hanging down over the corners of his mouth, his hollow cheeks covered

with white stubble, and his gray eyes peering under the raised brows
as he looked up to the bulwark of the ship. He was dressed in a gray
cloth cap and a dark, ill-fitting overcoat that looked too big for him,
as if his shrinking body could no longer fill it, the collar turned up
against the misty chill, the lapels folded over his chest and held together by a withered hand only partly visible under the too-long
sleeve. He looked like a cheating schoolboy caught in the act when
our bearded priest leaned over the bulwark and shouted down to him:
"Bob Glass, what are you doing here?"

I thought it was a rather unfriendly greeting, to which the old man
had no answer. But the priest was right. Bob Glass had no business
being in that boat, and his presence was an indication that perhaps he
had not yet quite given up his fondest dream, playing the role of headman for the Tristan community.

His full name was Robert Franklin Glass. He was the youngest son
of Thomas Glass, the "whaling boy" who had been one of Captain Hagan's henchmen in his unsuccessful bid for power. Bob was only thirteen years old when his father was lost in the lifeboat in 1885. A few
years later he left the island for a varied and adventurous life in South
Africa and on the high seas. He went whaling in the bark *Swallow*
and later sailed as third mate in the *Frances Allen* under Captain Joseph Fuller, his cousin. Just before the turn of the century he took
part in a large sealing expedition for the Ben-Susan Company of Cape
Town along with several other emigrated Tristan Islanders. On that
occasion they spent a winter on Gough Island. Returning to the Cape,
he fought in the Boer War, served as one of General Kitchener's
scouts, and won a medal for gallantry. By this time he had married
and had become a family man, and after the war he tried his hand at
farming and diamond mining in the Orange River Colony. Finally, he
decided to return to his native island of Tristan da Cunha with his
brother Joseph Fuller Glass and his cousin Jim Hagan, a son of Captain Hagan. The three of them had married three strong-minded sisters of Irish origin, whom they had met at the Cape, and with their
wives and families they comprised a formidable party of sixteen persons. With them also was a young man, Joe Hagan, one of Tilda Hagan's sons, returning after four years' absence.

The party arrived at Tristan in March 1908 in the schooner *Greyhound* of Cape Town. On board was also a Mr. Keytel, representing

the ship's owners and sent out to look into the possibility of a trade with the island in sheep and dried fish.

The invasion of such a large group of newcomers, even if some of them were not total strangers, could not fail to have an impact on the community as the population rose from seventy-eight to ninety-five in one day. Even more serious was the fact that the newcomers were of the overbearing Glass-Hagan set and apparently played their roles accordingly. Within a week the Arcadia was indeed converted into a scene of strife.

It soon became clear that the newcomers had designs on taking over the island. Their first target was Peter Green's house, the all-important symbol of prestige in the community. The young man, Joe Hagan, was born and raised in that house, and now he claimed it from the Repettos, actively supported by his uncle, Jim Hagan, and particularly by the two Glass brothers. They threatened to evict the Repettos and take possession by force if necessary. Repetto, however, refused to move out on the grounds that the young man was not able to present a letter or document from his mother to the effect that she wished them to give up occupation. It came very close to an exchange of blows when Joe Hagan challenged Repetto to a fight. Repetto, however, refused to let himself be provoked and, in true Tristan style, told the young man that if he wished, they would give up their bedroom to him. But they would not give up the house.

Three days later the newcomers started to take possession of the house by climbing onto the roof, ostensibly to mend it, and again it came very close to a fight. It is uncertain how the whole affair would have ended if it had not been for the intervention of the Reverend J. G. Barrow who was serving the congregation at the time. Mrs. Barrow relates the incident in her book, *Three Years in Tristan da Cunha*:

He [Mr. Barrow] told the young man if he could satisfy him that he had his mother's authority to take the house he should have it, after the Repettos had been given a reasonable time to find another. If he could not satisfy him then the Repettos would remain in possession. He went on to say he was here as a clergyman with the knowledge and consent of the Government; that it was his duty to do his best to prevent any breach of the peace and that he intended to do so.

He would see that justice was done just as a magistrate would. He warned him and all that if there were any further disturbance those causing it would run the risk of being sent from the island, for he should report the whole matter to the Government.

This was probably the first time in the whole history of the community that the outside authority of the British Government had been invoked to prevent an open breach of the peace.

The Hagan house, too, came under dispute. It was occupied at the time by Andrew Hagan, Jr., the only son of Captain Hagan who had stayed on the island, a quiet, unobtrusive man who had no design on a prominent position in the community. When the newcomers arrived, Jim Hagan with his whole family simply moved in with his brother and soon made life so intolerable for him, his wife, and their three children that they left the house and moved in with a widowed sister, Lucy Green. To top it all, Jim accused his brother of having stolen their stepmother's sheep, and threatened that there would be "blood and slaughter."

Island tradition points at Bob Glass as the instigator and "ring-leader" in these squabbles. There were numerous other troubles, too, and Bob Glass was invariably linked with them in one way or another. There had been thefts from the stores and mail brought by the *Greyhound;* naturally, the newcomers came under suspicion. Bob Glass was believed to have helped himself liberally and to have distributed stolen goods at will to win friends among the Islanders. On at least one occasion a boat's crew consisting of some of Bob Glass's henchmen went out to a ship but failed to surrender the bartered goods for general distribution, which in the eyes of the Islanders also amounted to theft.

Bob Glass, no doubt, had designs on great economic developments for Tristan da Cunha, which would give him a prominent position in the community as the manager of whatever business he might be able to start. He seems to have had a variety of ideas, none of which, however, got beyond the stage of a vague suggestion. Having worked, by his own account quite successfully, as a "boat-steerer" (harpooner) in a whale ship, it was obvious that one of his ideas had to be whaling, and I believe they once killed a whale. Another fairly obvious idea was seal hunting on Inaccessible. Completely without the capital to start anything at all, he appears to have made an attempt to cut himself in as a partner in Mr. Keytel's proposed business in sheep for the Cape market, and failing in this, he is supposed to have tried to make a deal with him for the sealskin business he hoped to start. Mr. Keytel, however, recognizing Bob Glass as a rogue, refused to have any dealings at all with him, whereupon Bob got together "a good boat's crew," went over to Inaccessible, and "deliberately" set fire to the tussock grass, supposedly to scare away the seal so that no one else should get them. The fire was burning for several days, and as it was the nesting season, it must have destroyed thousands of birds. He also told Mr. Keytel, who so rudely rebuffed him in his generous offer of cooperation and partnership, that "some day shortly there would be a big fight on the island" and gave menacing hints about having a revolver at his house, "which could be used on a certain person."

Violence was in the air, in sharp contrast to the usual harmony and tranquility of the island, and it is perhaps not surprising that in the traditions of these peaceful Islanders, Bob Glass has come to be pictured as a ruthless, crafty villain, who would not shy away from sneak murder to serve his selfish purposes. Although there is no evidence to support the rumors, he is supposed to have poisoned Andrea Repetto, and a story is told of how he tried to eliminate Henry Green, Frances Repetto's brother, by offering him a biscuit infested with rat poison, even daring him to eat it by taking a bite himself and pretending to swallow it. It is also hinted that he murdered his first wife with poison.

Although these stories are hard to believe, Bob Glass did at first, whether by bribes, persuasion, or threats, gain some followers among the Islanders, particularly among the sons and sons-in-law of Joshua Rogers, the other "whaling boy" who had supported Captain Hagan against Peter Green a generation before. Several of them had themselves been away from the island for shorter or longer periods and had learned the ways of the "Outside World." Besides, Bob Glass's schemes, however vague, did offer some hope for prosperity in a community which had not yet settled down after the devastating lifeboat disaster, and where the effects of increasing isolation were beginning to be severely felt. For awhile it looked as if the Glass-Hagan-Rogers coalition, with its philosophy of ruthless competition under a powerful boss, was going to crush the Cotton-Green tradition with its equality, freedom, and peaceful cooperation.

However, even in this severe crisis, the spirit of liberty and personal independence proved too strong to be crushed, although at a distinct disadvantage because, by principle, it recognized no leadership and had nothing to offer but freedom itself. It soon appeared that Bob Glass was losing his grip on the community. Little by little his followers, even his fellow newcomers, dropped away. Young Joe Hagan, regretting his part in the fight about Peter Green's house, offered apologies to his cousin, Frances Repetto, and got a passage back to Cape Town in the *Svend Foyn,* a Norwegian whaling steamer that took Mr. Barrow off the island in 1909. A year or two later Jim Hagan left with his family, and Joe Glass, although he stayed on Tristan, appears to have dissociated himself from his enterprising brother and his shady schemes.

In the meantime Andrea Repetto's position had been strengthened by his official appointment as lay reader, which not only placed the birth and death registers in his hand but also gave him authority to conduct marriage ceremonies. Bob Glass had asked Mr. Barrow to appoint *him* to that position, or at least to allow him to preach on Sundays as "the boys would like to hear how he would do," and when that was denied on the grounds that Bob was a notorious swearer, he suggested that maybe he could preach on Saturdays, as if to imply that this would be less sacrilegious. Apparently, Mr. Barrow did not see it that way and appointed Repetto instead.

But Bob Glass was not a man to give in at the first obstacle. Repetto died prematurely in 1911, only forty-four years old, and this gave Bob another chance. Somehow, he got his hand on the official registers, including a list of visiting ships which had been started in 1904 and faithfully kept up to date by Andrea Repetto until his death. From then on, Bob Glass took it upon himself to act, not only as a sort of town clerk, but also as a spokesman of the community on board passing ships. He kept written records of the contributions of each family to the communal barter and of goods received from each ship, and we must assume that he also organized and supervised the distribution of the bartered goods to the individual families.

Perhaps the best indication of the strength of the spirit of independence in Tristan da Cunha is that as long as Bob Glass drove a reasonably good bargain with passing ships and was "dealing fair" in the distribution of the goods received in exchange, no one really seemed to mind his acting as the spokesman of the community. None of the other men wanted the job anyway. Besides, he "got the larnin'," that is, he could read and write, which Henry Green, Old Sam Swain, and most of the other men could not, so the clerical function of keeping the records was happily left to him. In the absence of a priest, the community accepted him also as an unofficial marriage officer, although he never received authorization from the church. As far as he attempted to go beyond this in directing the lives of others, he was simply ignored.

So Bob Glass busied himself keeping records, which must have given him some sense of importance. When another resident missionary arrived in 1922, Bob had to surrender the birth, marriage, and death registers, but he continued to keep the shipping list. By this time, the communal trade with ships had ceased almost completely, so there was indeed very little else for a "Headman" to do except wait for those rare moments of glory when he could act as host and guide for officers who came ashore. An exceptional honor came to Bob Glass when the famous R.Y.S. *Quest,* with the Shackleton-Rowett Expedition on board, visited Tristan in May 1922 and Dr. A. H. Macklin, the naturalist of the expedition, spent several days as a guest in Bob Glass's house. It was perhaps he who induced Bob to start keeping records of wild life on the island. Thus we learn that over a period of five years, 1923–1927, almost 22,000 young "Mollyhoeks" (that is, yellow-nosed albatrosses) were killed by the Tristan Islanders; during the same period, an annual average of some 530 whales were "seen near our island."

As long as Bob Glass did not have any followers to support him, and as long as he limited himself to keeping records of this and that, he really posed no threat to the harmony of the community. Barring interference in their own personal lives, the Islanders had no objections to Bob Glass's activities in relation to visitors, and they could not care less about his ambitions to put himself on a level with the prestigious outsiders, which in their eyes only made him an outsider, too. They were slightly irritated but mostly amused by his vanity, which earned him the nickname "Height," and his boasting was taken with a grain of salt—as one of them explained, "He's done everything when he talks, but when you look into it, he's done nothing."

No one, of course, cared to put his foot forward to challenge Bob Glass in his self-assumed role as "Headman," nor could there, within the framework of an anarchical order based on equality and personal freedom, be any community action to curb his power-seeking efforts. In this community, each man stands alone in deciding his own course of action and maintaining his own personal independence without interference from the others, "each doing as seemeth right in his own eyes." It was indeed an "unstable equilibrium," as there would be nothing in such a community to keep it from falling into disunion and strife except a voluntary consensus.

In the community of Tristan da Cunha, the voluntary consensus had proven strong in the past. In times of crisis, it always seemed to be reinforced by an elite of steadfast characters, who refused to compromise the principle of individual freedom for personal grandeur, economic gains, or other selfish interests, and who enjoyed high esteem in the community exactly because in their lives and conduct they were the embodiment of its core values.

Such a steadfast character was Frances Repetto, Andrea Repetto's widow. She was the youngest of nine children born to William Green, Peter Green's eldest and apparently most prominent son. Her mother, Martha Green, who lived to be ninety-four, was a daughter of Alexander Cotton and was also a highly regarded person in the community. Born in 1876, Frances was only nine years old when the lifeboat disaster swept away nearly all of her male relatives. On that occasion she lost her father, three brothers, and eight uncles, and the only male relative she had left, besides her aging grandfather and a three-year-old cousin, was her brother, Henry Green, thirteen years her elder. In 1894, before she was eighteen, she was married to Andrea Repetto. At thirty-five she was a widow with seven children, the eldest being a girl of fifteen, and the youngest, a boy of two.

Frances Repetto was indeed a remarkable person. By all who met her, she was known as an exceptional and outstanding character, very intelligent, and "with the dignity of a queen." The first time I saw her, I did not know who she was. But the dynamic power of her personality was evident. It was only a couple of days after our arrival that

I just happened to meet her in the village. She was in her early sixties, but spry and active. Her graying hair was combed smoothly to the side under a colorful scarf and added to the impression of sternness imparted by her narrow mouth, the peculiarly long upper lip, and the slightly retracted chin. But her firm, hazel eyes were friendly, and she had the wrinkles of kindness on her face.

It was easy to sense that this was a person with influence in the community. In fact, she informed me quite frankly that she was the one who had told her son Willie—"we call him Chief"—to get the men together and help us bring our equipment and stores up from the beach, where they had been landed. From the casual and self-evident manner in which she presented this little piece of information, I gathered that this was the normal "line of command" on the island.

During our four months' stay on Tristan I had many a pleasant and interesting talk with Frances Repetto over a cup of tea in her spotless front room, so filled with mementoes of the bygone days of sailing ships and seamen's chests. Although she had never been away from the island of her birth (she had not even set foot on Nightingale or Inaccessible), her conversation disclosed great wisdom and knowledge of human nature and an amazingly broad outlook on life. She expressed herself well and with no hesitation, and keeping the conversation going was not the difficulty I had often experienced with other women on the island, with some of the men, too. In fact, I had a hard time getting a word in now and then myself. Her sense of justice was strong, and she held very definite opinions, well supported and frankly expressed, of what she considered right and proper in the affairs of Tristan as well as in the world at large. At the same time she was a warmhearted woman, kind and cheerful, and loved with reverence by all. What a rare person she was!

One of Frances Repetto's favorite statements was repeated so often that it became a well-known slogan on the island: "Every man on Tristan da Cunha can make his own living if he works on his potatoes, looks ahead, and saves for a rainy day."

The statement was always pronounced with emphasis on every stress —*every man* on *Tristan* da *Cunha* . . . —giving it a rhythmic effect that made it sound like a choral chant. I can still hear it ringing in my ears as it must have been ringing in the ears of every Islander. In Frances Repetto's mouth it was an admonition as well as a statement of fact. It was her straightforward and down-to-earth way of expressing her own allegiance, and that of every right-minded Islander, to the principle of personal independence for all, and her unfaltering faith in the prospect of maintaining such freedom on the island of Tristan da Cunha, even in the face of isolation and poverty. The statement was an argument, effectively used, against any pessimistic thought of having to give up the island or else submit to a corporate enterprise under a boss as the only road to survival. In due time, the spirit of that statement was to become a warding shield against any attempt to disenfranchise the people of Tristan da Cunha and turn them into pliable tools for modern industry.

Frances Repetto's influence, like that of Peter Green and Andrea Repetto before her, was due to the fact that she was not striving for personal dominance and glory. She was just an independent person holding her own, and it is evident that already as a young widow she had, by her example and her frankly expressed opinions, given significant moral support to the traditional values of the community. Of course, no more than anybody else would she attempt to replace Bob Glass as "Headman" of the community. Even if she had wanted to, she could never hope to act as a spokesman on board passing ships because the women never went out to them. All her life, however, she remained the focal point and moral support of an unshakable passive resistance to any usurper of power and authority in the community of Tristan da Cunha.

In the end, Bob Glass was indeed dethroned from a position that in reality he never held, but it took an outsider with rival ambitions and external authority to do it. After the *Shenandoah* affair in the 1860's, the British authorities had concerned themselves more with the possible evacuation of the island than with its formal administration, although the question of government had been raised several times as the island continued to be regarded as a British possession. As it appeared, however, to be the wish of the Islanders to be left alone, and their system of anarchy generally seemed to cause no problem or strife, the authorities seldom interfered.

Various attempts at establishing at least a rudimentary form of administration were made by some of the resident clergymen sent out by the Society for the Propagation of the Gospel. All of them had certainly experienced the difficulty of living among these independent people and trying to get something done that might involve the whole community. Despite the fact that the ministers were held in high esteem, not only because of their holy office, but particularly because they represented the prestigious Outside World, they were utterly frustrated in any attempt at a communal enterprise.

The Reverend Henry Martyn Rogers did endeavor during his three years' stay on Tristan (1922–1925) to develop some system of local government "which should induce a sense of corporate responsibility among the men of the island, which seemed to us to be a good deal lacking." He instituted an official Meeting of all the Heads of Families, which he called "Our Parliament," with himself as chairman. "He was listened to very respectfully," says Mrs. Rogers, "and good work resulted." Indeed Mr. Rogers was the one who finally succeeded in getting the Islanders together in the communal enterprise of building a church. However, the "Parliament" was only occasionally in session as it was "never called except for really important matters touching public morals or public business," and it was hardly more than a sounding board for the minister as all initiative remained with him, not only in calling the meetings, but also in bringing matters before the assembly, and it hardly ever went beyond confirming the chairman's opinion. When Mr. Rogers left, "Our Parliament" faded into oblivion. During the term of his successor, the Reverend R. A. C. Pooley (1927–1929), no governmental institutions were in operation.

The first serious attempt to establish a formal local administration with authority from His Majesty's Government was made by the Reverend A. G. Partridge (1929–1932). He has left the impression among the Islanders of being a man of ambitions, not only for the island and its community but for himself as well—as they expressed it, "he was trying to make a name for himself," in their opinion a most deplorable if not contemptible occupation. This, of course, was their judgment of Bob Glass also, indeed of anyone who tried to put his foot forward to assume a leading position in the community. With such ambitions Mr. Partridge apparently saw in Bob Glass an annoying rival, and whatever came of his efforts to establish himself as a Magistrate of Tristan da Cunha, he did the Islanders the service of getting rid of this usurper from among their own ranks. Under the date December 10, 1929, across two pages in the register of ships that had been kept since 1904 by Andrea Repetto and after him by Bob Glass, we find the following declaration:

This book was taken from R. F. Glass by the Revd A. G. Partridge, Priest in Charge, with the unanimous consent of all the men of the Island.

This meeting decided that Captains and officers of all vessels visiting this Island are to be informed that the said R. F. Glass (Bob Glass) has *no* locus standi or position of any sort.

> [signed] A. G. Partridge
> Priest in Charge
> Philip C. Lindsay
> Lay Missioner

This was the end of Bob Glass's self-established regime. Unfortunately, it was the end of the shipping list as well. After this, only two ships' visits have been entered in the records, the last one being that of the Danish ketch *Monsunen,* Captain Knud Andersen, owner, bound from Buenos Aires to Cape Town, which "came to visit Island (on March 17, 1930) for private pleasure and unofficial information."

A few years after the demotion of Bob Glass, when the Bishop of Saint Helena, the Right Reverend C. C. Watts, visited the island, Mr. Partridge persuaded him to include the following recommendation in his report:

It is absolutely essential to the well-being of the islanders that a strong, sympathetic, and capable missionary be permanently resident on the island. This missionary should be provided with a written authority from the Imperial Government appointing him as Magistrate of the island. Previous missionaries have stressed this point as it would give him authority and obviate possible disputes.

In accordance with this recommendation Mr. Partridge was indeed appointed His Majesty's Commissioner for Tristan da Cunha. And as if to put the Glass "dynasty" and its social set entirely out of commission, he surrounded himself with an "island council" consisting mainly of men who were closely related to the Repettos by blood or by marriage, and with Joe Repetto, a son of Frances, as "First Officer." Recognizing, however, where the real power in the community rested, Commissioner Partridge soon replaced Joe with his brother Willie, who was unmarried and lived with his mother in Peter Green's old house. It was on this occasion that Willie Repetto was named "Chief Man," while Frances Repetto was designated "Chief of the Women." These appointments were made with the Islanders' consent and were, in fact, only a formal confirmation of a situation that had developed spontaneously on the basis of Frances Repetto's outstanding personality.

After his demotion Bob Glass led a life of relative retirement. When I saw him in 1938 he was suffering from high blood pressure and an ulcer, rare maladies on this island of unusual health, and he seemed much older than his age. Yet, he was tall and slim and had preserved much of the self-confident dignity of a man of the world. He often came down to our camp for visits, especially on Sundays, and then always dressed up in what appeared to be his well-worn Sunday best, with baggy gray trousers under a dark, old-fashioned coat and a battered felt hat. Around his neck, neatly folded in front under his vest, he wore a checkered silk scarf fastened in the center by a large golden pin, and his chest was adorned by the shiny medal won in the Boer War, which he always wore on Sundays and for special occasions. He would usually greet us with a healthy *"Goeie morê,"* mainly directed to our South African geologist, with whom he would exchange a few sentences in Afrikaans before conceding to the linguistic ignorance of the rest of us by switching to English. Like an old hermit hungry for an audience, he would give us pieces of his life as well as of his view of life, all very interesting and somewhat puzzling.

Here was a man, like so many old men, living in a world of dreams, wonderful dreams that never really came true but in his ruminations sounded as if they almost did. But they were dreams entirely his own, as if he were setting himself apart from the little community, which was his whole world of reality. His memories lingered with the twenty years he had spent away from the island, on the high seas, in the war, and in the diamond mines of the Orange River Colony, as if those were the only years he had really lived, and among his most cherished mementoes, besides his Boer War medal, was an old sextant from the days when he sailed as third mate in the *Frances Allen.*

Only occasionally, when prodded, would he offer comments and opinions about the community in which he lived, but always as if he were not a part of it, like a stranger looking upon it from outside. He was critical of the Islanders' conservatism and of what he saw as lack of ambition, their limited outlook, and their stubborn independence:

"They don't listen to anybody!"

There was contempt and bitter resignation in his voice.

6   Heritage of the Seven Seas

As long as trade winds pushing canvas remained the principal means of ocean transport, the waters around Tristan da Cunha were among the most heavily traveled sailing lanes of the open seas. The island, with its characteristic conical profile, was a landmark as well known to mariners of all nations as any familiar feature on a frequently trodden road, at the same time a threatening menace and an alluring haven, approachable only with the utmost care in the strong and treacherous currents of the Westerlies, but delectable as a resort for body and soul after the sulky calm of the Doldrums and the baffling variables of the Horse Latitudes.

There are no running records of the number of ships that called at Tristan through the nineteenth century, but the traffic was considerable. We have already noted that the Reverend William Taylor counted some seventy ships sighted near Tristan during a twenty-one-month period in the 1850's, forty-five of which came in for provisions. Many of them were whalers. But even after the whaling traffic had passed its peak and diminished considerably, when Captain Brine of H.M.S. *Wolverene* visited Tristan in 1876, he was informed that an average of twenty ships called annually off the Settlement for water and supplies.

A fair indication of the amount of traffic in the vicinity of Tristan during the nineteenth century is the number of shipwrecks that occurred there. By this token the traffic appears to have been increasing toward the end of the century, in spite of the gradual disappearance of the whalers. After the wreck of the *Emily* in 1836, which brought Peter Green to the island, twenty years passed before there was another shipwreck. Then in 1856 the three-masted full-rigger *Joseph Somes,* bound for Australia with a cargo of gunpowder, caught fire in the South Atlantic. As the ship was approaching Tristan, the fire was out of control, and Captain Jones, as island tradition names him (other sources have him down as Captain Elmstone), decided to abandon her. The captain and crew got safely on shore and watched in awe as their ship exploded and sank.

Eight years later, in 1864, the American brig *Lark,* famous as a smuggler and privateer of the American Civil War, foundered at Tristan in a hurricane, and then followed in rapid succession the *Bogata* in 1869; the *Sir Ralph Abercrombie* in 1870; the *Beacon Light* in 1871, with the loss of six lives; the *Czarina* and the *Olympia,* both in 1872. The next was the *Mabel Clark* in 1878, and seven more wrecks were to occur before the end of the century, making a total of twenty shipwrecks at or near Tristan. More than half of them took place after 1870, four of them in the 1890's.

Indeed, Tristan da Cunha was in the mainstream of ocean traffic and had an important role to fill in the household of a larger world. Jonathan Lambert's old dream of making Tristan a refreshment station for sailing ships of all nations had come true after all. Besides, the island had taken on a part that Lambert never dreamed of: a rescue station for shipwrecks.

Throughout the nineteenth century, in joy and in tragedy, the Tristan community remained a living part of that distinct and peculiar way of life which flourished under the bulging canvas and in the gloomy forecastles of the sailing ships—the Heritage of the Seven Seas. Born as it was out of the loneliness of the endless ocean, this heritage was a world of its own, strange to the landlubber and mysterious to kings and princes, yet luring and beckoning to the young with a bent for adventure. It was a way of life with its own moods and sentiments to match the shifting tempers of the mighty Main, with its own virtues and vices, its own heroes and villains, its myths and legends and songs, and above all with a singular pride in a life as free as the ocean itself.

Today this heritage has all but vanished from the busy decks and engine rooms of the modern, fast-moving tankers and freighters. But its mood and spirit, and some of its customs and symbols, have lingered in places that, for whatever reason, were bypassed by one of the greatest cultural revolutions in the history of mankind. In a machine age, some of these forgotten places have become living relics of the days of sail.

One such place was Tristan da Cunha. As the mighty clippers and lesser transports vanished from the open seas along with the whalers, nothing came to take their place—not in those waters. Transoceanic traffic was surely growing at a rapid rate but was now taken over by the more efficient steamships and motor vessels, which followed new and more direct routes, independent of the trade winds. Today, none of the main shipping lanes passes within a distance of about twelve hundred miles from Tristan da Cunha.

By 1915 the sailing ships had practically disappeared, and for about a quarter of a century Tristan was in almost complete isolation from the rest of the world, with an occasional steamer stopping by for an hour or so, mostly out of curiosity but in no need of fresh supplies from the Islanders' stock, and only a rare stray sailing ship still gratefully heaving to for moral as well as material refreshment after some sixty to ninety days or more at sea. During this period as many as fifteen months might pass without a sail or a mast being sighted.

Finding itself no longer in the mainstream of traffic and commerce, the Tristan community was thrown upon its own resources in more than just a material sense. Stuck in a "cultural backwater," as people from more "progressive" areas are pleased to call it, cultural impulses from the outside, both technical and aesthetic, became as scarce as driftwood and brandy, and old established customs, standards, and symbols were doubly prized, rigidly adhered to like a bulwark against moral depravation and cultural decay.

Even at the time of the Norwegian expedition in 1938, entering the village of Tristan da Cunha was like stepping several generations back in time, into a forgotten nineteenth century. Here indeed was a living relic of the days of sail. To a visitor from a modern age the village itself, the low stone huts with their thatched roofs, the shaky carts on their solid wooden wheels pulled by torpid oxen under rough yokes, the women with their long skirts fluttering in the wind, the sedate tempo of beasts and people, everything appeared like pictures from the past, almost unreal. To the Islanders they were symbols of their own identity, as real and unchanging as the mighty Goatridge, rising behind the village, and the other familiar landmarks.

Even today, some of the early houses are still standing, taller and bigger than the rest, as enduring evidence of former prosperity. They are built of very large stone blocks neatly fitted together, a fair indication that explosives must have been available to quarry the stone. Their interiors show every evidence of having benefited from the traffic of sailing ships. They are well equipped with wainscots, partitions, and lofts, and some of them have white-scoured floors of solid planks. Well-built cabinets are usually found in the corners, and among the furniture one will frequently see an old sea chest. Almost everything in these houses, from the heavy lumber in walls and floors to the brass hook on the door, bears evidence of having come from a ship, giving the house itself, as it were, a salty atmosphere.

Chief was living in a house like that, as behooved his status and his descendancy from the old salt Peter Green. This is in fact Peter Green's house, which for more than half a century served as the social center of the community. During Mr. Taylor's ministry in the 1850's it had been used as a church and schoolhouse and was then taken over by Peter Green. According to tradition it was built by Charlie Taylor, the mason who was brought ashore from a whaler to die but recovered and married a daughter of Governor Glass. In spite of his illness he must have brought with him to the island not only his skill but also the tools of his trade, for the stone shell of Peter Green's house may well be described as an excellent piece of masonry.

It is again the interiors, however, that give the clearest evidence of the once ever-present blessings of the sailing ships, but also of the dangers of those treacherous waters to any wind-driven vessel. As you step through the door of Peter Green's house, a decoration on the opposite wall, a long board with the letters MABEL CLARK neatly carved into its surface, catches the eye. It is the actual nameboard of the American bark that foundered on the west side of the island in 1878. During the days and weeks following the wreck, as the unfortunate ship gradually disintegrated on the rocks, the Islanders had reaped a rich harvest of salvaged canvas, rope, and hardware, but particularly of precious wood from this newly built ship. Even two of the ship's bells were retrieved, one of which was later mounted on the gable end of the church to serve a double purpose, calling the people to dance as well as to divine service. There are still two or three houses on Tristan today where the owner can point to a door, a cabinet, or a sea chest and say: "It came from the *Mabel Clark*." Chief would tell you that most of the wood in his house, including the solid deck planks in the floor, came from that ship.

Then, of course, there is the house that Captain Andrew Hagan had built for himself. With its tall gables and smooth masonry work of huge soft-stone blocks, it even now looks almost stately in the surroundings, and to this day it is the only house on Tristan furnished with a cellar. This house, too, was built by Charlie Taylor, the mason, and it was later fitted with wood from the *Mabel Clark*. David Hagan, the grandson of Captain Hagan, who now owns and occupies the house, will point with pride to another nameboard from the American bark, similar to the one in Peter Green's house and likewise mounted on the wall in the front room. But he will take particular pleasure in pointing out the mighty yards from the hapless square-rigger, now serving as beams under his loft.

These old houses are not only a source of immense pride to their owners, they serve as significant historical monuments to the whole community, as symbols of a heritage that during the long years of isolation was the Islanders' only source of identity, dignity, and self-respect. It was as though the two nameboards of the *Mabel Clark*, the sail yards under David Hagan's loft, the ship's bell on the church gable, and every sea chest from any named shipwreck were constant reminders of the deeds and virtues of the forefathers, their courage and boatmanship, their generosity and kindness, their compassion for people in distress, and their dignity and pride as free men and women in a community where freedom for all is taken for granted. Perhaps, with time and shifting generations, the deeds and virtues were exaggerated and idealized, even glorified, as tales and symbols gave form and nourishment to an ideal image of what it meant to be a "Trisst'n." And perhaps the image was vague and inarticulate with most. But John Hagan, of Cape Town, who was born and raised on Tristan, certainly knew what strings to play when, on request, he wrote a letter of introduction for members of our expedition:

Dear Frances Repetto,
I take this liberty of addressing you, and hope you will pardon me for doing so. The bearer is one of the Norwegian Scientific Expedition to Tristan, and is anxious to get in touch with the people there. Being strangers, I trust you will assist and do everything in your power to make their stay as pleasant as possible. By doing so,

you will keep up the good reputation of our dear late grandfather
Green, whose good deeds, and kind actions to shipwreck crews regardless of colour, nationality, or creeds, are known through out the
wide world. I am sure you will show the same kind of spirit . . . .

I remain your cousin,

J. H. P. Hagan

So in work as in play, in sorrow as in joy, in their religious belief
with its unshakable faith in divine providence, as well as in their
moral convictions stressing generous dignity and kindness in all their
conduct, the Tristan Islanders, like any human community, drew on
their own time-honored traditions, only more so because, in their isolation from the world, this was their only source of identity.

More than in anything else, this identity and heritage came to expression in their boats and boatwork. For most of the settlers, boating
was an intrinsic part of their lives even before they came to Tristan,
and on the island the boats remained essential to their livelihood.
This is no less true today than it was a hundred years ago. Now as
then, there are fish in the ocean, and the other islands, Inaccessible
and Nightingale, separated from the main island by twenty-five miles
of open sea, are important hunting grounds. As both fish and birds
have always been major elements in the Islanders' food supply, the
boat has become a necessary instrument of survival. Besides, there are
pastures and orchards and even wild berries on the other side of the
main island, which can be reached over land only by a stiff walk of
several hours over the mountain or, at low tide in smooth weather, by
running the bluffs between breakers along the beaches. Most of the Islanders are excellent walkers, and carrying a hind quarter of beef on
his back does not seem to slow a man down perceptibly, even if he has
to climb up a three-thousand-foot cliff and down again on the other
side. But the Islanders prefer to go by boat, especially when there are
loads of meat or apples to bring home. Even more important is the
fact that since the island has no port for seagoing craft, the boats are
the only link with the outside world—that is, if the outside world
comes close enough to give them a chance. It is hardly an accident,
therefore, that the one area in which these land-bound seafarers created something uniquely their own was in the building and handling

of boats; nor is it surprising to find that boatmanship is not only their most outstanding skill but also the one most highly prized among themselves.

During the days of sail, the Islanders obtained their boats from ships and shipwrecks. These rather heavy and rigid wooden craft, however, were easily damaged in the surf, as Jonathan Lambert and William Glass had experienced. As a result the Islanders sometimes had difficulty keeping an adequate supply of seaworthy boats. Repairing a punctured hull with bits of skin from the sea elephant or the seal was a trick they probably learned from the whalers, and it was said that Peter Green once had a dilapidated lifeboat completely covered with sealskin.

It was probably in the 1890's that the Islanders started building their own boats out of canvas stretched over a slender and flexible framework of wood. The innovation seems to have originated with an Italian sailor, Gaetano Lavarello, a regular old tar who had run away from his home town of Genoa at the age of ten, had gone through several shipwrecks, and finally ended up on Tristan by the wreck of the *Italia* in 1892. Determined that this would be his last shipwreck, he and his shipmate, Andrea Repetto, decided to settle down on the island, and each married a Tristan girl.

The first mention of the Tristan-made canvas boats is found in a report from Captain H. V. Elliot, Commander of H.M.S. *Beagle,* who visited the island in November 1901. And Lieutenant H. L. Watts-Jones, Commander of H.M.S. *Thrush,* describes them with admiration in his report of 1903. Initially, the boats probably did not differ much in shape and appearance from the type of "whaleboat" used in the naval service. Little by little, however, adaptations were made until the prototype had gone through so many significant changes that we may well talk about the Tristan long-boat as a distinct boat type of its own. Because of its slender bow and slightly fuller stern, its high free-board of the quarter, but especially because of its light weight and flexible structure, it has proven itself an excellent craft, particularly suited for passing through that critical belt of surf separating the beach from the calmer sea beyond.

To the Tristan Islanders, however, the boat is much more than a tool of transportation or even an instrument of survival. Each boat is built and owned jointly by a select group of men, just large enough to

Tristan da Cunha.

The Settlement in 1938.

Little Beach before the eruption.

Nightingale Island.

Meeting the Islanders, December 7, 1937. In the stern are Fred Swain (at the tiller), Chief Willie Repetto (cap in hand), and Bob Glass.

Augustus Earle's drawing of William Glass standing in front of his house, 1824.

Bob Glass and his wife, Charlotte, out for a Sunday stroll, 1938.

David Hagan's house, built for his grandfather about 1850 by the American whaler and stonemason Charlie Taylor.

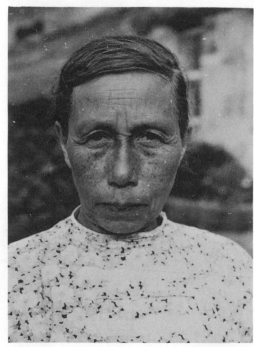

Frances Repetto, 1938.

Chief Willie Repetto, 1938.

104

Kitchen in one of the poorer houses, 1938.

Building a longboat, 1965.

The *Canton* (right) challenging the *Pincher* to a race.

Landing the longboats at Nightingale.

Thatching.

Left, the new volcano and lava field. To the right, behind the village, is a scar from the big landslide.

Exiled, 1962.

Left, Tristan Islanders waiting for the bus in Fawley, 1962. Johnny Repetto is second from right.

Adaptation to modern civilization in England, 1962.

The Settlement in 1965.

At a Tristan wedding, 1965.

111

A modern kitchen in one of the newer houses, 1965.

At the washing stone, 1965.

The harbor, completed in 1968.

Longboat under sail.

form a full crew, that is, six or seven in each of the longboats and usually four in the smaller dinghies, which are used for fishing and for shorter trips around the beaches. But each of the co-owners does not hesitate to refer to the boat as "my boat." There is a strong sense of identity with the boat and, although the Islanders seldom boast about their own boatmanship, their faces light up in pride and joy when they tell about their boats, how "smart" and seaworthy they are, their speed, their beauty, and their ease of handling through the surf. The praise for good performance always goes to the boat. Their own incredible skill as boatmen is taken for granted.

As is often the case with people whose lives are tied up with boats and boating, each boat is regarded as having an identity of its own, its own prestige level, and even a personality. The longboats, and some of the dinghies, have names, which are often painted on the bow or on the "stern chease," as the Islanders call the sheets, a small poop deck that serves as the helmsman's seat. The names have usually been picked from ships that have touched at the island, particularly from those that have had some special importance to the Islanders, and it is obvious from the names of some of the longboats that as late as the turn of the century, New England whalers were still among the most important visitors—such as the *Canton,* the *Morning Star,* and the *Daisy,* all of New Bedford. The *Morning Star* was, in fact, the last square-rigged American whaler to visit Tristan; she made her final call on November 22, 1913. Just about that time a new Tristan longboat was being built and was named after her. The mighty windjammers have long since disappeared from the high seas. But for many years their memory was kept alive on Tristan, and the name of one of them, the *Canton,* is still cutting the wind and plowing the sea on the keel of a smart Tristan longboat.

A new and more patriotic trend in naming the boats was started by the *British Trader,* the boat that Bob Glass built for himself and his sons and named after the British exhibition ship which was scheduled to call at Tristan on her itinerary around the world in 1922 but never showed up. The Tristan Islanders have always considered themselves British and are very proud of it. When H.M.S. *Carlisle* made a couple of visits to Tristan in the 1930's, bringing mail and much needed stores, Henry Green and the other owners of the *Daisy* decided to re-name their boat in honor of the proud warship. In the Tristan vernacular it came out as the *Carline*. The trend did not really catch on, however, until the Second World War, when a detachment of the Royal Navy was stationed on the island and a small militia of Tristan Islanders was formed and put in training. These events and the awareness of Britain being at war apparently stirred the Islanders into giving expression to their strong British loyalties, and there could be no better way of doing it than through the established identity of their longboats, which are so much a part of themselves. The *British Trader* and the *Carline* had set the example, and from then on to this day the Tristan longboats have carried such proud names as *British Lion, British Flag*, and after the visit in 1957 of the Royal Yacht with His Royal Highness Prince Philip on board, *Britannia*, promptly shortened to *Tanny*. Also, they proudly fly the Union Jack from the top of the gaff boom when under sail, and one boat has the flag painted on her stern chease.

The identity of a longboat may remain unchanged over generations, through shifting crews, as shares are handed down from father to son, and through several complete rebuildings of the boat, each of which would make it longer and perhaps smarter. Even a complete replacement of a boat did not seem to disturb the sense of continuity in the boat's identity as long as the crew remained the same. One time, the *Morning Star* was lost at sea and replaced by an entirely new boat. A resident missionary provided much of the wood, and he suggested naming it *Lorna*—"he probably had a girl by that name," was the Islanders' joking explanation. But it is still known as the boat that Andrew Swain had built some ten years earlier with his sons and the Repetto lads, partly to provide for the widowed mother of the Repettos. Johnny Repetto, who was just a little boy when the boat was lost, and not yet a member of the crew, may now be heard to say, "It was *my* boat that was lost that time." It is as though crew and boat were a mystic entity, forever the same, even though its physical manifestations, its size and shape and all its component parts, human as well as material, have been replaced.

The best example of this continuity in the identity of a Tristan longboat is perhaps the *British Flag*, or the *Longboat* as she is more commonly called. This boat has a history that points back to Gaetano Lavarello himself. Gaetano was a boatman as passionate as they come. He had a share in the *Wild Rose* with his brother-in-law, John Glass, and John's other two brothers-in-law, and with his skill and experience Gaetano became the regular coxswain of that boat. But she was little more than a dinghy, only about sixteen to eighteen feet long, only four oars. Gaetano's shipmate, Andrea Repetto, had joined *his* brother-in-law, Henry Green, in the *Daisy,* and they had built their boat twenty-two feet long, for five oars, "the largest yet made," says Mrs. Barrow. This was a challenge to the old tar Gaetano, and as soon as his two oldest boys were big enough to pull an oar, he took them in as members of the crew and built the *Wild Rose* twenty-four feet long, with six oars. To the rest of the Islanders it must have been a magnificent sight to behold. They immediately dubbed her *Longboat,* and that name stuck to her forever after. Of course, it was a name to Gaetano's liking, and he did his best to live up to it. As his other sons grew up, they were given shares in the boat until they had an oversized crew of nine, six of them Lavarellos. And as the other boats were built to the measures of the *Longboat,* Gaetano and his crew had their boat rebuilt, too, and always a couple of feet longer than the rest. This tradition was kept up faithfully and proudly by his sons long after Gaetano had retired from boating and even after his death, at the age of eighty-five, in 1952. Today the *Longboat* has reached an overall length of thirty feet.

In the meantime the crew had split up and a new boat was built. It was on this occasion that the "real" name of the *Longboat* was changed from *Wild Rose* to *British Flag.* But in everybody's mind and heart she was still the *Longboat.* John-the-Baptist Lavarello, Gaetano's eldest son, went into the other boat because his recognized skill as a coxswain was needed there, but his heart remained in the *Longboat.* Twenty years later I met him in England—it was during the evacuation of Tristan after the volcanic eruption. John was an old man then, gentle, shy, and modest, and with a kindness of heart which was unusual even for Tristan and had earned him the nickname "Brother." Talking to strangers was not his strongest point, and getting information from him was like pulling teeth. But when the conversation turned to the *Longboat,* his face lit up, and his tongue loosened. Although he was vague on other dates and events during his long life, he knew the history of the *Longboat* through all her refittings, rebuildings, and changes of crews. By that time probably not a slab or timber from the original boat remained, and the only one left of the original crew was his brother Robert, too old now even to go in the boat. But to John it was still the same old boat: "For forty-six years, that one has been going!" Of course, the *Canton* and the *Daisy* had gone longer than that—but it would have been very unkind to remind Johnny of it.

This is something more than fondness for a boat. It is complete identity with it. One can hardly wonder, therefore, that to these people the boat has become the most important instrument of genuine self-expression. Whenever a Tristan Islander is engaged in any kind of boating work—whether he is building a boat, taking it through the surf, or sailing it on the high seas, whether he is the coxswain himself or just a member of the crew in charge of the jib—he is an artist at work, striving for the kind of perfection that even the best of artists see only in their dreams. Here he is tested and proven for what he is worth, not only in his own eyes but also in the eyes of his fellows.

On this island, therefore, where time is no concern and most things move in a leisurely tempo, every boating activity is a contest of skills, where each boat's crew is leveled against the other, and every man is matched against his teammates. Although the boats are never launched for the sake of pleasure alone or just for the purpose of having a race, whenever two or more longboats go together, there is implicit if not explicit competition, and nothing makes a Tristan Islander more happy and proud than to have his crew win a race or to surf-ride his longboat high and dry to a perfect landing.

This, obviously, is one of the reasons a trip to Nightingale is such an important social event, quite apart from its economic significance. For here the whole community is involved. On these trips, whether for the collection of eggs, guano, or birds, several longboats go together, and the event turns into a regular regatta with the whole community as onlookers.

Most important of all these excursions is the "fatting trip" in March or April, when usually all the longboats go "for fat," that is, for cooking oil extracted from the rich blubber of the young petrels. This is one trip on which women go, too, as each crew member is allowed one helper and usually takes his wife or sweetheart along—which, of course, adds to the holiday spirit that permeates every boat trip on Tristan but especially this one. On the day of departure the whole community converges on the beach. Everybody, whether he is going on the trip or not, is excitedly busy helping to bring down the "gear," including everything from oars and sails to blankets, pots and pans, and a little extra for "lunch." Soon the women appear on the beach in smashing new dresses, often made especially for the occasion. There are farewell kisses and good wishes as one longboat is launched after the other and is paddled out beyond the breakers to wait for the rest. And when the last boat has been "shove' off" and has joined the others, the men stand up in their boats and give three cheers before they row off to "catch the breeze."

From that moment the contest is on, but secretly at first. By mutual consent there are safety rules to observe, and one of them is that the boats stay together over the stretch of open sea between the islands, even if it means that some of the boats will have to lower their sails to wait for a slower sailer. But no one wants to be the laggard and probably be reminded of it for weeks and months to come, so from the start, without ever letting on to what everybody knows anyway, each crew is watching the others carefully, trying to maneuver their boat into an advantageous position. And as soon as the sails are hoisted, the boats are given full cloth, for it is better to take the lead and have to wait for others than to reduce sail.

No boat-lover from the outside world who has had the good fortune to sail in a Tristan longboat on one of these trips can ever forget the deep, serene excitement of dashing across the water at a lively speed with the foaming wake splashing along the sides of the slender hull. Gently the ground swell cradles the boat on its mighty rollers, letting it down in its troughs so deep that the other boats, even the one next over—mast, sail, and all—are lost from view for a few long seconds before they again emerge, slowly, seemingly from the abyss of the ocean itself, as the speeding craft is softly raised by the next roller. Sailing on the high seas in an open boat gives a strange feeling of oneness with the wind and the waves, with the sea itself, with the albatross and giant fulmar soaring overhead or riding the waves, undisturbed by the rushing boats passing by. And even the Tristan Islanders, in their own quiet way, fully share this serene feeling and quickening excitement every time they sail a longboat across the sea, although most of them have surely made this voyage a hundred times before.

I once went along on one of these trips. The sky was clear, and the wind was brisk and good, straining the canvas of jib and mainsail, making the sea rush by at the very gunnel of the raking craft. Our helmsman, a seasoned old salt, was intently watching his projected course to take advantage of every gust of wind, careful to hit every wave just right, keeping the boat as high to the wind as she would run. An occasional glance went to the other longboats around us, in particular to the one dead astern, who was closing in and trying in vain to fetch up on our windward side. One of our crewmen had settled down in the bilge of the boat, with nothing but the thin canvas between him and the gurgling wake, his arm resting on the gunwale, where the splashing foam licked his elbow while the salty spray was swishing into his face. He let his eyes roam over the endless ocean as if to take in the whole expanse to the fading horizon and beyond. Then he muttered, "Ah, this is life!"

But the excitement doubles when the boats return home. If it is a "day," which means that there is a favorable wind and sea for the trip, the people at home will know that the boats may be expected. Young men are sent out to the Bluff to watch for the returning fleet, and as soon as the news is spread that the boats have been sighted, everything else is dropped, and the whole community is again geared to this one overriding event: The boats are coming! Young boys run to the pastures to round up bullocks and donkeys, women get busy preparing their tea to bring down to the beach for the homecomers, and people gather in groups at various vantage points along the bank to watch the race. For as soon as the boats have Anchorstock Point on their starboard beam, there is no more waiting for laggards. The last five-mile lap along the shore of the island is a free-for-all race, and as the boats dash along in close formation, teasing challenges are shouted from one boat to another:

"Come on, there! Grab this rope, I'll give you a tow!"

"I can beat you swimmin'!"

"Me and you 'as a race for Martha!"

Excited shouts of delight and triumph are heard from a boat where the coxswain has been lucky and clever enough to catch a cresting wave for a surf-ride that may literally bring his boat up to the velocity of the wind, making the sails hang limp from the mast for a short thrilling moment while the rushing foam from the breaking crest is frothing around the boat's buoyant stern, and the slender bow cleaves the water into spray. The Islanders call it a "sleigh ride" in vague reminiscence of the wild "Nantucket sleigh rides" of the whale catchers being towed by a harpooned whale. Such a "sleigh ride" may make the difference between winning or loosing the race. Willing bets are being made in the boats as well as on shore, and as soon as the boats are "up," making a turn into the wind while the sails are lowered, there is the same confounded scene as the whole community again converges on the beach and the longboats, one after the other, are being surfed to a landing amid shouts and ribbing and a happy welcome home to everybody, especially the winning crew.

So, every time the longboats return from Nightingale, it is a time to rejoice. And to give an extra festive stamp to the occasion, there is always something special to refresh the "inner man." The tender meat of the young shearwater and yellow-nosed albatross is considered a special treat on Tristan, not only because of its tart flavor of wild game but particularly because it is a seasonal break in an otherwise rather monotonous diet. It is inconceivable that anyone would ever return from a trip to Nightingale in the bird season, be it a "guano trip" or a "fatting trip," without bringing home a quantity of "buds," not only for himself and his family but also for parents and grandparents, sisters, brothers, and cousins, and soon the delicious aroma of bird meat fried in its own fat will rise from every house and envelope the whole village.

But there is another reason to rejoice, never mentioned, although the Tristan Islanders are well aware of it. They know that on every one of these boat trips they are pitched against a more formidable adversary than the teasing members of another crew, and in that contest their own lives are at stake. At the time of our visit in 1938 old people could still remember that sorrowful day in November 1885 when a new lifeboat vanished without a trace with fifteen men on board. The weather around Tristan is indeed treacherous and often unpredictable. A fair wind may suddenly turn into a violent gale from the opposite quarter, whipping the sea into a churning maelstrom as wind and waves meet head-on, often accompanied by torrential rains that would envelop any hapless boat who might be out there in blinding darkness.

It has happened more than once that the Tristan longboats have been caught in such a sudden switch in weather and "nighted," that is, forced to spend the night on the water. As the gale broke loose, they had to "run for the lee," although in weather like that, even the seven-thousand-foot-high land mass of Tristan da Cunha does not offer much of a lee. There are usable beaches on the southeast side of the island, but as landing would be impossible because of wind, swell, and blinding rain, the longboats would tie up to the kelp, a long and sturdy seaweed that grows in a belt around the island some distance from the shore. There they would spend the night awaiting the abatement of the storm.

On one occasion two of the boats did not make it to the kelp. One of them had her mainsail ripped in one flash from top to bottom, and the other one lost her rudder. Both were blown off to sea, and separated from each other, they were tossed around on the ocean for five days and nights without food or water before, by the incredible seamanship of their crews, they found their way back to the island.

There have been other accidents from time to time. Andrew Swain, the village fiddler, was a hunchback because his boat, the *Phoenix,* had overturned during an emergency landing and had struck him in the back. The place where it happened is still known as Phoenix Beach, although both the *Phoenix* and Andrew Swain are gone now, and a huge rockslide has completely covered the beach. The *Morning Star,* which was Andrew Swain's next boat after the *Phoenix* was smashed to pieces on the beach by a heavy surf, was on her way to Nightingale with the other longboats when suddenly her canvas shell was ripped open, presumably by an attacking swordfish. Men and gear were saved by the other longboats, but the boat was lost.

Like all good seamen, the Tristan Islanders have the deepest respect for the sea, an attitude that comes naturally with intimate knowledge. They are cautious but fearless, and if human lives are at stake, they will readily risk their own, as was demonstrated on many occasions when ships were wrecked on their shores. But the foolhardy, the daredevils, and the braggarts reap no honor or praise among them.

One day in April 1963, shortly after an advance party of Islanders had landed to prepare the island for resettlement after the volcanic eruption, a ship appeared off the Settlement. A couple of days of stormy weather had whipped the sea into a fury, and to launch a boat seemed impossible. But a bullhorn from the ship announced that there was mail on board, and a dinghy was pushed into the seething surf. It was indeed too rough. The first wave twisted the boat askew and out of control, the next threatened to swamp it, and the two oarsmen dived for their lives and swam ashore. The abandoned dinghy, though half filled with water, stayed on its keel and was bobbing on the cresting waves just outside the surf, the oars still dangling in the rowlocks. Suddenly a young Islander stripped to his underpants, swam out to the boat, and climbed aboard. Seeing another wave about to hit the boat broadside, threatening to overturn it, he dived into the breaker but soon again reappeared and grabbed hold of the flat stern of the dinghy to hoist himself aboard a second time. The men were anxiously watching from the beach, and Chief, with more anger than worry in his voice, boomed at the top of his lungs: "Leave 'er be, you fool!"

This time the young man succeeded in getting the boat safely out into smoother waters, and as soon as he had bailed out, he proceeded to row single-handedly out to the ship, where he was rewarded with a dry set of clothes and a meal before he returned to the shore with the mail.

The incident happened before the eyes of reporters, who had accompanied the advance party of Islanders to cover the resettlement for their British and American newspapers and magazines, and the story was flashed over the world as an example of the heroic courage and seamanship of the Tristan Islanders. Among the Islanders, however, the young daredevil's deed was regarded as nothing but foolhardy, and he himself was considered a nut, foolish for having put his life in jeopardy for an abandoned dinghy and a bag of mail.

Courage and seamanship are taken for granted on Tristan when the situation calls for it. But the sea is not a thing to be played with for the sake of the thrill alone or to show off one's prowess. Miscalculations and accidents do occur, with an occasional broken bone and a few narrow escapes. It is, however, a record very much to the credit of the Tristan Islanders that in the whole history of the community there are only two incidents where lives have been lost in a boat. The first one was the tragic and mysterious disappearance of the lifeboat in 1885, and the second occurred in April 1968, when a motorboat belonging to the South African fishing company now operating on Tristan was lost and one of the Islanders on board was drowned. Not one life has ever been lost in a Tristan-built longboat.

7 *Patterns of Poverty*

The most obvious economic effect of the increasing isolation of the Tristan community was that it was thrown upon its own local resources to a greater degree than ever before. And, from the hand of Nature, Tristan is not at all well endowed with a variety of things that Western man had learned to take for granted. For the Tristan Islanders, the first decade of this century was the initial and most difficult period of a transition by which the barter economy of the earlier days was gradually replaced by a subsistence economy based on hunting, gathering, and such farming and fishing as weather and primitive tools and methods would permit. By the 1930's, when our Norwegian expedition visited the island, the transition was as complete as the local resources would allow.

The problem of clothing was typical of the situation. The Islanders had sheep, and the wool was carded, spun on homemade spinning wheels, and knitted into various garments, of which we had noted the characteristic Tristan stockings with stripes, or "marks," of brightly colored wool just below the ribbings. Homemade sweaters similarly decorated were also in evidence. But the Islanders had neither the means nor the technique to dye the wool; the all-important "marks" had to be made from imported yarn. Weaving was unknown. Two looms brought to the island by an enterprising missionary were standing idle in a storeroom because no one knew how to use them. We had also noted the cowhide moccasins, which were worn by all, big or small, as a substitute for shoes. For the rest, the Islanders still depended on barter with passing ships, and at times the supplies were very short indeed.

Another serious problem during this period of extreme isolation, as was evident from the appearance of the boats and of some of the houses, was an inadequate supply of wood and lumber as well as nails, canvas, paint, rope, and all sorts of tools. The only endemic kind of tree that grows on the island is a stunted, wind-twisted evergreen, which is well suited for firewood as it will burn in a green state, but so hard and gnarled that it is not very useful for other purposes. Small groves of willow and apple trees have been planted in sheltered places here and there around the island, and the springy branches of the willow, especially, do good service as ribs in the boats. Otherwise, lumber for building purposes had to come from outside, and that Tristan had seen better days in this respect was quite evident from a closer look at the houses, especially their interiors.

For most of their woodwork during this period, the Islanders depended on flotsam washed ashore around the island, and "goin' 'round the beaches" to look for driftwood was part of their routine. Excursions were sometimes made to Inaccessible, twenty-five miles over open sea, exclusively for this purpose, as this most westerly island in the group seemed to catch a good deal of the debris drifting in with the prevailing currents. As total shipwrecks were now a thing of the past, not much was to be found, surely, and what little there was had often suffered in quality from floating in the sea for God knows how long. If it was not rotten or waterlogged, it was often perforated in every direction by a wood-carving mussel. But every piece found, large or small, was tried on the spot by hitting it against a rock and, if it gave a "healthy" sound, carefully taken charge of. Some Islanders had even trained their dogs to swim out and retrieve a piece of wood floating in the sea. Everything found was put to use in one way or another. A crate or packing box was a most wonderful thing for anyone to get his hands on; for if it could not be used directly as a table or stool or cupboard, the wood it was made of was probably better than most wood available.

These "patterns of poverty," as we may well call them, were firmly established at the beginning of this century. When the Rev. J. G. Barrow arrived in 1906 to serve the congregation for three years, he and his wife and a maid were put up in Betty Cotton's house while she moved in with a relative. The house, however, was badly in need of repairs, although it was one of the older houses, which had obviously benefited from the traffic of sailing ships in the past:

Our cases are being used to re-floor the bedrooms and passage, which had a large hole in it . . . . The walls of the bedrooms are covered with illustrated papers, which here take the place of wall-paper. . . . The doors have the most primitive and varied fastenings, and one a bit of rope in the place of a handle. Many panes in the windows are cracked, and one or two have departed altogether.

Building a church under these conditions was not an easy task, as related by Mrs. Rose Annie Rogers, the wife of the minister serving at that time. This was in 1922:

The building of the church was really wonderful for Tristan da Cunha. It was a true monument of faith overcoming mountains of difficulty . . . . There had been discussions as to "ways and means," for getting anything done at Tristan seemed nearly hopeless. Foundations must be dug, but again tools were insufficient. Spades, shovels, picks, barrows, crow-bars were hopelessly few. Most had to be lookers-on while others worked. Then we had neither woodwork, glass, paint, nails, nor roofing material. But we started as a venture of faith indeed . . . .

Somehow, after a year, the church was completed and put to use after proper dedication ceremonies, although the interior decorations were not finished until several years later.

Keeping the boats in proper shape and seaworthy was a most serious problem with the shortage of wood and other materials, and building a "new" boat usually meant rebuilding an old one, with new ribs, or "timbers," furnished by the local willow trees. One boat was being renewed during our stay on the island. It was taken apart bit by bit, with great caution being taken not to break or damage any reusable part. Every salvageable piece, every tack or nail, was carefully saved for use in the "new" boat. While the building was going on, one man did nothing for a couple of days but straighten out old rusty nails with a hammer on a moderately flat rock. Even the keel, already a spliced piece, was dismantled into its several parts and then put together again with one or two pieces replaced with fresh wood that happened to be available and, I might add, badly needed. New canvas was out of the question; the old one had to be patched up with pieces from an old mailbag and reused. And as paint was short, the inside of the canvas was given a coat of homemade penguin oil.

The decline in the sailing traffic had a particularly devastating effect on the island's food supply. Imported foods, such as rice, oatmeal, flour, and bread, sugar, molasses, coffee, and tea, became increasingly scarce and were soon regarded as "luxuries." The Islanders still had their domestic resources to fall back upon. However, these were limited, especially since every attempt to grow wheat and other grains on the island had failed, partly because of the strong winds, and partly because of rats and mice, which had invaded the island from shipwrecks and were thriving gloriously on eggs and young birds on the mountain slopes. And the few riches that were to be found on the island were gradually depleted under the more intensive exploitation that followed.

Perhaps the most damaging depletion took place, ironically, as a result of a reduced exploitation. In the great exodus that followed the lifeboat disaster of 1885, many of the widows took their families and left for South Africa or for the whaling communities in New England, where most of them had relatives from earlier emigrations. Some of the young men of the island also left to seek their fortune elsewhere. Most of the people who left had cattle and sheep in the common pastures that surround the village and extend to the Bluff some five miles to the west, an estimated twelve hundred acres of grassland. Already the combined flocks were probably more than sufficient to meet domestic needs, and they were increasing as the sale to passing ships declined below the natural growth of the herds, although a small trade in cattle had been established with Saint Helena. Whether because they expected possibly to return some day or because they did not know what to do with their sheep and cattle, the emigrants usually left their stock, as well as their houses and other property, in the care of some relative, who would get the milk from the cows and the wool from the sheep but apparently did not feel free to kill for meat. A few of those who left did indeed return and repossessed their property. But a large part of the herd was left to increase unchecked, and soon the stock exceeded by far the capacity of the pastures.

By 1905 there were about seven hundred head of cattle and some eight hundred sheep on the island, all grazing in the same pasture. Milk and butter were plentiful in those days. It is said that Betty Cotton, who had returned from South Africa to take care of her aging mother when the rest of the Cottons left, and who was an aunt to practically everybody on the island, once had the care and use of thirty milch cows and used to send buckets of butter as presents to her relatives in South Africa.

Obviously the pastures were overtaxed and were soon depleted. Cattle had been lost occasionally before, but during the winter of 1906 there was a near disaster. The preceding summer had been exceptionally dry, the grass was short, and that winter almost four hundred head of cattle, more than half the herd, died from starvation. In spite of increasing utilization of the much smaller pastures at Stony Beach and Sandy Point, the loss was never regained. From year to year new losses occurred, and during the winter of 1937 another 60 head of cattle perished, reducing the herd on the northwestern plain to 154 head. By that time the population had increased to 185.

Now that even meat and butter were removed from their everyday fare, the Islanders turned with greater vigor to the seabirds, and for a short period the mountain slopes of the main island were of the greatest importance to the subsistence of the community. These slopes used to be densely populated with seabirds, particularly the three species of albatross known to the Islanders as the gony, the molly, and the peeyoo, which were sought for their eggs as well as for their young ones. The biggest of them, the gony, was probably gone before the turn of the century. But in the 1920's the molly, or yellow-nosed albatross, was still plentiful, even on the mountain slopes directly above the Settlement, and thousands of eggs and young ones were taken annually and eaten by the Islanders. As all albatrosses have a very slow rate of regeneration, only one young per couple each year, it was not long before even the molly and the peeyoo were threatened with extinction. Today they are mainly found on the more inaccessible eastern slopes of the mountain and on the precipitous cliff face where even the agile Islanders cannot get to them. Soon Inaccessible Island suffered a similar fate and was almost completely cleaned out.

Nightingale, the smallest island in the group, was still teeming with seabirds: penguin, molly, and particularly the wailing shearwater, or petrel, as the Islanders call it. During the breeding season, huge numbers of this bird converge upon the tiny island from the whole of the Atlantic Ocean, digging their burrows wherever they can find soft and

fairly dry ground. Even today, after some forty years of exploitation by
the Islanders, latecomers are unable to find a vacant spot to dig a nest
and have to drop their eggs on the bare ground. Although there is no
fit drinking water as the existing brooks and trickles are saturated
with guano, and no landing beach—the boats have to be pulled up on
a flat rock some three feet above the water—it now became the only
remaining hunting ground of importance. The number of birds and
eggs brought home from Nightingale, however, is limited by the loading capacity of the boats. Besides, the seasons are short.

Fish had always been plentiful in the surrounding sea but, with the
simplest tools and fishing methods, not always easy to catch as fishing
luck is no more predictable on Tristan than anywhere else. Besides,
even in the summer the beaches of Tristan may be unworkable for
days on end because of swell and surf, and during the winter there
may be weeks when it is impossible to shove off a boat. During such
periods, many families on Tristan had nothing but potatoes to eat,
and if the potato crop was cut down, as happened occasionally, by
windstorms or blight, there was starvation in many a house.

Sometimes you didn't have a thing to eat—wait till the boats come
ashore from fishing. Well, we use' to play about 'n' kick about on the
grass and never forget we was hungry. So, when the boats come ashore,
my mother would soon get a kettle o' fish cookin', and off we go and
eat that and be quite thankful.

These were the words of old Mary Swain, Chief's sister, reminiscing
about her childhood. And conditions were not any better when the
Norwegian expedition visited Tristan in 1938. That year the potato
crop was a failure. Violent hailstorms had cut down the young plants,
and no sooner had they recovered when the "potato grub" took over, a
large moth larva, which was abundantly present everywhere and in
certain years would descend on the potatoes, eating literally every leaf
off the plants. One Islander told me that for his family of eight, two
hundred bushels of potatoes were not too much for the winter, "but
this year," he added with a smile, "I'll have about eighty." The others
were not any better off. To make things worse, the previous winter
had been bad for cattle, resulting in the loss of almost a third of the
already reduced herds, and during the following winter, storms kept

the boats on shore most of the time. An Islander described the situation in a letter to Dr. Henriksen, the medical man of the Norwegian expedition: "July and August and September were rather bad weather for fish. In July we got seven days fishing and in August we got eight and in September we got eleven days, so you see we had very bad for fish."

These were what even the Tristan Islanders would call "hard times," when many families would go for days with hardly any food at all, and as Dr. Henriksen remarks, "the Tristanites have probably experienced many equally bad years in the course of time."

There was, of course, always the tenacious hope that the next day would bring a ship. It used to be said, with some exaggeration perhaps, that the only thing that could excite the otherwise calm and dignified Tristan Islanders was the sight of a ship on the horizon. They had developed a fabulous eyesight for just that sort of thing.

One day during the stay of the Norwegian expedition, we noticed from our campsite a great commotion up in the village. People were running and shouting, dogs were barking furiously, and young boys were climbing the gable ends of their houses and were standing up on top of the chimneys, looking out to sea. Scanning the horizon with our binoculars we could see nothing but the unbroken line of the endless ocean. With their naked eyes the Islanders had discovered the top of a mast. By the time we had laid eyes on that infinitesimal jag on the line between ocean and sky, they had determined what kind of ship it was, and estimated its course and speed!

Whenever a ship was sighted, everything was dropped on the spot. The cry of "Sail-oh!" rang over the village, and women and children ran from house to house with the news. A couple of young lads would jump on the nearest donkeys; riding bareback, they would whip their drowsy mounts into a gallop to alert anybody who might be working in the Patches unaware of the approaching ship. As likely as not, those in the fields had also seen the ship and were on their hurried way home. Men would come from all directions, grab their trade bags, which were always kept in readiness, and scramble to the beach to clear the boats for launching, while women with fluttering skirts would try to catch a honking goose or a cackling hen to be offered for sale on the ship. The commotion would soon converge on the beach, where twelve to fifteen men would crowd into each boat rather than try to get all the boats in the water, and there was no waiting for late-comers. As soon as the first boat was ready, it was given a running launch through the foaming surf, and the men put their full weight to the oars. If the wind was right, they would hoist a sail, laying their course for the best possible chance of intercepting the ship, even though it might take them several miles out to sea.

As often as not, the whole effort was in vain. One fine sunny day during our stay on the island, a ship came in fairly close. She was approaching from the southwest, where the view from the village is blocked by the Hillpiece and Hottentot Point, and no one had seen the ship until she rounded the point and was almost upon us. With amazing swiftness a couple of boats were launched. I scrambled into one of them as it was already moving into the surf and was hauled aboard by helping hands, just missing a breaker. Before I could settle down on a thwart, we were through the surf and speeding toward the ship, the men pulling at the heavy oars with all their might. We got close enough to the ship to make out the last part of the name on her bow: . . . *Maru,* a Japanese of the "Maru Line." There was no doubt that our boats were observed from the ship, but she did not stop, and the men turned around, downhearted and disappointed. These gentle men never swear. In deep silence they rowed slowly back to the beach, and one of them muttered: "What a shame! And such a fine day!"

These were times of scarcity and want in every respect. It was obviously during this period of isolation and poverty that they developed the incredible frugality that is still a prominent trait among them and, as I have been told, a puzzle to the nutrition experts, since the Islanders seemed to survive quite successfully on a diet which, in regard to calories at least, was far below what the medical sciences considered a minimum to support life. In those days there was no village dump on Tristan because nothing was ever thrown away. Everything was taken care of and put aside for future use, from odd pieces of wrapping paper and string and ribbon to every scrap of wood or metal and every nut or bolt or crooked nail. And there was no need to worry that the storing space or hiding place would ever become cluttered. "Looking ahead and saving for a rainy day" was one of the favorite slogans of the Islanders. Thrift and providence became virtues of necessity reduced to habit.

This was the time when the self-image of the Tristan Islanders reached its lowest ebb and they developed that deep respect, to the point of deference, for the "Outside World," which seems so peculiarly incongruous with the spirit of anarchical independence. No matter how isolated a human community is—geographically or socially—it always stands in some relationship to a larger cultural system or, as Robert Redfield used to call it, a "greater tradition." When this larger world is associated with affluence, prestige, and power (as it often is), it takes on the appearance of a "superculture," which may be imposed upon the little community from outside but usually remains more or less aloof from the local tradition.

The Tristan Islanders had always looked upon themselves as the most loyal subjects of the British Crown, represented in their own experience mainly by the Admiralty and the British men-of-war that occasionally visited the island. Up through the whole of the nineteenth century, this was their "superculture." As isolation increased, however, a new generation of Tristan Islanders grew up with vaguer ideas about authority and outside power. By the time of the 1930's, the whole of the "Outside World" had become a single, undifferentiated superculture, mysterious and remote, which made sporadic and intermittent appearances in the form of passing ships, resident missionaries, and visiting dignitaries. In this world, the "Admiralty," the "Colonial Office," and the "S.P.G." had merged in the Islanders' minds with everything else from the outside into a single, vaguely conceived superpower vested with awesome authority emanating like rays of mana from the Crown, and every stranger visiting the island was somehow believed to be a part of it and was addressed with a humble "Sir," whether he be an Admiral of the Royal Navy or a coalheaver from a passing freighter. In relation to this mysterious Outside World, they themselves were "only low and poor people," and this most humble spirit was as much a part of the dignity of being a "Trisst'n" as the cheerful generosity, the kindness, and the frugality instilled in them from childhood.

Awareness of their own increasing poverty, reinforced by patronizing efforts on the part of outsiders to bring charity to the island, was undoubtedly at the root of this attitude of humility. But an important contributing factor may have been the attitude of prestigious outsiders to the mixed racial origin of the Islanders. Although the great majority of the Tristan Islanders are quite Caucasian in appearance and many of them show definite Nordic traits, their mixed racial background has resulted in a great diversity in the degree of skin pigmentation and other racial traits among them. There is no doubt that, in the past, official visitors to Tristan had regarded the Islanders as "Colored." Racial appearance is seldom mentioned in official reports, but in one instance, Lieutenant Watts-Jones, who visited the island as Commander of H.M.S. *Thrush* in 1903, states:

The majority of the islanders, though rather sunburnt and weather beaten, are practically "white." Some, however, show, by more or less distinct negroid characteristics of feature or colour, their descent from Cape or St. Helena women. This is chiefly to be found in [certain] families, especially among the older members, [one member] being but little removed from a Kaffir in appearance.

We also recall Captain G. Stanley Bosanquet's statement after his visit to the island in 1875, that most of the Islanders were "of plastic materials," being "half-castes," and therefore, by implication, weak in character and unfit to govern themselves. It was, of course, inevitable that this condescending attitude on the part of official visitors, however "friendly" they otherwise might have been, should be noticed by the Islanders.

In the early days of the settlement, the Islanders might not have accepted such a condescending view of themselves as valid. We have seen that racial prejudices possibly played a part in the split between sailors and whalers, which ended in the removal of the all-White American whalers from the island and the confirmation of the proud independence of the "half-caste" sailors. But now, with an increasing number of Whites with prestige and authority visiting the community, the Islanders seemed ready to accept the notion that they were "low and poor people," not only because of their poverty, but because they were "black," which was indeed part of their self-image at the time of my first visit to the island in 1938.

This submissive attitude of the Tristan Islanders to the superculture of the Outside World was indeed an important power base for a couple of rather imperious ministers who served the island during the 1930's. Plain fear was undoubtedly part of it, for the devoted ministers would not shy away from invoking the authority of the British Government, issuing threats of severe punishments for insubordination, including deportation and even total evacuation of the island by Government decree. We have already met one of them, the Reverend Mr. Partridge, who had himself appointed His Majesty's Commissioner for Tristan da Cunha, and who set up a pillory on the island, in which a woman was placed for not keeping her house clean. His successor did not inherit the title of H.M. Commissioner. This, however, did not prevent him from presenting himself to the Islanders as a delegated representative of the British Government, and in many ways he ruled the island with a harder hand than his predecessor. Among his many enterprises was a "Five-Year Plan" to colonize Inaccessible, which turned out a complete failure. Another pet project was a storehouse, for which he confiscated all stores acquired collectively by the community, either as gifts or by barter, and from which he issued weekly rations "to keep the island from starvation," besides a few extra gifts to anyone who might support him by turning an informer. Quite candidly he once remarked that "the way to rule Tristan is to have your storehouse full and keep the key."

There were indeed a couple of open protests against the minister and some of his policies. The storehouse, in particular, was the source of much annoyance, partly because it interfered with the Islanders' social life by depriving them of the freedom of an occasional extravagance, but mainly, it seems, because it was felt to represent a patronizing guardianship. The protests, however, never got beyond the point where a man would refuse to accept his rations for a while, as if in a stubborn effort to prove the truth of Frances Repetto's often repeated statements that the storehouse could not support forty-two families and that "every man on Tristan da Cunha can make his own living." Due to the general attitude of minding one's own business, the protesters never got more than a moral support from the others. Besides, to these generous and peace-loving people, a conflict—no matter for what cause—was in itself a painful mental strain which they could never long endure. In the end, in face-to-face confrontation, the minister was usually given a humble "Yes, Father," partly out of powerless fear, partly out of genuine respect for his high and holy office.

Yet even in this situation, the Tristan Islanders kept their dignity and poise; and the spirit of anarchical independence, though often frustrated, remained as strong as ever among them. Any interference in their private lives was deeply resented. Powerless as they were of open resistance and fearful of the consequences of such action, the Tristan Islanders have developed the art of passive resistance to a high degree of refinement. In most situations they would go along with the orders and decrees of their imperious rulers as far as they thought necessary to avoid open conflict, but would ignore them whenever they thought they could get away with it, a situation that the ministers on their part found highly frustrating. Generally, they looked upon the antics of some of their ministers with considerable amusement. They have always been deeply religious people and devout members of the Church of England, with a somewhat "high church" emphasis on ceremony and ritual coupled with an unshakable faith in God's benevolent providence. They were genuinely thankful to have a man of the cloth among them to perform the services, to minister the sacraments, and to teach the children a little reading and writing. But as far as the other matters were concerned, such as parliaments and councils, even five-year plans and storehouses, they seemed to regard them merely as playthings for the minister, at worst as instruments of self-aggrandizement. And when they went along with them (as far as they did), it was, no doubt, in part because, out of kindness, they did not want to spoil the fun for the man. For the most part, in their usual cheerful generosity, they let the minister have his way. After all, in two or three years he would be replaced, a new minister would come with new ideas and new pet projects, and there was not a thing they could do about it.

There was one partial escape from the mental and spiritual dominance of the imperious minister, and this became an important form of passive resistance. One could quit the Anglican Church and join the little Roman Catholic congregation that had sprung up on the island in response to the situation. The three Smith sisters, the Irish women who came to Tristan in 1908 as wives of the newcomers, were Roman Catholics, and those of their children who were born at the Cape had also been baptized and brought up in the Catholic faith. No issue was made of it at the time—without renouncing their faith, the newcomers simply joined in the services and functions of the existing Anglican congregation, and no one thought a thing of it. Twenty-four years later, however, in 1932, some of the original Catholics separated themselves from the Anglican Church and organized their own congregation, induced to do so by a Roman Catholic priest who visited Tristan in H.M.S. *Carlisle*.

By this time, only Agnes, the youngest of the three Smith sisters, remained on the island. Annie, the oldest, had returned to the Cape with her husband, Jim Hagan; and Lizzie, Bob Glass's wife, had died. Joe Glass, Aggie's husband, died in 1915, but a few years later she married Blind William Rogers, with whom she had a family of seven children. Agnes Rogers now became the organizer and leader of the newly organized Roman Catholic congregation, a service for which she eventually received a medal from the Pope.

At first, the congregation consisted of only two families. But it soon grew in size until, around 1940, it reached a peak of some fifty members—about one fourth of the population. There can be little doubt that to most of them, joining the Roman Catholic congregation was a welcome escape from the imperious Anglican minister. As soon as he left, the Catholic congregation started to dwindle. It is still in existence and remained under Agnes Rogers' devoted guidance until, at the age of eighty-two, she passed away on Easter Eve, 1970. But the congregation is again reduced to a small number, mostly of "Granny Aggie's" own children and grandchildren, and there is no doubt that it has played out its role in the community.

If the culture of poverty is a "culture of resignation," as some social scientists claim, the Tristan Islanders are certainly an exception. Even in material things, the Islanders did their best to live up to standards that were set at a time when life was brighter and easier. Any change in the monotonous diet of potatoes and fish was, of course, appreciated, and when opportunity presented itself there was usually no stinting. During the egg season in September and October and the apple and bird season in March, the Islanders delighted in their temporary abundance of perishable food and made the best of it while it lasted—in two or three weeks it would be gone. In the egg season, many families ate by choice nothing but eggs, and large quantities of them. These were "fat times" and happy days.

As is often the case with people who live from hand to mouth the greater part of the year but with seasonal plenty, the Tristan Islanders enjoyed being generous, even extravagant, when occasion called for it. Meat was a luxury that only few could afford once in a while. But on special occasions it was indispensable. Comparatively luxurious dinners were given at weddings and on the more important birthdays, such as the twenty-first or the fiftieth, or when some special piece of work had been finished, like building a house or thatching a roof. At Christmas time, the Islanders would eat mutton or beef and new potatoes every day for a week or two, an enormous extravagance considering their meager diet most of the year.

In their everyday life, the Islanders refused to let poverty interfere with their standards of dignity in grooming and conduct. The styles, of course, were those of the turn of the century, and especially the women were quite particular about the propriety of their clothing—ankle-length skirts and lace-trimmed blouses with high necks and long sleeves—even if it meant that a dress of a more modern cut, obtained with great difficulty from the outside, had to be made over or entirely discarded. Although their work clothes might be patched and sometimes torn, we were surprised to find that for Sunday and special occasions nearly all the Islanders were able to produce well-kept suits for the men, brightly colored dresses in the prescribed style for the women, and imported shoes.

Similarly, in their houses, the great majority of the Islanders refused to accept the dirt floor and the bare stone walls as the normal state of affairs. Obviously, it took years to collect enough wood to furnish a house according to the standards set by some of the older dwellings, and many a newly married couple had to be satisfied to move into an unfinished home at first, with old newspapers to cover the walls, and then try to equip the house gradually as bits and pieces of wood might drift ashore. Under the circumstances, it was actually surprising to find that so many of the houses, by the owners' yearlong concern, industry, and perseverance, had indeed been equipped with complete floors, ceilings, wainscots, and partitions. And most of the houses were kept neat and clean. If there was a wooden floor, it was scrubbed every day. Shelves and windowsills were decorated, in Victorian middle-class style, with paper nicely cut in tongues and lace patterns draped over the edges, although it might have to be torn from an illustrated magazine or cut from a piece of old wrapping paper. And even if a tottering partition of box boards and driftwood was swaying like a superannuated board fence and the floor was nothing but hard-trampled dirt, there were always fresh flowers on the table and on the mantelpiece.

8   *The Will to Survive*

Many outsiders have had little understanding and less sympathy for the Tristan Islanders' love of a way of life that offered freedom but little in the way of material comfort. In fact, to most visitors, especially to those who were wearing a white collar, either backward or forward, the island of Tristan da Cunha has always appeared barren, void of any promise of "development," and therefore utterly uninhabitable, suggesting that it would be an act of humanitarian mercy if the Islanders were removed to a more prosperous locality, where they could become useful parts of the greater society. The view seems to be that unless "progress" is made, particularly in material things, life is empty and survival questionable.

These are the ideas and values of the Economic Man, probably the most rational, but hardly the most humane, image of Man created by any culture. Once an ideal, or perhaps just an idea, this image of Man, always in pursuit of "happiness" in terms of wealth, profit, and economic advancement, has in our Western civilization been brought to real life and has, in some highly admired instances, reached near perfection. Whether he "really" exists in the flesh, however, is beside the point; the image of the Economic Man is always with us, and his ethos has permeated our lives to the extent that, where "progress" and "economic advancement" are concerned, it is taken for granted that other values must yield.

Although the Tristan Islanders are Western in origin, they have from the outset deviated in many ways from the ethos of the Economic Man. And they were living under conditions that to most outsiders, and particularly to the authorities, appeared as a constant state of economic distress. Throughout the history of the community they have been exposed to persuasions, pleaded with, and threatened in attempts to make them give up their insular life. Time and again they have received offers, sometimes quite generous offers, from the British government that would enable them to leave the island and settle somewhere else. But each time they have declined, politely but firmly, and with increasing unanimity and determination.

The question of complete evacuation of the island of Tristan da Cunha had been raised already by the Reverend William Taylor, the first resident clergyman on the island. In 1855 he thought it would be "a happy day when this little lonely spot is once more left to those who probably always were, and now, in its present barren condition, certainly are, its only fit inhabitants—the wild birds of the ocean." He was warmly supported in his view by the Bishop of Cape Town, Dr. Gray, who visited the island in March 1856 in H.M.S. *Frolic,* dispatched in response to Mr. Taylor's alarming reports of economic distress. The bishop "found that the people were almost unanimous in desiring to quit the island," a bit of information obviously obtained from Mr. Taylor, whose endeavors to persuade the Islanders to leave were highly praised by his superior: "Nothing could be more satisfactory than Mr. Taylor's whole work. I hope that in a few days a large ship will be sent to bring them all away. I have offered him employment." No one, apparently, cared to ask the Islanders' opinion.

The following year—action having been delayed by the threat of a Kaffir war—H.M.S. *Geyser* (one of the first paddle steamships to visit Tristan) was indeed sent to the island prepared to evacuate the whole population. It was on this occasion that four families, comprising thirty-five persons, left the island for Riversdale, South Africa, reducing the population to about half its former size but still leaving behind a hard core of sailors, like Alexander Cotton and Peter Green and their families, who were determined to stay in order to preserve their anarchical independence.

No less pessimistic than his predecessor in his view of Tristan's economic prospects was the next resident clergyman, the Reverend E. H. Dodgson, a brother of Charles L. Dodgson who later, under the pen name Lewis Carroll, became world famous as the author of *Alice in Wonderland.* Mr. Dodgson arrived at Tristan in March 1881 and remained until December 1884, when he returned to England because of ill health. Again the authorities in London were told that Tristan da Cunha was unfit for human habitation, and that the only permanent solution to the problem of survival was the complete removal of the entire population. Like Mr. Taylor before him, Dodgson argued that the decline in the sailing traffic had removed the only economic base for a viable community on Tristan. He emphasized that there was an imminent danger of overpopulation and added that since the invasion of rats from a wrecked ship, which occurred during his stay on the island, the situation had reached catastrophic dimensions. In addition, the zealous parson had a few not very flattering things to say about the people of Tristan, apparently to demonstrate that they were deteriorating both physically and mentally and were unfit to survive on their own.

Mr. Dodgson's report to the Society for the Propagation of the Gospel was obviously not intended for the Islanders' perusal. The Society, however, put the report in print, and, by an ironic fluke of fate, H.M.S. *Opal,* the very ship that took Mr. Dodgson off the island, brought a bag of mail containing a copy of the parson's report. Peter Green was quick to reply, and his anger brought his earthy wit to a pitch. On the same day that the *Opal* left Tristan, he started a lengthy letter to the Admiralty. It was finished at least three weeks later:

Tristan d'Acunha, December 29, 1884

H.M.S. "Opal," Captain Brooke, R.N., arrived here and landed a life-boat, mast, sails, oars, anchor, chain, boat's gear, cordage, paints, flags (2 sets), one package, etc., likewise the International Commercial Code of Signals. The signals were directed to the Rev. E. H. Dodgson. As he left Tristan in H.M.S. "Opal," I shall take care of the said signals.

. . . but the Rev. E. H. Dodgson is going to break up this settlement. He has made up the account of our cattle, sheep, donkeys, fowls, etc. . . .

Can the Rev. E. H. Dodgson take our people away without the consent of Government, or the Admiralty to have something to say about it? . . .

We received a bag of mails, papers, books, etc. In the said bag was a publication about us sinners at Tristan, by the Rev. E. H. Dodgson. The said publication said that we are going to the devil, . . . I would rather remain here as a British subject than to go and leave Tristan with the reputation of a Satanic subject. He says there are a few exceptions to this rule; but who is the exception?

We are going to make a new link in the Darwinian chain be-

tween the man and ape. I consider that me or mine claim no more
of the monkey than Mr. Dodgson . . . but if this theory about the
apes is true, we may say eat, drink, and be merry, for to-morrow we
will be apes.

Peter Green pointed out that there was still a considerable traffic of
sailing ships around Tristan, with several ships calling at the Settlement for refreshments. He also drew attention to the fact that the days
of shipwrecks were by no means past:

Since 1870 we have had five shipwrecks on Tristan, two at Inaccessible, and one at Gough's Island, all a total loss. We received several ships' crews from ships abandoned at sea, so if I may suggest, I
should think it necessary to have a good boat's crew at Tristan, not
supernumeraries, like myself and some more of my confreres, but
men.

It was less than a year after this that the event occurred which has
had such a decisive impact on the Tristan community in so many
ways, the lifeboat disaster of November 28, 1885. The incident is still
shrouded in mystery. Contemporary reports are contradictory. Old
Sam Swain, who was eighty years old when I met him in 1938, remembered the day well. He was a grown man at the time of the disaster,
just past twenty-eight, but had avoided the tragic fate of the others by
being away on a hunting trip. "I'll never forget it," he said, "the
women wailing and crying, no work being done, everybody just waiting, hoping, and praying." He recalled that it was a warm, sunny day
with moderate sea, and he saw no possibility of the boat having been
swamped or wrecked unless it had been run down by the ship. He was
convinced, as were most of the Islanders, that the men had been
shanghaied.

Old Sam's memory, particularly concerning the weather on that fateful day, is confirmed by Peter Green's contemporary report to the Admiralty, which seems to be a fairly accurate account of what was observed from the Settlement:

Tristan d'Acunha, November 28, 1885

On this day a ship came to Tristan. She could not fetch up to the
settlement. When she got in shore she was about three miles from

us to the eastward. Our life-boat went off to her with sheep, potatoes, geese, etc. When the boat got near the ship she hove aback;
the boat was alongside the ship some time, then the ship stood out
from the land. We could see our life-boat towing astern of the ship.
She stood out about four miles. When she came in again she got so
far to the eastward that she was lost to our view. We were watching
for the boat all that night, but no boat made her appearance. Next
morning two parties went round the island by land. They could see
nothing of the boat. The wind was moderate, the sea was moderate,
and a good new life-boat which we received from H.M.S. "Opal,"
Captain Brooke, R.N., as a present from the Board of Trade, one
thing is certain, she never reached the island. She had all our best
boatmen in her, rather too many, 15 in number, 10 of them married. If the boat and crew is lost it will make Tristan an island of
widows. . . . But I am still in hopes that the boat's crew is still on
board the ship. I have lost boats alongside of a ship myself, but the
captain of the ship gave us a little boat to go ashore. I had three
sons and three grandsons, three brothers-in-law, and one son-in-law
in the life-boat. Our minister, the Rev. E. H. Dodgson, left us in
H.M.S. "Opal;" he was going to break up this settlement. If the
boat's crew is lost it will be broke up with a vengeance. I shall have
to send this letter as it is so far, for we see a ship standing in for the
settlement.

I remain, etc.
[signed] Peter W. Green

Essentially the same story was told by other Islanders to the Captain
of the *City of Sparta,* a Glasgow full-rigger that touched at the island a
month later. Much more dramatic, however, and differing from the Islanders' accounts on practically every detail, including the date of the
accident, was a report said to have come from the captain of the ship
involved. It was published in an Australian newspaper:

AN EXCITING INCIDENT AT SEA

Captain William Thomas, of the iron barque "West Riding," which
arrived yesterday from Bristol, gives the following report of an extraordinary incident that occurred during the voyage. On November 27th,
at 4 a.m., saw the island of Tristan d'Acunha, S.E. by S. true, there
being at the time strong squalls with a heavy sea, though the weather

was clear. The settlement on the island bore S.W. distant nine miles, and a large fire was observed on shore in the vicinity. Soon afterwards a sailing-boat was sighted steering for the vessel, being then distant about six miles from the settlement. Captain Thomas immediately took in sail, and had his ship brought to the wind on the port tack. At 7.40 a.m., when the boat was on the barque's port quarter, distant one and a half miles, its sailing mast suddenly disappeared. The boat was afterwards seen, apparently making towards the vessel with paddles. Thinking some accident had happened, Captain Thomas made sail, and stood towards the supposed spot where the boat was first seen; but although the ship cruised in the vicinity for two hours, with the captain and mate in the mizen-top with telescopes, she failed to discover any vestige of it or its occupants. As the wind was from S.W. and the vessel was rolling dreadfully, broadside on to the sea, having a heavy cargo on board, and there being a north-easterly current and heavy sea, it was found impossible to communicate with the island, Captain Thomas not deeming it prudent to launch a boat, at 10 a.m., believing that nothing more could be done to assist anyone, Captain Thomas kept the vessel away on her course. Seeing that the inhabitants were so eager to communicate, during the prevalence of strong winds and a heavy sea, in a small boat, with a vessel nine or ten miles direct to leeward of the settlement, it is conjectured that some shipwrecked people have probably got ashore on the island.

It was this report that fell into the hands of Mr. Dodgson. With its dramatic account of a large fire on shore, which was immediately interpreted as having been a distress signal to attract the attention of ships, and with its report of strong winds and heavy sea, having the boat vanish without a trace before the very eyes of the captain and crew of the ship, it alarmed him greatly. After his return to England Mr. Dodgson had never given up his hope of persuading the authorities to remove the Islanders from this barren rock in the sea. Now he concluded, in a letter to the Admiralty of March 13, 1886, that "the people must be already in great straits, for under ordinary circumstances they would have regarded it as an act of madness to attempt to board a vessel nine miles to leeward in such dangerous weather." With renewed energy and persuasion he implored the authorities to send a relief ship to investigate the situation, offering, in spite of his continued ill health, his own services for another tour of duty to Tristan.

However, he remained, now more than ever, convinced that there was no solution to the problem of Tristan da Cunha save total evacuation. This he expressed most forcefully in a letter of May 18, 1886, to Mr. John Bramston, Under-Secretary of State for the Colonies:

. . . they will be in danger of absolute starvation unless some arrangements are entered upon for removing the people with their cattle en masse to some other part of the world where they may be able to make a living. Owing to the terrible plague of rats with which the whole island is now infested, and also owing to the loss by drowning of nearly all the able-bodied men, their life at Tristan *is no longer possible.*

Mr. Dodgson's deep concern, his zeal and energy, were very convincing, and he came very close to persuading the authorities that Tristan da Cunha should be depopulated. The Admiralty offered the service of one of Her Majesty's ships for the purpose, and the evacuation was all but decided. A delay was caused mainly by the failure to find a suitable place for resettlement. The Cape Government had been approached by telegram, asking if they could provide accommodations and take charge; but the reply was negative, stating that "during the present depression . . . the number of persons out of employment in the Colony is so great that the chances of fresh arrivals obtaining a livelihood by work is hopeless."

In the meantime, Captain Day H. Bosanquet, of H.M.S. *Thalia,* scheduled to sail from England for Australia via the Cape of Good Hope, was directed to call at Tristan da Cunha with relief stores. Mr. Dodgson was granted a passage in the ship, which arrived at Tristan in August 1886.

Captain Bosanquet's report was a solace to all authorities concerned. On the ship's arrival at the Cape, the Governor of the Cape Colony telegraphed the Secretary of State for the Colonies: ". . . inhabitants well, no sign of distress." And Rear Admiral Sir Walter Hunt-Grubbe, Commander-in-Chief of the Cape Naval Station, forwarded the captain's full report to the Admiralty with the curt remark: "Captain Bosanquet's Report is very interesting, and is perfectly reassuring as regards the distress from which the inhabitants were supposed to be suffering. Tea and sugar appears to be the only thing wanted . . . ."

Captain Bosanquet had in fact reported that he "found the condition of the islanders by no means so bad as had been reported in England, but bad enough to give rise to uneasiness for their future." Mr. Dodgson, however, was not easily persuaded that everything was all right. He now went to work on the Islanders themselves to convince them that it would be impossible for them to stay on Tristan any longer, and that they would be better off at the Cape. Less than two weeks after he had been landed on Tristan, before Captain Bosanquet had even submitted his report, the zealous parson informed Captain Musgrave, of H.M.S. *Rapid,* who made a chance visit to the island, ". . . that the whole of the inhabitants were very desirous of being removed from the island, even at the sacrifice of their cattle . . . if they could be given a small grant, viz., 5 *l.* each for a start."

Recognizing the source of the information, Rear Admiral Hunt-Grubbe forwarded Captain Musgrave's report to the Admiralty,

. . . observing that the Rev. Mr. Dodgson appears to have, in a few days, imbued the islanders with the idea that they would like to leave if given a 5 *l.* gratuity; and I cannot believe that all would go, leaving the quantity of stock described to be on the island . . . .

They are certainly, in many respects, better off than the Scotch crofters, and incomparably so as regards the poor in the west of Ireland.

The Rear Admiral was right in his skepticism in regard to Mr. Dodgson's report to Captain Musgrave. The Tristan community still contained a substantial hard core who staunchly resisted any attempts on the part of their would-be benefactors to save them from their own chosen way of life. Peter Green was one of them. However, as the Rear Admiral and Peter Green agreed, the influence of Mr. Dodgson, like that of Mr. Taylor before him, was considerable and may well have increased the unrest in the community that naturally followed the upsetting event of the lifeboat incident. Although only ten persons accompanied Dodgson when he left Tristan the second time in 1889, during the years following the lifeboat disaster, as we have seen, a large number of Islanders pulled up stakes on their own to try their luck elsewhere, mostly in South Africa. By the loss of the lifeboat and the emigration that followed, the population of Tristan da Cunha was reduced from 108 in 1884 to 63 in 1891. Many of the emigrants later returned to Tristan, some of them only to leave a second time. In fact, it took the community more than twenty years to settle down to fairly stable conditions again.

Following Captain Bosanquet's reassuring report, the idea of total evacuation of Tristan da Cunha was put to rest for the time being. Instead, it was decided that there would be an annual visit by one of Her Majesty's ships from the Naval Station at the Cape, which was not much more than a perpetuation of something that had been going on fairly regularly since 1873, when H.M.S. *Challenger* touched at the island on her famous voyage of oceanographic exploration. After the visit by H.M.S. *Thrush* in 1898, however, this traffic was interrupted by the Boer War, and when the war was over, there was a new Commander-in-Chief at the Cape of Good Hope Station who wished to discontinue the service. Consequently, in 1903, when the *Thrush* was sent out again, this time under the command of Lieutenant H. L. Watts-Jones, the main purpose of the mission was to take up with the Islanders once again the question of total evacuation.

By this time Peter Green had passed away, and it is evident from Lieutenant Watts-Jones's report that, with this staunch champion of anarchical independence no longer among them, the Islanders' resistance to their would-be benefactors had weakened. The report—as interpreted by the authorities in London—was, in fact, so encouraging with regard to the prospect of total evacuation that the Secretary of State again approached the Governor of the Cape Colony on the matter of resettlement.

This time the Cape Government was ready to cooperate. The outcome was that when H.M.S. *Odin* proceeded on an official visit to Tristan da Cunha in January 1904 she had on board Mr. William Hammond Tooke, Under-Secretary for Agriculture of the Cape Colony, who was to act as the Commissioner of the Cape Government and present to the Islanders a definite offer for their resettlement in South Africa. On his arrival at Tristan, a meeting of all family heads was called, and the proposal was presented to them. The details of the plan were as follows:

Should all the inhabitants wish to leave the Island, the Cape and Home Governments would provide them with a free passage, purchase their live stock from them and settle them within 100 miles of Cape Town, allowing them about two acres of land on rent, and also advance them money on loan to start their homes, etc.

They were also told that they would be near the seacoast, where they would be able to start fisheries to supply the people of Cape Town, and that they could not rely on a yearly visit by a man-of-war in the future should they choose to remain on Tristan.

The Islanders were given twenty-four hours to think it over. The following day there was another meeting. However, as only three out of eleven families elected to go, the offer was withdrawn as previously agreed. In his extensive and thoughtful report, which included a survey of the history of the community, its economic resources, and its social organization, Mr. Hammond Tooke expressed the opinion that

. . . if we regard solely their own interests the decision that they took was a wise one. Not only is there much to be said in favour of the life they are now leading, but there is room for grave doubt, I will not say whether they would improve their condition by coming to the Colony, but whether they would be able to maintain themselves in the ease and comfort they now enjoy.

He also argued strongly against the abandonment of the island from the standpoint of British interests and seems, in fact, to have been the first one to do so, contending that the cost of sending a man-of-war periodically to look after the Islanders' welfare was negligible compared to the real and potential advantages of keeping a community of British subjects on the island. He argued that abandoning the island would be to invite some other power to take possession.

On receipt of the Commissioner's report, the Governor of the Cape informed the Secretary of State that "it is not the intention of the [Cape] Government to take any further action in inducing the islanders to remove."

This, however, was not the end of the evacuation issue. Within a couple of years it was to be raised again, not by the Islanders but, as always, by outsiders with a concern for the real or imagined plight of this lonely community in the sea. And they were supported by official authorities eager to get permanently rid of what appeared to be a perennial problem of exaggerated distress reports and needless but costly relief expeditions. What triggered the oversensitive alarm system this time were some private letters from Tristan describing conditions on the island.

The year 1906 was indeed a time of grave concern for the Islanders.

It was the year of the great livestock crisis, when almost four hundred head of cattle were lost because of the depletion of the pastures. The lack of rain (indeed a rare occurrence on Tristan) had also resulted in a small crop of potatoes, and by midwinter they were running low. Besides, since the annual visit of warships had been discontinued, the decrease in sailing traffic was beginning to be severely felt. Mr. Barrow had arrived in the S.S. *Surrey* on April 8, a day so rough at the Settlement that the landing of his baggage and stores (including a harmonium for the church) had to be made further east, at a place still known on the island as Down-where-the-Minister-land'-his-things. After that there was no communication with the outside until July, when the Danish bark *Hans* and the British bark *Loch Katrine* touched at the island, although several full-rigged ships and one bark had been sighted on days too rough to launch a boat. It was a situation that certainly gave cause for concern on the part of the Islanders, and it is hardly to be expected that it should not be mentioned and described in letters that the Islanders sent to their friends and pen pals in England.

One such letter was brought to the attention of the Colonial Office by a Mr. B. R. T. Balfour, of Drogheda, who writes on October 26, 1906:

I have recently received a letter from Mr. Repetto, written the 22nd July, in which he says that the islanders this year are "more in need of provisions than in the past year, as the wind blights their plantations." His letter expresses great pleasure at the arrival of the Rev. Mr. Barrow, and at the improvement in the children since he arrived on the Island . . . .

From another source I hear that Mr. Barrow's own supplies are falling short. I hope, therefore, that some means will be found of sending a mail to Tristan this season.

The "other source" of Mr. Balfour's information may have been a Miss M. H. Moginie, apparently a relative of Mr. Barrow, who presented three similar letters to the Colonial Office in October 1906. One of the letters was from Mr. Barrow himself, who was still hoping that a warship might be sent out to Tristan in response to a request previously made by him:

. . . We are ordering things from the Army and Navy Stores, and also from Cape Town in order to make sure of having them by the man-of-war. If no man-of-war comes we shall be up a tree indeed, for we should have no supplies. Those we brought will only last to about the end of January. As it is, we do not have bread every day for want of sufficient flour.

Another letter, from an Islander, describes the situation in a letter style that is still typical on the island. It is dated July 16, 1906:

Dear Friend,

I thank you very much for the print that you send me by the "Surrey" Mrs. Barrow gave it to me and I were so please with it, and to think that you are such a true friend; we were all so please to have a clergyman come to stay with us and to teach the dear little children; we had plenty to do when he came—the house to make ready, but happy to say he is nicely settled now by himself, his wife, and maid, all in a house by themselves; we will do all we can to make them comfortable—not one but all. He arrived on the 8th of April, and we have only had one ship since he came. I do hope that some more will come soon, as we had a very poor crop of potatoes this year, and now we are having plenty of rain and are losing some cattle, but I am happy to tell you that all on the island are well and in the best of health, hoping you are the same, so I will now say good-bye and believe me to remain,

Your truly friend,
Andrew Swain

And Frances Repetto, who was then becoming a prominent person in the community, writes:

. . . We are so anxious for a ship to come so that we may get some comforts; it seems very hard to be on an Island like this, with no necessary things. I pray God we may soon have a vessel call. We are having some great misfortunes this year; we have had a great loss of cattle and heavy floods, which wash away the roads and give plenty of work for the men.

These letters were hardly intended as distress signals. All they express is the hope that a ship would call soon so that the Islanders could barter some provisions, something that under the circumstances was naturally foremost in their minds. It might be added that floods washing away the roads are almost an annual affair on Tristan, especially where the roads cross the deep gulches, like Hottentot Gulch and Big Sandy Gulch, which are dry during the summer. And the damage is easily repaired. This, of course, was unknown to Miss Moginie, who probably visualized something disastrous. Moreover, Mr. Barrow was clearly referring to his own private supplies, not to the general provisions of the community as understood by Miss Moginie, who obviously was unfamiliar with the conditions of a subsistence economy and concluded that the Islanders were on the brink of general starvation. On the whole, she interpreted the letters to say that there was "distress among the Islanders" and implored the Colonial Office to do something for their relief, "as they cannot be left without provisions."

The Colonial Office accepted Miss Moginie's interpretation and reacted with amazing swiftness. After having found from the Admiralty that none of His Majesty's ships was available for mail and cargo service to Tristan, the Secretary of State telegraphed the Governor of the Cape: "Letters received from Tristan da Cunha indicate probability of failure of supplies next January. I am endeavoring to ascertain best means of arranging for relief . . . . Propose to take opportunity to urge strongly on inhabitants advisability of removal from Tristan da Cunha at an early date . . . ."

Within a month the three-masted schooner *Greyhound* was chartered and scheduled to sail from Cape Town by the end of January 1907, carrying £150 worth of relief stores for Tristan, and with orders to convey, at Government expense, any passengers who might wish to leave Tristan da Cunha for the Cape. With the ship was also to go a letter of instructions from the Colonial Office to Mr. Barrow concerning the total evacuation of the island.

The "relief ship" came as a surprise to everybody on Tristan, including the writers of the letters that had brought it about. Mrs. Barrow, in her published diary, *Three Years in Tristan da Cunha*, gives a lively description of the arrival of the ship:

Monday, March 4, 1907.—It is difficult to sit down and collect one's thoughts to write. Saturday was a most eventful day. Early in the

morning a ship was seen on the horizon. It was coming from the east.
This is the first time a ship has come from that direction since we have
been here. The excitement was great. She was seen to be tacking for
the island. The excitement increased. We felt something was in store
for us, possibly a mail. In due time Graham [i.e., Mr. Barrow] and
the islanders started forth; there was a breeze and the sea was decidedly rough. As we were returning from seeing them off the women
said they could see a flag on the mast-head, which meant that somebody special was on board. We at once decided it must be the Bishop,
and hurried home and buckled to, for there was plenty to be done.
We saw the boats reach the ship, and to our surprise in about fifteen
minutes they were off again. We then felt sure the ship was going to
stay and was landing some one. When the boats were getting fairly
near the shore we went down. A tremendously heavy shower came on
which drove us to seek shelter in a diminutive cave. The sea had become rougher. We watched the boats working their way in from the
east; they were being tossed and pitched about like corks and the
spray was dashing all over them. Our interest grew as they neared the
shore. How we scanned them to see who was on board. As they drew
near us we could see there was no bishop, but the people soon recognized two Tristanites, Willie Swain, son of Susan Swain, and Charlie
Green, son of Lucy Green, who had been away for two or three years.
They both will be welcome, as they are needed at home to work for
their widowed mothers. . . .

It was soon revealed that this was a "relief expedition." Everybody
was puzzled since no one on the island had requested one. But the surprise turned to amusement when it was found that the stores provided
by the Government, besides large amounts of flour and other food-
stuff, which, of course, was highly appreciated, contained such items as
several boxes of crockery, including a dozen earthenware teapots and
six dozen cups and saucers—"a most useful gift," concluded Mrs. Barrow, but hardly the kind of thing one would expect to find among the
"relief stores" to a people in "distress," whose total removal from the
island was supposed to be imminent.

The letter of instructions from the Colonial Office to Mr. Barrow
read in part:

So long as the inhabitants remain on the island, there will always be
a risk of a recurrence of scarcity of provisions. His Majesty's Govern-

ment cannot, however, undertake to arrange for the despatch of relief whenever a scarcity of provisions is apprehended, and they would accordingly invite you to use your best endeavours to induce the inhabitants to consider seriously the alternative of removal to the Cape Colony. You should impress on them that His Majesty's ships are no longer available for the purpose of visiting the island, and that the expenses attendant on the charter of vessels for the purpose appear to be out of all proportions to the size of the community or to any object to be attained by their presence on Tristan da Cunha. A free passage to South Africa is offered to any of the inhabitants for whom there may be accommodation on the vessel which takes this letter, and you will no doubt do your best to induce as many persons as possible to avail themselves of the facilities offered.

The removal of the whole community would presumably require a vessel having more accommodation than the relief ship now sent, and would involve more time for preparation than can be given on this occasion. The relief ship will, however, remain long enough at the island for you to discuss the question with the inhabitants, and it is hoped that you will do so and subsequently report to this Department whether, if His Majesty's Government decide to remove the remaining inhabitants in a body and provide transport for the purpose, there would be any insuperable objection on their part to the project. His Majesty's Government will await your report before coming to a final decision in the matter.

There was indeed an "insuperable objection" to the project: an emphatic and unanimous *No* from the Islanders, this time not only from the family heads but from everybody, men and women, down to the age of fifteen: "We'd rather starve here than at the Cape!"

In his report to the Colonial Office, Mr. Barrow stated, as Mr. Hammond Tooke had done before, that he thought the Islanders' decision was a wise one. In this, Mr. Barrow differed strongly from the views of his two predecessors, Taylor and Dodgson:

With all their privations they are much better off than many a working-man we have known at home. It should be borne in mind that there is always a need for provisions here, *i.e.*, of such things as flour, rice, tea, coffee, and sugar. Scarcely a month passes by without witnessing a lack of these in one or other of the families. This is privation—a privation to be much regretted—but it does not cause distress.

From 8th April, 1906, to this day [March 5, 1907], the period of our residence here, the islanders have been without these provisions for months together. Worse still, owing to blight by wind the potato crop had been so poor that for three months (September, October, and November) of 1906 some families had no potatoes of their own, though they got a few from more fortunate neighbours. Also, through those months and the two previous ones there was scarcely any milk— for weeks none at all. This was due to the death of cattle . . . .

This scarcity of potatoes and of milk intensified the privation which is always present, but did not cause distress, and there has been no danger of starvation.

After this the Islanders were left alone, so much so that there was hardly any communication with the island at all for many years. Occasional sailing ships continued to call for water and provisions, but they were few and far between. The last American whaler touched at the island in November 1913. Although there was a temporary increase in steamship traffic, as if the habit of following the familiar sailing lanes was hard to break, there were no scheduled calls. Mr. Barrow, who returned to England in 1909, had offered his services for another tour of duty on Tristan but had to give up the idea for lack of a passage to the island, although he traveled first to South America and then to South Africa in search of one. It took more than eight months before the Islanders learned that World War I had come to an end: the news was brought in July 1919 by H.M.S. *Yarmouth,* the first British man-of-war to visit the island in fifteen years. In February 1921 the Reverend Henry Martyn Rogers responded to an appeal for a missionary to go to Tristan but had to wait for more than a year before he finally obtained a passage to the island by having the Japanese liner S.S. *Tacoma Maru* diverted about three hundred miles from her course between the Cape and Rio de Janeiro. This was the first Japanese ship ever to visit Tristan, and when she arrived April 1, 1922, she was the first ship of any kind to call at the island in almost sixteen months.

The question of evacuation came up again in connection with the visit by H.M.S. *Dublin* in March 1923. The visit had been arranged in response to an appeal made by Mr. Douglas M. Gane, a London solicitor who had taken a warm interest in Tristan da Cunha after a fleeting visit to the island in 1884. On August 22, 1916, a letter appeared in *The Times*, stating that there had been no mail to the island for ten years. The letter was written by Mr. Balfour, another lasting friend of the Tristan Islanders. Spurred by this letter, Mr. Gane started a movement on behalf of the Tristan community, established a Tristan da Cunha Fund from voluntary contributions, and continued for the rest of his life to work for the welfare of the Islanders. He argued strongly against evacuation and carried on a perpetual campaign to convince the British authorities that Tristan da Cunha had a "place in the Empire."

The Tristan da Cunha Fund was placed under the trusteeship of such venerable and influential bodies as the Royal Geographical Society and the Royal Colonial Institute (later renamed the Royal Empire Society, now the Royal Commonwealth Society). The main objective of the fund was to improve the means of communication with the island "with a view to bringing about a regular periodic intercourse with it," but also to "mitigate the hardships of life on the island by consignment of necessary food, clothing, tools, utensils, and other goods and articles of whatever nature."

The first shipment of stores on behalf of the Tristan da Cunha Fund was sent to the island in 1918 in a Norwegian whaler. Later on, Mr. Gane succeeded in persuading the British government to provide transportation, resulting in the visits of H.M.S. *Yarmouth* in 1919, H.M.S. *Dartmouth* in 1920, and H.M.S. *Dublin* in 1923—remembered by the Islanders as "the first, the second, and third man-of-war."

It was obviously not Mr. Gane's intention to put the Tristan community on relief. All he wanted was to restore an opportunity for the Islanders to trade with the outside world and to convince the British Government of its responsibilities in the matter. It was considered desirable, therefore, that the stores and goods sent to Tristan by the fund should be subject to exchange "when the means of communication and other circumstances allow." As it turned out, however, the stores were regularly presented to the Islanders as gratuitous gifts. Nothing was demanded in exchange. As a result Mr. Gane's well-intended efforts indirectly confirmed the lingering doubt of the authorities that here, indeed, was a community that could not support itself and should therefore be abandoned and the people removed.

Captain Shipway, the Commander of the *Dublin*, had received no orders from the British Home Government to take up the issue of evacuation at this time. But the ship carried some very important passengers. Besides Bishop Holbech of Saint Helena there was a Surgeon-Commander Rickard, who had been sent out by the Union Government of South Africa to furnish a report on the conditions of the community, "which would be of use in determining their future." On board the ship was also a Mr. Lawrence Green from the Cape Town newspaper *Cape Argus*.

Mr. Green's correspondence to his paper was not very favorable to the Islanders' wish to remain on the island. He strongly urged evacuation. The official reports, however, were more sympathetic and added a humanitarian touch, which was new in a discussion that so far had been carried on almost exclusively on the basis of economic and political considerations:

Unlike other British settlements, the Settlement of Tristan da Cunha was founded with the express sanction of the Government, and the people have since made it their home, and their ancestors are buried there.

Ministers of the Crown can never willingly introduce the principle of coercion into colonial administration, even by so thin an end of the wedge as this. Two or three precedents of the kind, and we might have had the authorities compelling Ulster to enter the Irish Free State.

The emigration of peoples has always been attended by sorrow and suffering, and the Islanders are conscious of this. As they say, they would sooner starve on Tristan than at the Cape.

The evacuation would be ineffective, for the island would soon attract other settlers . . . In any case, the wishes of the people should prevail . . . .

And the wishes of the people were, now as before, to stay on Tristan. Surgeon-Commander Rickard adds this note to his own personal report: "As regards the community and settling them in more civilized and less remote parts and what effect it will have upon them, the history of most movements of the kind shows that they nearly always lead to disaster for the individuals concerned."

Two years later, in 1925, when Mr. Rogers left the island after having completed his tour of duty, he brought with him a petition signed by himself and all the grown male inhabitants, forty-one in number. The petition was directed "to The Rt. Hon. The Secretary of State for the Colonies," to whom it was submitted by Mr. Gane. It was another appeal for an annual mail to the island. The petition stated explicitly that "the island produces sufficient food to maintain life" but pointed to the impossibility of obtaining a variety of food such as flour, rice, tea, and sugar.

In response to this petition the famous Royal Research Ship *Discovery* was directed to Tristan, where she arrived in January 1926. For several years following, the Government did indeed provide a yearly means of transportation to the island, mostly by chartered ships. Moreover, the public relations campaigns launched by the Tristan da Cunha Fund to solicit contributions had apparently created a general interest in this unique community in the ocean, inducing some of the steamship companies to include Tristan da Cunha in their world cruises. As a result a few large cruise ships started to make scheduled calls at the island, such as the *Asturias* in 1927, the *Empress of France* in 1928, and the *Duchess of Athol* in 1929. It seemed as though Tristan da Cunha had entered a new era with regular mail and even tourist traffic, if one ship a year can be described as "traffic."

With each mail ship, however, there were gratuitous supplies from the Tristan da Cunha Fund and other donors. And every time a cruise ship called at the island, a collection of money was taken among the passengers for the benefit of the Islanders, usually resulting in a sizable gift from the ship's stores. So the Tristan Islanders were constantly cast in the role of recipients of charity, a fact that greatly contributed to the maintenance of the notion that the Tristan community was perpetually in distress and on the brink of starvation. It was inevitable that the question of evacuation should be taken up again by the authorities, who never felt assured that the Islanders had made a wise choice in remaining on the island under such deplorable conditions.

In January 1932 H.M.S. *Carlisle* was dispatched from the Naval Station at Simonstown on what amounted to a research expedition to Tristan da Cunha. The expedition included at least three surgeons of the Royal Navy, a dental surgeon, and a representative of the newly formed Tristan da Cunha Welfare Committee in Cape Town, besides a reporter from Reuters. The main purpose of the expedition was to make a medical and dental survey of the Tristan population. But an important part of the mission was to promote an "experimental scheme" developed by the Tristan da Cunha Fund and designed to create a "migration movement" from Tristan to South Africa. Conceded that the population as a whole did not want to quit the island, it was assumed, nevertheless, that many of the young people, at least, would want to leave if given a chance. Under the new scheme young people of Tristan "desirous of fresh scope for their endeavours" would be accepted for training on the mainland to prepare them for entry into the labor force on a competitive basis. It was for this purpose that the Welfare Committee had been established. Surgeon-Commander Bee traveled with the expedition as a representative of the British Government with a particular view to the promotion of emigration. A passenger in the *Carlisle* was also the new Bishop of Saint Helena, the Right Reverend C. C. Watts.

According to plan, Surgeon-Commander Bee addressed a meeting of all the Islanders, holding out the prospect of overpopulation as a threat that eventually would put the island in a serious position as the supplies of food and stores from outside would be decreasing. He declared that "especially the young men would have to look for fresh fields in other parts of the world," and offered to take the names of those who would like to leave so that proper preparations could be made for their future elsewhere.

This was a new approach to the issue of evacuation. But it did not work. There was not a single volunteer.

In contradiction to some of the pessimistic statements made by Surgeon-Commander Bee to the assembled Islanders, Bishop Watts remarked in a separate report:

Wholesale evacuation of the Islanders is quite unnecessary and would be cruel. There is no starvation in sight, and as a rule the people are well fed. During the winter, times are hard, but real starvation does not exist. . . .

The Islanders as a whole are unanimous in their desire to remain on the island. And I am of the opinion that their view is the right one. They are better off there than they would be anywhere else. . . .

Even he agreed, however, that "if possible, some of the younger ones should be taken away" as "in some ten years" the cultivatable land would be insufficient. And he concluded that gratuitous supplies from outside would continue to be necessary: "Oars, canvas, paint, clothing, flour, soap, and other necessaries to the amount of £150 per annum must be supplied from outside sources to the islanders. They cannot obtain them themselves and they are necessary for life."

So the Islanders continued to receive gratuitous supplies from outside. More importantly, they continued to be regarded, even by their sympathizers, as proper objects of charity. And with this, the prospect of evacuation continued to hang over their heads like a Damoclean sword. At least one imperious missionary, as we have seen, used it quite deliberately as a threat in order to command submission to his authority in secular as well as spiritual matters. And it is characteristic of the Islanders' attitude to the question that it was about the most effective threat he could use.

Whether the Tristan community could have survived without the gratuitous relief supplies is a moot question. It appears likely that without the cruise ships and the chartered supply ships, not a single vessel would have called at Tristan during the three years of 1931, 1932, and 1933. Invariably, however, the reports of economic distress and of impending hunger and starvation on Tristan were exaggerated, and supposedly well-founded statements about the willingness, even desire, of all or most of the Islanders to leave Tristan da Cunha repeatedly proved false. Yet, such reports and statements were willingly listened to, while reports to the contrary—such as those of Captain Bosanquet in 1886, of Mr. Hammond Tooke in 1904, of Mr. Barrow in 1907, of Captain Shipway and Surgeon-Commander Rickard in 1923, of Bishop Watts in 1932—were consistently ignored. It really makes one wonder whether the tenacious persistence of the evacuation issue was based not so much on the deteriorating conditions of Tristan da Cunha as on the insecurity of an affluent "superculture" faced with a people—however small, insignificant, and powerless—who consistently refused to accept its value system.

As far as the Islanders were concerned, they stubbornly maintained that gratuitous support of their community was unnecessary. All they needed, and all they had ever asked for, was a regular communication with the outside world just once a year, so that they could barter their surplus and exchange parcels and letters with people outside. Proudly,

Frances Repetto pounded it in: "Every man on Tristan da Cunha can make his own living." And this was the conviction of all.

Of course, as long as the supplies continued to arrive, they were accepted with deep and honest appreciation by the Islanders as another manifestation of the inscrutable workings of the minds of outsiders, who appeared to oscillate between benevolence and the wish to deprive the Islanders of their homes. Besides, they were too gentle and polite to turn down a gift. And so the "Big Mail" became an institution on Tristan, an annual event anticipated with great expectations and clean scrubbed houses, like a Christmas party, complete with packages and gifts and all the excitement of unwrapping, comparing, and enjoying new things. But, as Frances Repetto told me, she would have been happier if she were given the opportunity to buy the stuff.

The supplies sent to the island in this manner were generous as far as the British Government and the Tristan da Cunha Fund were concerned. But they did not substantially alter the economic condition of the community or eliminate the periodic hardships of isolation and poverty. The Islanders knew this. They were not adverse to hardship, however, especially when the only alternative seemed to be to give up their life of freedom and independence. When they chose a life of poverty, they did it with open eyes. To the Tristan Islanders, then as now, survival means more than merely a physical sustenance. In their hierarchy of values, material comfort and affluence clearly come in second place to personal integrity and freedom as they know it.

9   A Social Experiment

The Utopia of Tristan da Cunha had had its brushes with civilization and the thoughtways of the Economic Man, but had survived each crisis by clinging to its secluded territory in the ocean. It was inevitable, however, that sooner or later modern civilization would invade the island itself, for in spite of their poverty in material resources, the Tristan Islands had one asset that could not avoid inviting exploitation by modern industry. There were plenty of fish in the ocean, and scooping them out and bringing them to market was only a question of technology, organizational skill, and capital.

The Second World War finally brought an end to the extreme isolation that Tristan da Cunha had fallen into when the sailing ships disappeared. Reports had been received that the famous German "pocket battleship" *Graf Spee* as well as U-boats had been sighted off the shores of Tristan, and in 1942, although the *Graf Spee* had been successfully hunted down by then, a detachment of the Royal Navy was landed on the island along with a party of South African engineers. They established a naval garrison officially known as "H.M.S. Atlantic Isle" but described by the Islanders simply as "the Station." The detachment included a chaplain and an officer surgeon. Most of the officers brought their families along, which led to the establishment of a regular school, with a teacher added to the number of "station people," and with compulsory attendance by the Tristan children as well. A wireless station was built, whose main function was to send weather reports to the South African meteorological service. And with all this, of course, there had to be a canteen, which served as a regular country store, and looked like one, too.

For the Islanders this meant a new and closer contact with the Outside World, both socially and economically. Odd jobs were available in construction and maintenance work around the Station, and for the first time in a generation or more, the Islanders had an opportunity to earn a little money that could be spent in the canteen for "luxuries." The wages were low (a shilling a day), but so were the prices (flour could be bought in the canteen for a penny a pound).

After the war the military establishment was abandoned. But the renewed contact with the outside world had far-reaching consequences for the Tristan community. Not only did the South African Government decide to maintain a meteorological station on the island with civilian personnel, thus insuring continued radio contact with Cape Town and regular visits by supply ships. More important for the future of the Tristan community was the industrial development that resulted. An enterprising Navy Chaplain, the Reverend C. P. Lawrence, who had served on Tristan during the war and had been entranced by the unbelievable riches of the fishing grounds around the island, was impressed by the fact that the Tristan community was living on such a narrow subsistence margin, in fact on a submarginal level by the standards of the outside world, with these incredible riches remaining practically unexploited right at its doorstep. Particularly the South Atlantic crawfish—or crayfish, as the Islanders call it—which was the basis of a prosperous fishing industry in South Africa and had already captured the American market under the label "rock lobster," was abundant around Tristan and easy to catch. Weather permitting, the Tristan Islanders supplied themselves with plenty of this delectable crustacean by the most primitive fishing methods. A wooden box, weighted, and lowered to the bottom in shallow water, with no bait at all, could be filled up in a couple of minutes. Out of sheer curiosity, it seemed, the crayfish would crawl in.

Since the unhappy adventure of William Glass and his companions with the schooner *Jane* in the 1820's, few attempts had been made to establish a regular trade between Tristan and the outside world, and none of them successful. In the 1880's a trade had been established with Saint Helena in cattle, sheep, and geese, carried by occasional tramp schooners, which were loaded by swimming the cattle out to the ship with pieces of wood supporting the animals' heads. Peter Green mentions this trade in his letter to the Admiralty of December 29, 1884:

We sent two cargoes to St. Helena, but the third time it was a Yankee barquentine. She came to anchor about six miles to the eastward of the settlement. Somehow they made out to bump her on a nice sandy beach, high and dry, and left us her cargo of rats. The next was an English schooner; she brought the Rev. E. H. Dodgson to Tristan. She let three fine days slip by, then she came in with a northerly wind. The captain was ashore; our boat went off with the captain, but it was too late, she got ashore abreast of the settlement, a total loss. We had one English schooner since. She took her cargo in one day, and was off. We have much bad weather, but those two cases of shipwreck was rather carelessness.

Stories were told on Tristan implying that the two shipwrecks were due to more than carelessness. The "Yankee barquentine," the *Henry B. Paul*, was said to have been willfully stranded so that the captain, known locally as "Brand Bread" from the way he fed his men, could steal the money given him by a Saint Helena firm to buy cattle on Tristan, claiming that it had gone down with the ship. This was indeed the ship that brought the rats to Tristan, but Peter Green seems to imply that the cargo of the next ship, the English schooner *Edward Vittery*, was hardly more desirable—"she brought the Rev. E. H. Dodgson to Tristan." Her wreck was believed to have been arranged to collect insurance. Anyway, because of the two shipwrecks, owners were reluctant to send their ships to Tristan, insurance rates went up, and the traffic ceased.

No more successful was an attempt in 1883 to start a business in guano, similar to the one carried on at that time with great profits from the Ichaboe Islands and several other small islands near the South African coast. An unnamed American schooner arrived at Tristan in November of that year and hired twelve Islanders to collect guano on Nightingale. The schooner was to return the following year to pick up the cargo but never showed up. She was reported wrecked somewhere else.

After the lifeboat disaster the question of establishing a trade that could be profitable to the Islanders had been discussed several times by visiting officials as an alternative to evacuation, although the authorities paid little attention to it. In his report of 1903, Lieutenant Watts-Jones says:

I would suggest that if something could be done to revive the schooner trade, it would be possible to discontinue the visits of men-of-war.

. . . In addition to cattle, the island can produce a fair amount of wool, while if enough salt were taken to the island, a load of salt fish could easily be ready for the next year. There are also the donkeys which, I believe, are now valuable at the Cape.

There is also the guano from Nightingale Island, which the islanders could store at Tristan Island until the schooner arrived. I am therefore of the opinion that if once started the trade could be made to pay its way. Occasional help might be wanted, but the cost of starting the trade, and the occasonal help would probably be much less than the yearly coal bill of the man-of-war.

The following year Captain Pearce of the *Odin* suggested that guano, whaling, and fish-curing might be suitable industries for development on Tristan, and Under-Secretary Hammond Tooke concurred, going into great detail about the guano deposits, samples of which were taken to Cape Town for analysis.

Encouraged by these reports, the owners of the *Greyhound* used the opportunity when their ship was chartered by the Colonial Office for a relief expedition to Tristan da Cunha in 1907 to send Mr. P. C. Keytel as their own representative to investigate the possibilities of starting a trade. Mr. Keytel was strongly encouraged in his efforts by the Reverend Mr. Barrow, and the following year, in March 1908, after it had been ascertained that the Islanders did not want to leave the island, he returned to Tristan to start an export of sheep and dried fish to the Cape. It was on this occasion that he brought Bob Glass and company back to Tristan.

This time Mr. Keytel stayed for a year while the *Greyhound* returned to Cape Town with a cargo of two hundred live sheep. He got the fish-drying business started, with the men fishing and the women cleaning, splitting, and salting the fish. Soon, however, he ran into difficulties. The sheep on the island proved to be infested with scab, and he had to throw away much of the fish because it had become fly-blown and mildewed. But the greatest obstacle to his ventures was the Islanders' stubborn independence. They agreed to work for the enterprise all right, but then turned up for work only when it suited them.

It appears that a labor contract as it is known in the outside world was not only a new and unfamiliar concept to them, it was evidently felt to be in conflict with their sense of freedom.

The *Greyhound* was scheduled to return to Tristan in March 1909 for another cargo. But when April came around without her appearance, Mr. Keytel left in the *Svend Foyn* with the Barrows. The schooner arrived three weeks later, but finding Mr. Keytel gone and no cargo available, she returned to Cape Town.

Then followed the period of extreme isolation, during which no attempts were made to establish any kind of trade with Tristan da Cunha on a commercial basis. When the Reverend H. M. Rogers left the island in 1925, he endeavored to interest the manager of the Union Whaling Company at Durban in trying to develop an industry in whaling and crawfishing at Tristan, but the project was considered hopeless, and it was not until after the Second World War, when Mr. Lawrence developed his plan, that the question was taken up again.

Mr. Lawrence was apparently a man of action, but with a broad streak of idealism, and with a genuine concern for the welfare of the Tristan Islanders. He developed a plan to transform the economy of the community and bring it up to a higher level of affluence by pulling in outside interest and capital to exploit the abundant fishing grounds on a commercial basis in an enterprise whose prime consideration would be the welfare of the Islanders. He succeeded in arousing the interest of several fishing companies in Cape Town, and in January 1948 an exploratory expedition was sent to Tristan in the *Pequena,* a converted minesweeper that belonged to one of the interested companies and was completely refitted for the purpose.

The expedition was initiated by Mr. C. H. Gaggins, then Managing Director of the Lamberts Bay Canning Company. The leader of the expedition was Mr. Lawrence. It also had the blessing and support of the Union Government of South Africa and the Colonial Office in London and was described at the time as "one of the best-equipped scientific expeditions ever organized by South Africans." It included three marine biologists, a fish oil expert, an agricultural chemist, and a medical pathologist. The *Pequena* reached Tristan on February 6 and stayed around the islands for about a month. She returned to Cape Town in March with extremely favorable reports, and within a few months the Tristan da Cunha Development Company was formed, with a capital of £100,000, and was granted exclusive rights to establish a permanent fishing industry on the island.

It was clear from the outset that this was more than an ordinary commercial enterprise. The plan, developed and promoted primarily by Mr. Lawrence but with full support from Mr. Gaggins, who now was the managing director of the new company, was described as a "social experiment" and included a broad program of social services and economic reorganization. The object was to make the community of Tristan da Cunha economically self-supporting by establishing a profitable industry in which there would be maximum involvement on the part of the Islanders, and the hope was to give the community a social as well as economic "uplift" and bring it "back to a stage of complete self-reliance and a way of life that gave prospects for the future." Fishing seemed to be the logical industry to embark upon, not only because of the location of the community and the incredible abundance of the fishing grounds, but particularly because the Islanders' equally incredible skill as boatmen promised to make them valuable and self-reliant participants in the venture. The tenet of the whole project was well summed up in the "Editorial Viewpoint" expressed in *The South African Shipping News and Fishing Industry Review* shortly after the return of the *Pequena* expedition:

The sponsors [of the Tristan expedition], with great wisdom, spent a good deal of money in a rather broader field than is usual in a commercial enterprise. Any industrial development at Tristan will, however, require for its own purpose a general re-organisation of the island economy, and the sponsors of the expedition are now armed with the most comprehensive information for dealing with engineering, agricultural and medical problems. Tristan by its very isolation provides a unique opportunity for combining an industrial undertaking with a social experiment. Any crawfish industry there can be conducted with a proper scientific regard for conservation, and with no history of neglect; while the social programme will start off with the inestimable advantage that this new deal for Tristan is rooted in the traditional and principal occupation of the islanders—fishing.

The original plans were quite ambitious and included the building of two canning factories, one at the Settlement and one at Sandy Point, with a permanent road (possibly even a railroad) to connect them, the development of hydroelectric power from three sizable crater lakes near the northern edge of the base, and the establishment of subsidiary industries, such as the production of fileted bluefish (a large fish endemic to Tristan), of fertilizer from the refuse of the fishing industry, and extraction of alginic acid from the macrocystis seaweed. But the main basis for the whole enterprise was to be the crawfish industry, with export of canned and frozen "rock lobster" tails for the American market. An initial "easy target" was set at an annual production of 50,000 cases, or 1,600,000 crawfish tails.

In the planning of the enterprise, great emphasis was given to the "sociological" problems involved. To release the local labor force for the industries, a complete reorganization of the island economy was visualized. The existing subsistence economy was to be replaced by a specialized cash economy. This, of course, would involve some radical changes, which it was hoped would lead to an "uplift" of the Islanders' diet as well as of their whole outlook and way of life. In particular it was anticipated that the fishing company would have to assume responsibility for food production on a large scale for local consumption to release most of the Islanders from their farming activities. In view of the depletion of the soil, particularly the pastures, it was deemed essential to "regenerate" the whole system of agriculture on a "scientific" basis. Chemical analysis revealed that "the island's soil is rich and, if carefully handled by an expert, could be made sufficiently productive quite speedily to support both the islanders and the Company's employees." The most radical recommendation in this regard came from Mr. L. L. Eksteen, the soil expert of the *Pequena* expedition, who suggested converting the existing subsistence farming into an "agricultural industry" by having "the entire system of farming reorganized and managed by only *one* responsible person." At the least, to carry out the social as well as economic program, it was felt "to be absolutely essential that the Company should employ a doctor, an agricultural expert, and two teachers."

In the contract drawn up with the Colonial Office, in which the Company was granted exclusive fishing rights for the whole Tristan da Cunha group of islands (including Gough Island, 250 miles south of Tristan), it was again emphasized that this was more than an ordinary commercial enterprise. According to the contract, the Company would provide the Islanders with "full medical, educational, and social amenities." Furthermore, by the terms of the contract, each wage earner was guaranteed a minimum annual income of £100 in cash or in kind, and the Company would pay £1,500 a year plus a proportion of its net profit to the Crown Agents for the Colonies, one third of which would be set aside in a trust fund to provide public buildings, stipends for youngsters to receive a higher education off the island, grants to aid special cases, and other social services not directly under the responsibility of the Company. The trust fund would be administered by a trust council, which would meet in Cape Town. Finally, the Company would pay a levy to the community on all cases of canned goods and frozen crayfish tails produced.

The economic program of this "social experiment" was never carried out to the full extent suggested in the original plan. As it turned out, the Company had its hands (and capital) fully engaged with the crayfish. The building of a canning factory was started near the Settlement, and fishing operations were carried on from the *Pequena,* which had a refrigerated hold for immediate freezing of the crayfish tails. In October 1949 the *Pequena,* a small vessel of 181 tons gross, returned to Cape Town from her first season at Tristan with 60,000 frozen crayfish tails (about 2,000 cases) and 20,000 penguin eggs.

Although this was far below the initial "easy target" of 50,000 cases, it was encouraging enough in view of the limited operations to expand the industry. Mainly through the investment of £130,000 by the British Colonial Development Corporation, the Company's capital was more than doubled, from the initial £100,000 to £250,000. The canning factory was brought to completion and started production, fed by shore-based fishing operations; and the pelagic fisheries of the *Pequena* were augmented by the purchase of a larger ship, a former escort vessel of 628 tons, later known as the *Tristania,* which was rebuilt and specially fitted for the purpose. Her equipment included a radio telephone capable of direct connection between the island and the mainland.

For various reasons the planned reorganization of agriculture under Company auspices was not put into effect. Nevertheless, it was hoped that a voluntary introduction of more rational farming methods and an expansion of the cultivated areas would put the Tristan economy on a sounder base by increasing the surplus margin of the agriculture. It was further hoped that this would encourage a voluntary division of labor among the Islanders, thereby releasing sufficient manpower from the farming and hunting efforts to allow the fishing industry to operate entirely with the available Tristan labor.

To this end the Company eventually did employ an agricultural expert, who served as an adviser and instructor to the Islanders. A tractor furnished with modern plows was provided and made available to any Islander who cared to make use of it. In due time several important improvements were successfully introduced. Sprays were applied against the potato blight and the "potato-grub," samples of which had been sent to the University of Cape Town to test out the best possible insecticide. More rational grazing methods were introduced by erecting extensive fences, separating sheep from cattle and allowing a rotation of the pastures. An experimental farming area was set up at Sandy Point, growing various kinds of vegetables, partly to supply the Station but mainly to demonstrate the feasibility of expanding farming operations beyond the staple crop of potatoes. A small sheltered area was planted with pine trees for a future supply of lumber.

Success was the keynote of the first report dispatched by Mr. Lawrence, who stayed with the enterprise during the first year, acting as a liaison officer between the Islanders and the Company. "The immediate results are obvious in both uplift and health," he reported, and a "bumper crop" was predicted for the following year.

But the expected results in terms of released labor available for the fishing industry failed to materialize. A labor problem was probably what the Company management least expected from these poverty-stricken people who, it was assumed, would need every penny they could earn. Nevertheless, this is what they were faced with, like Mr. Keytel before. It appeared that most of the Islanders were simply not prepared to stick to a labor contract that demanded they turn up regularly for work. In their minds the activities of their traditional subsistence economy clearly took precedence over working for somebody else. The excuse given most of the time for not turning up for work, if an excuse was given at all, was that they had to tend to their potato patches, their cattle or sheep, or that they had to go for eggs or birds. Particularly devastating to the operations of the Company were the expeditions to Nightingale, especially the "fatting trip" in March. Such a trip might take a couple of weeks, depending on wind and weather. During that time the village would be practically deserted, and the

Company had no choice but to shut down or run with sharply reduced manpower, which meant the loss of that many precious fishing days.

Typically, in accordance with the thoughtways of the Economic Man, the Company management explained the situation in strictly economic terms. It was realized that a single industry of limited capacity simply could not support the whole community of some 250 people. The reason, they thought, was not so much to be found in low wages, which were compensated for, at least in part, by the continuation of the canteen as a nonprofit utility store. More important was the fact that the Company could not offer continuous full employment because of weather conditions. During the days and weeks when the beaches were unworkable on account of swell and surf, the shore base would be idle, and the factory would have to shut down. The trouble was that these periods were ill suited for the activities of the subsistence economy as well, and so the Company came out on the short end of the rope in either case—in good weather because the full labor force was not available, in bad weather because all economic activities on the island were more or less idled.

So the fact was recognized that the fishing industry could only supplement but not supplant the traditional subsistence economy of Tristan da Cunha, that it would be impossible for most of the Islanders to enter into a binding contract that would make them available whenever the interests of the Company demanded it without jeopardizing the subsistence of the respective households and thereby upsetting the whole economy of the community. It was partly on this basis that it was decided to convert the canning factory, which had mainly employed women while the men were fishing, into a freezing plant, which required less labor for its operation and maintenance. At the same time more emphasis was given to ship-based fishing operations. The old *Pequena* was replaced by another converted minesweeper of some three hundred tons, which was renamed the *Frances Repetto* in honor of the recently deceased "Queen" of the island. Cape Coloured and African fishermen were brought out from the Cape to work from the ships.

The Company yielded reluctantly to the pressure from the subsistence economy as the superior skill of the Tristan Islanders, both as boatmen and as fishermen, was well recognized. But it was also recognized that the success or failure of the whole experiment depended entirely on the support and cooperation of the Islanders. The Company could certainly run its business without the Islanders. Even the shore base could be kept in operation with imported South African labor if they were allowed on shore. Precedents for such procedures are plentiful where industry has moved into an "underdeveloped" area, usually with devastating effects for the local population. But the whole idea of this social experiment on Tristan da Cunha, to which the Company was committed both by its contract with the Colonial Office and by the conviction of Mr. Gaggins, was to get the Tristan Islanders involved in such a way that it would benefit the economy of the Tristan community.

Arrangements were made, therefore, to give the Islanders an opportunity to participate in the fishing operations on a more flexible basis without having to bind themselves to a labor contract that would interfere with their traditional subsistence economy and way of life. The arrangements were that the Company kept a number of dinghies and fishing nets at the shore base, and whenever there was a "fishing day," that is, when the beach was workable and the sea was calm enough for fishing near the Settlement, the "fishing bell," an old torpedo shell left by the Royal Navy and hung from a tripod in the middle of the village, was sounded in the early morning, and those of the Islanders who were available (and had the inclination) would turn up on the beach and sign up for a dinghy or for a job as a beach worker or checker for the day. Two motorboats, also owned by the Company, were on hand to tow the dinghies to their chosen fishing grounds, and the fishermen were paid by the catch. Also, an opportunity was given for those Islanders who were so inclined to sign up as fishermen in one of the ships for half a season, usually the "big season" (as it is called) from September till Christmas, thus being able to get off the ship for the Christmas celebrations, which are very important in the social life of the Islanders, and before the busy season in the traditional subsistence economy. Only about a dozen Islanders, who were prepared to accept a binding contract, were continuously employed in what was known as the "permanent staff," which included, among others, a beach foreman, a storekeeper, a man in charge of machines and engines, and eventually even an "assistant manager."

The system appeared to work well, especially since the peak of the fisheries during the "big season" coincided with a relatively slack period in the routine of the subsistence economy. On a good fishing day during this period practically all the men would turn up, and the Company could soon report that occasionally it would muster a labor force of about seventy-five men and fifteen youths. During the "small season" (January through March), which is the busiest season in the lives of the Islanders with potato digging and numerous excursions to outlying areas, including Nightingale, the available labor force was sharply reduced, at least periodically. During this time the Company relied for continued operation more predominantly on the pelagic fisheries from the two refrigerated fishing vessels, the *Tristania* and the *Frances Repetto,* with their South African fishermen.

Despite the curtailments of the original plans and the adjustments that had to be made to keep the subsistence economy of the island intact, the establishment of a permanent industry on Tristan da Cunha had, of course, far-reaching consequences affecting the economic and social, even the political, life of the community.

In the first place it was obviously no longer possible to comply with the Islanders' wish to remain in a state of absolute anarchy. To the more bureaucratic minds of the Colonial Office this state of affairs had always been a vexing anomaly anyhow.

Now, with the presence of a permanent colony of "expatriates" and especially with South African private interests being granted exclusive concessions on the shores as well as in the territorial waters of this British possession, it was felt that the British Crown should be officially represented locally.

Administrative powers were at first, as a temporary arrangement, delegated to the resident chaplain or doctor. But in January 1950 the first duly appointed Administrator of Tristan da Cunha sailed for the island to serve for a designated period of three years. His principal duty, as announced in the newspapers, was "to act for the people of Tristan" in their relations with the Company. To assist the Administrator in determining the interests of the community, an Island Council was immediately appointed, consisting of Chief Willie Repetto and ten other men of the island, plus two representatives of the Company. Two years later the Island Council was made an elective body, with ten men and five women to represent the community, and with the Administrator, the Resident Chaplain, the Head Man, and the Head Woman as members *ex officio.*

On the face of it this is government by representation. However, when the provisions were spelled out in an ordinance of March 10, 1952, the absolute power of the Administrator was formally established. In this ordinance the Administrator was given exclusive power to make "bye-laws," that is, community ordinances, which were "to have the force of law in Tristan da Cunha or any part thereof." Among the matters explicitly to be covered by such bylaws were land use, the organization of public work, and the assessment of taxes. The Administrator was also given the power to prescribe penalties for any infraction of his bylaws (as determined by him) and to hear any "contravention" in a summary way, acting as magistrate. As far as the Island Council was concerned, its duties "shall be to advise the Administrator" in regard to the exercise of his powers. But it is explicitly stated that the Administrator "shall not be bound to act in accordance with such advice."

From the letter of this document it is clear that the powers of the Administrator went far beyond "acting for the people of Tristan" in their relations with the Company. When Tristan got its Administrator, the island was in effect reduced to its present status of a protectorate in which the local population has no more say about their own fate and destiny than it pleases the Administrator to grant them. He alone is lawmaker, judge, and executive, all in one person. This is the tragic fact behind Chief Willie Repetto's pathetic words when, on a later occasion, he was asked in an interview to explain his functions as Chief Man: "When the Administrators come to the island, you see, they took over."

The real basis, however, for the enormous power that the Administrator in fact had, whether he wanted to use it or not, lay not so much in this legal document as in the attitude of the Islanders. For they continued to regard authority from outside with deference and awe. To them, the power of the Crown was absolute, unquestionable, like a divine force, but benevolent and full of grace. And this power and grace of the Crown was the source of all established authority, particularly that of the Administrator. As a person, they recognized, the "Admin" had his limitations like everybody else. He might be wrong on occasion, and the Islanders might grumble at some of his decisions and regulations. They might even hold a particular officer in considerable contempt, convinced that had the Queen only known, she would have been utterly displeased. But no one doubted for a moment the right of

the Administrator to act as he saw fit and to demand complete obedi-
ence from the Islanders. They seemed content to accept without question the administrative machinery that was descending upon them as a
thing beyond their comprehension. Moreover, it never entered their
minds that they should have anything to say about it. They seemed to
regard the authority of the Administrator as something beyond ethical
norms, and a concept of general "human rights" over and above established authority was completely unknown to them.

In a situation like that, of course, a lot depends on the kind of person who is holding the position of Administrator at any given time. It
is probably fair to say that most of those who have served in the capacity over the last two decades have had the welfare of the community
genuinely at heart and have conscientiously sought to represent the real
or imagined interests of the Islanders. The trouble was that the welfare of the community and the interests of the Islanders were invariably interpreted in terms of the values of the Outside World with their
emphasis on Progress and Development as measured by material affluence alone. Since the Administrators themselves were the products and
agents of a highly industrialized and bureaucratized civilization, it was
inevitable that many of them should have little understanding of the
values of the Islanders' traditional way of life. To most of them the
fishing industry was an unqualified blessing, a solution to all the Islanders' problems, and the promotion of a solvent and profitable industry became a matter of policy believed to be in the best interest of
the Islanders, even at the sacrifice of some of their accustomed free-
doms. So it happened that the Administrator came to stand in the eyes
of the Islanders as an agent and ally of the Company rather than as a
buffer and a protector of traditional values.

The Islanders tried to put up with this new power holder in their
midst as best they could, continuing their old strategy of playing
along, doing whatever they were told to do without a question, as if in
a game whose rules they did not know and whose goals were determined somewhere beyond their reach. They even played at sitting in
the Island Council, going through the motions of elections and meetings, making a few decisions of minor importance, knowing full well,
as at least some of them did, that the Administrator controlled the
agenda and that any really important decision concerning the island
and its future would come from the Administrator's office or from his

distant superiors in the Colonial Office, regardless of the Islanders' own wishes.

As far as Chief was concerned, his position did not change a whole lot with the introduction of a new administration. He was still regarded by the Islanders as their "Chief Man," and his most important, if not only, function was still to act as their spokesman in front of outsiders. The most conspicuous "outsider" in the new situation was, of course, the Administrator, and so it happened that Chief's role developed into that of a liaison between the Administrator and the community. As such, he could probably have exercised considerable influence by making himself a spokesman for the Islanders' gripes and complaints, and on occasion he did perform that function. Being a peaceful, kind, and modest man, however, he did it with reluctance. Nor did the Islanders seem to expect him to play such a role, although there were undoubtedly some who wished he had had a little more of his mother's strong personality. Instead, he often found himself charged with the unpleasant task of announcing and implementing the Administrator's provisions and decrees opposite the Islanders.

The Administrator had indeed "taken over." Of course, the presence of a heteronomous authority, which it became increasingly difficult to ignore, was a serious limitation of the Islanders' much cherished freedom. They resented it deeply, but partly out of fear of reprisals, partly out of deference to the authority of the Crown, they felt powerless to resist. Perhaps it seemed a little less disagreeable to them in the light of the material improvements that were indeed a result of the new state of affairs.

Several programs of public service introduced by the new administration and financed by the newly established trust fund contributed greatly to the improvement of the Islanders' health, welfare, and general level of living. Health had not been one of the major problems of the Tristan community, especially since its isolated position had spared it most of the serious infectious diseases of the civilized world. This, on the other hand, meant that the population was extremely vulnerable should such diseases ever be introduced since no natural resistance had had a chance to develop. The arrival of the *Pequena* expedition in 1948, although careful precautions had been taken in this regard, triggered the outbreak of a severe influenza epidemic—"the *Pequena* sickness" the Islanders called it—causing several deaths, including that of Frances Repetto and of her brother, Henry Green. The population, moreover, was heavily infested with roundworms and had probably been so for generations. This was attributed in large part to the water supply, which was taken from open brooks shared by geese, sheep, donkeys, and cattle.

The most extensive public services introduced under the auspices of the trust fund, therefore, were naturally concerned with the prevention and cure of disease. In addition to the continued free service of a resident physician, they included the maintenance of a small but fairly well equipped hospital, housed in one of the abandoned navy barracks, with a nurse on daily duty. A modern sewerage and water supply system was installed, with water piped in and flush toilets set up in every house. A communal bath and washroom was erected but has since been torn down since all the houses at the Station and several of the village houses now have private baths.

From an economic point of view the most important change resulting from the establishment of industry on Tristan was the introduction of money and a cash economy to supplement the traditional subsistence economy, on a much larger scale than had been the case under the military occupation during the war. Throughout the nineteenth century, most of the trade with passing ships had been by barter. Various currencies, however, had been in limited use, especially when dealing with outsiders. The Spanish dollar was the currency in which Lambert had promised (but failed) to pay his men. William Glass's transaction with William Hollett of Cape Town were made partly in Dutch rix-dollars, partly in British pound sterling. The American dollar came into use with the American whalers. But with increasing isolation, money went out of use. Already in 1884 a report stated that money was not acceptable as a means of exchange for supplies to ships, presumably because there was no way of spending it. In 1904, when the British Government offered to send a school master to Tristan if the inhabitants would contribute £75 a year toward his salary, the answer was given that such a payment was impossible as only five shillings had come to the island during the whole of that year. By the time of the Norwegian Scientific Expedition (1937–1938), money was nonexistent and practically unknown on Tristan.

The fishing industry now offered the opportunity for every Islander to earn some money, either as an independent fisherman or as a member of the permanent staff. Besides, there were odd jobs available around the factory and at the Station, and the very presence of a colony of salaried outsiders gave a chance for Islanders to sell fresh meat, vegetables, milk, eggs, and fish at the Station as well as for a limited number of young girls to get employment as domestic servants. This, in connection with the continued maintenance of a fairly well stocked canteen run by the Company on a nonprofit basis, introduced an entirely new element in the Tristan economy. The Islanders now had the occasion to use money to buy imported goods of almost every description and even to order things to be sent in the next ship.

The amount of money earned by the Tristan Islanders under their new economic system was by no means exuberant, at least not by outside standards. Certainly, in the eyes of the Islanders there was "really good money" in fishing, and a skillful fisherman could, in fact, take in as much as five pounds or more on a good fishing day. But this was rare. An average fishing day was more likely to bring in no more than about fifteen shillings (two dollars) for each fisherman, and considering the fact that even the average fishing days were relatively few and sometimes far between, it did not amount to a great deal of money. And while beach workers and checkers were paid from fourteen shillings to one pound for a day that could run fifteen hours or more (as they had to wait for the last dinghy to return from fishing), occasional workers in odd jobs received only a shilling an hour, or eight shillings a day. As far as the permanent staff was concerned, their basic monthly pay varied from thirteen pounds to sixteen pounds, and even the assistant manager received a salary of no more than thirty pounds a month. On the whole the average cash income of a Tristan household could be estimated to be considerably less than two hundred pounds (about six hundred dollars) per year.

Since this cash income, however, was a net addition to the naturalia produced by the subsistence economy, it meant an enormous improvement in the economic level of every Tristan household. This becomes quite evident from a comparison of the conditions prevailing in 1938, at the time of my first visit to Tristan da Cunha, and those of today. There is a new affluence in the Tristan community, which is most conspicuously evident in the condition of the houses, both exterior and interior.

Some of the more recently erected houses show a definite improvement in the stone work—witness to the fact that explosives are again available to quarry the stone. And the new access to imported materials is shown by the use of cement (bought from the canteen) both in the walls and in the walks in front of the dwellings. A few houses have been built in part from concrete blocks instead of soft-stone, and some of them have even exchanged the traditional thatch for corrugated zinc on the roof, which is not necessarily an aesthetic improvement but shows a definite increase in affluence.

It is particularly in the interior of the houses, however, that the new level of the economy is apparent. Today there is not a single house on Tristan that does not have a finished interior with good carpentry work in lofts, wainscots, and floors, made from adequate lumber and nicely painted. Some of the houses have the interior walls completely paneled in masonite, and most of them have rugs and carpets on the living room floor. In most houses the homemade furniture has been replaced by modern imported chairs and tables, and upholstered sofas and easy chairs are not uncommon. Kitchens and pantries are usually well equipped with cabinets, sink, and counters, especially in the newer houses, and most of the cooking is now done on paraffin stoves rather than in the open fireplace. Paraffin-driven refrigerators are found in some houses as well as battery-driven transistor radios, record players with small selections of records, and even tape recorders. A few houses have added a bath with a "geyser" (hot-water heater) to the other luxuries.

This new affluence is, of course, noticeable also in the Islanders' diet and food habits, in their clothing and grooming, in the quality of their homemade canvas boats, and in practically every aspect of their economic and social life. Things that the Islanders learned to regard as "luxuries" during the period of isolation, such as wheat flour and other cereals, sugar, tea, and coffee, are now again taken for granted along with a number of items from the stock of modern mass production, particularly canned foods of every description, which were previously unknown on Tristan but are now available at the Island Store.

From a social and cultural point of view it was of the greatest significance to the Tristan community that the Station (as it is still called) continued as a permanent colony of transient outsiders and their families. Most importantly, it meant the continuation of a regular school, which is maintained, with some financial assistance from the Company, by the Society for the Propagation of the Gospel. Ministers had been sent out to the little congregation by the S.P.G. intermittently since the 1850's and as a permanent service since the late 1920's. Part of the minister's duties, often performed by his wife, was to teach the island children. Since the establishment of a permanent industry on Tristan, however, a regular school has been maintained with a certified teacher from England as Head Master and two or three of the more gifted young Islanders as assistant teachers.

The Station also remained an important channel to the Outside World, not only by providing regular connections by ship and by radio to Cape Town and the world at large but also by offering an opportunity for young people of the island to leave their limited habitat and seek their fortune in other lands. During the thirty years from 1911 to 1940, only one Islander had left the island, although there was no lack of opportunity, especially during the late 1920's and the 1930's. But since the establishment of the Station on Tristan (until the volcanic eruption in 1961, when the whole population was evacuated), either young girls have left for England, where some of them were given a start as domestic servants in the homes of former Tristan officials, or for Saint Helena, where they received training as nurses. A few young men and couples, by arrangements of the authorities, went to the Falkland Islands to work on sheep farms. It is characteristic, however, of the Islanders' affinity for their island and their way of life that most of them eventually returned to Tristan.

On the whole, the development of a permanent industry on the island, however modest it turned out to be in the end, pulled the Tristan community back into the commerce of the civilized world and made it again a living part of Western society, complete with a movie house and a public bar. On the other hand, the presence of a permanent colony of outsiders and the extended contacts with the Outside World gave the Islanders a new awareness, even a new concept of their own collective identity as "Islanders" or "Villagers" as opposed to "Stations" as well as to the ships' officers and the South African fishermen and sailors. In fact, the Islanders learned again what they had apparently forgotten during the long period of isolation, that the "Outside World" was not an indiscriminate body of awesome authority, prestige, and power, in relation to which they themselves were "only low and poor people." They rediscovered that in the "Outside World," in contrast to their own egalitarian community, there were hierarchies of power, which sometimes put serious limitations on what a man could or could not do. In other words, they learned again to distinguish between "important" and "unimportant" people. Most significantly, they learned that a Tristan Islander is not necessarily inferior to *everybody* in the "Outside World."

This new self-awareness of the Islanders was strongly confirmed by the privileged position that they enjoyed on board the fishing ships. Here the line of command, which is always in evidence on a ship, was greatly emphasized by the obvious social distance that existed between the White officers and the Colored and African crew. And here the Islanders saw really "black" people for the first time and found themselves, in comparison, to resemble the White officers much more than the crew. Anyway, they quite happily took an intermediate position in the racial caste system of the South African ships, but much closer to the officers than to the crew. Their ability to do so was obviously connected with the fact that their knowledge of beaches and weather conditions around the islands, as well as their superior skills as boatmen, were very useful to the ships' officers, who often relied on the Islanders' judgment before deciding to put the fishing dinghies over the side. When serving on board the ships, the Islanders demanded, and were given, separate quarters from the rest of the crew. They were always on first names with the officers, and in some cases personal friendships developed, which permitted the Islanders, when off duty, to come to the bridge for a friendly visit, or to drop in on an officer in his cabin for a drink. And the relationship was a mutual one. When officers came on shore, they were more often seen visiting in the Village than at the Station.

All this, of course, meant a great deal to the Islanders' self-esteem. The pride they take in their boatmanship has always been great. But here they were for the first time associating as friends with people who, as professional seamen, really could appreciate their skills. And their dignity as human beings received an immense lift from their ability to communicate with at least some outsiders as respected equals. It was really in these associations that the Islanders learned to raise their heads from the traditional deference to all outsiders, and to say with pride: "I's an Islander."

10 Conflicting Values

When modern commercial industry moves in on a folk society, it usually comes with two powerful arguments in its favor: it comes with the prestige of a "superculture," and it brings material affluence. Besides, it is strongly supported by the ethos of rationality as well as by technical superiority and organizational skill. These are values that Man, the rational animal, cannot easily dismiss or refute, no matter what other values his own cultural tradition may have given him in terms of integrity, emotional security, dignity, and self-fulfillment. The ethos of the Economic Man, therefore, always comes as a serious challenge to any cultural tradition that does not place calculating rationality and material affluence at the top of its hierarchy of values. Moreover, as so often happens in social and cultural change, fringe values are easily compromised and even sacrificed; but the involvement of core values, usually more general in scope and more vaguely atriculated, becomes apparent only after the change has already been implemented and there is no way back.

All this was no less true in the case of Tristan da Cunha than in any "underdeveloped" society where modern technology and industry have recently made their appearance. Because the new affluence that the fishing industry brought to the Tristan community was recognized by all as something desirable, and because it was not apparent on the surface of things that this would seriously interfere with the basic core values of the community in terms of liberty, equality, and individual integrity, the new enterprise of the South African fishing industry was at first received with enthusiasm by the Islanders. Adjustments and compromises were indeed made on both sides. However, it soon became clear—to the Islanders if not to the Company and its representatives—that some of the demands and expectations of the fishing industry were infringing upon established relationships and patterns of conduct within the community, which were intrinsically tied to manifest expressions of traditional core values. A conflict of values ensued, in which the ethos of the Tristan Man was pitched against that of the Economic Man.

However "atomistic" the Tristan community turned out to be, it is, like most agrarian and fishing communities anywhere in the world, tied together by a network of cooperation and mutual aid. Economically, each household is in principle independent of the rest. Every married man has, as a rule, his own house, his own little plots of land where he cultivates his potatoes and vegetables, his own cattle and sheep, and all his work is primarily geared to his one overriding responsibility to provide for his own household. In spite of their individualism, however, the Islanders are gregarious people. They like to do things together, not as a community, but in small select groups that may vary in size depending on the nature of the work, and the tendency is to turn practically every job of any significance into a cooperative affair.

Much of this cooperation is prompted by practical considerations, by the nature of the job at hand and, particularly, by the fact that in so much of their work the Islanders are dependent on boats. It takes a crew to handle a boat, especially through the surf on an open beach with the whole Atlantic rolling in, and so it is for practical as well as social reasons that each boat is built and owned jointly by a select group of men just large enough to form a full crew.

Likewise for practical as well as social reasons, the wild cattle at Seal Bay and Stony Beach are owned mostly by small groups of joint owners, usually two to four in number, with some men belonging to two, three, or even four different groups. This results in a rather complex pattern of selective but overlapping and interlocking relationships. The same applies to the orchards at Stony Beach and Sandy Point, where each single apple tree is usually owned jointly by two to four persons, and to huts and shacks built for shelter on Nightingale and in other outlying areas.

But the pattern of joint ownership also applies in many cases to situations where circumstances do not seem to demand it for practical reasons. In particular, a large portion of the cattle on the easily accessible northwestern plain is also owned by similar small selective partnerships. In a few cases it may be a matter of economy, as when two men share a team of oxen and the cart as well because they cannot afford a team each. But economy does not explain all or even most of the partnerships that do exist.

Also, there is extensive mutual aid. Even here, the pattern is sometimes but not always prompted by the nature of the job at hand, and even here it is always selective. If a man has a job to do that is more than he can handle alone, he summons the assistance, not of the whole community or of an indiscriminate number of volunteers, but of specific persons whom he "calls"—it almost takes the form of an invitation. He is having a "working day," as it used to be called, and the only material reward he gives his helpers is the meals for the day and the prospect of a return service as occasion may arise. There is, for example, the thatching gang, in which as many as twenty men may be working on a neighbor's roof, replacing the old thatch with fresh, green flax, with an additional two or three older men or young boys driving teams of oxen, some of them borrowed from other neighbors, to bring more freshly cut flax from still another neighbor's garden, while women are working inside the house, or bringing dishes of food from their own houses, to feed the gang. Less conspicuous because it is an indoor job, but no less important as a form of mutual aid, is the carding gang, for which a housewife "calls" a number of women to card and spin her wool.

Thatching and carding are special occasions, both because they are relatively infrequent and particularly because of the number of people involved. On a smaller scale, however, the same sort of thing is going on all the time. Any man who has a special job may call in an assistant, or any number of assistants, whether he is painting or remodeling the interior of his house, adding another room, building a cabinet, shearing his sheep, fencing his garden or a new potato patch, breaking in a young bullock, or whatever it may be. In some types of work, two or three families may join forces in a perennial arrangement of mutual assistance, as when digging potatoes or trying out bird fat on Nightingale. More occasionally composed groups may get together to go fishing or hunting, to fetch wood from the hillside, or to go for apples. And when a boat is seen approaching the beach for a landing, a whole series of mutual aid patterns are activated, some people taking a bullock cart and a donkey or two down to the beach to bring up the load, others going down just to help land the boat.

Tied in closely with these patterns of mutual aid is an extensive sharing and exchange of gifts. When a man kills a bullock, he distributes probably more than half of the meat in gifts to other members of the community. Likewise, when there has been a good fishing day with possibly three or more boats returning home with good catches, there is in the evening a busy traffic of children crisscrossing the village from one end to the other with plates covered with clean towels, going to this house or that with "a bit o'fish for your supper." And when people return from the orchards in the apple season, or from Nightingale in the egg season or the bird season, most everybody gets a share in the spoils. Gifts are given on all kinds of special occasions and often without any occasion at all. The list could be continued to include practically every kind of activity in which the Islanders are engaged, and hardly a day passes in the life of an Islander unless he is involved in some cooperation with, or service to, another person.

What makes these acts of cooperation, aid, and service particularly important in the social life of the slanders is the fact that they are selective and reciprocal. There is no feeling of obligation to the community as a whole, and a Tristan Islander does not cooperate or exchange services and gifts with just any other person at random or because he is a neighbor. "Neighborliness" in this sense does indeed exist on Tristan but usually comes into play only under exceptional circumstances, such as bereavement or the like. The acts of cooperation and service that are socially important are the ones that are selective and reciprocal because they are symbolic expressions and confirmations of specific interpersonal relations. In this sense the Tristan community conforms exactly to the definition of an "atomistic" community, which "recognizes only individual allegiances and ties."

The all-important basis for these individual allegiances is kinship, which in this case, as in most Western societies, is bilateral, that is, with equal importance given to relations through mother and father. It is recognized in some cases as far as second cousin once removed. These kinship ties, however, are reinforced or counteracted, as the case may be, by a number of other factors, such as marriage and in-law relationships, comparative prestige, and even personality and compatibility. And kinship does not always prevail. In one or two cases, even such a strong and demanding kinship relationship as that between brothers appears to have been overruled and practically eclipsed by counteracting in-law relationships and established friendships.

Since kinship relations are recognized bilaterally, they do not result in the formation of clearly defined and mutually exclusive groups or "clans" but are diffused throughout the community in such a way that everyone is at least a relative of a relative of everybody else. Thus every person on Tristan da Cunha stands at birth in a potential relationship, not to a specific "clan" or "kinship group," but to a fairly large number of individual relatives within a diffuse segment of the community, which may cut across a number of vaguely defined kinship congeries and "social sets," but tapers off as kinship becomes more distant. It is within this range of potential relationships, later supplemented and enlarged by friendship ties established during childhood and adolescence, and by courtships and marriage, that the individual selects those relationships which he chooses to recognize and emphasize. This selection is extremely important because it is through this process of selective mutuality that a Tristan Islander finds his position and, in fact, his individual identity within the social structure of the community. The all-important instrument in this search for identity is the selective reciprocity of cooperation and mutual services and gifts, by which the chosen relationships are expressed and thereby confirmed and reinforced, while others may be played down or completely ignored and eventually fade away.

This is the overwhelming importance of the selective reciprocity that permeates all activities connected with the traditional subsistence economy of the Tristan community. Moreover, this is what makes the loosely organized aggregate of independent households a "community" in more than an ecological sense, firmly structured and integrated as it is by a network of selective but overlapping and interlocking relationships that leaves no one untouched, where a person belongs, not at the expense of his individuality, but on the contrary by virtue of a personal identity which is expressed and confirmed in those relationships that he chooses to reinforce in a pattern of selective reciprocity.

This atomistic integrity of the community (for this is how it must be described) is perhaps most clearly expressed in the one annual event in which the community comes as close as ever to a concerted community action. That is the "fatting trip" in March, when usually all the longboats—there are nine of them at present—go to Nightingale "for fat." This, as we have seen, is undoubtedly the most important social event in the life of the Tristan Islanders, and one should think that here, at least, is one situation where individual identities would merge into one solid, homogeneous community. To some degree this is the case. Social distances that may exist in everyday life are temporarily ignored in a situation like that. However, a Tristan Islander never loses his individual identity, for even here the established network of selective reciprocal relationships is in operation.

For one thing, definite established relationships determine in which boat each man goes, which is a matter of some importance because each longboat has its particular prestige and social status. For anyone who owns a share in a longboat, the situation is fairly well structured: either he goes in his own boat; or he sends someone to go for him, usually a son or a son-in-law; or he may yield his place in the boat, leaving it to the rest of the crew to select someone else to take his place on the basis of established reciprocal relationships. For one who does not have a share in a longboat, therefore, it is of the greatest importance that he has an established mutual relationship to a longboat owner, for this is the only way he can obtain a place in a longboat. If he plans to go on a trip, he will select the relationship appropriate to his status well ahead of time and reinforce it by offering his energetic assistance in preparing the boat for the season, a job that generally is done at Christmastime.

Likewise, each man's relative position and role in the boat, during launching and landing as well as under sail, is determined by his established relations to the rest of the crew: who takes the tiller, who handles the jib or the mainsail sheet and halyard, and who plays the passive role of the passenger. This, in turn, determines a whole series of other activities, what each man's role is in the loading, trimming, and unloading of the boats, from whom he may receive and to whom he may give directions, and so on. Even the ones who stay at home have specific roles to perform in relation to specific others, which determine who helps whom with the "gear," for whom he brings a bullock cart or a donkey, and in the case of a woman, for whom she brings the tea as the boats return.

On the whole, at sea as well as on the beach, even with all the boats going together, each boat's crew with its adjunct of helpers on shore seems to operate as a fairly independent, well-integrated unit, in which each member's status and role are defined by established personal relationships. All these things fall into well-structured patterns without much direction being given at all. Leadership, if it exists in the proper sense of the term, is discreet and inconspicuous, partly because no one wants to put himself forward to take the role of a leader, but mainly because leadership is unnecessary in a situation where each individual knows where he stands and what he is expected to do in relation to every other individual in the group. This seems to be the explanation why a word of command is seldom heard in these boats. While the man at the helm is in complete control as long as the boat is under sail, he never issues orders. He only offers suggestions so softspoken that an outsider is unable to distinguish them from the usual small talk: "She might run a little higher, Johnny, if we pull in a little on that jib."

Thus even in the confounding activity of a boat trip to Nightingale, which to a casual observer might appear as a loosely structured, or even completely unstructured, collective enterprise, each individual has his very definite place and clearly defined identity within the totality, and it is by virtue of this identity that he belongs as he plays it out in his specific reciprocal relationships. In the same way, every thatching gang or carding gang, every hunting trip to Stony Beach or Nightingale, every potato digging crew, is an active confirmation and reinforcement of this integrating structure of selective personal reciprocity as well as of every individual identity within it. This is what makes every major operation connected with the traditional subsistence economy a social event of the greatest importance, a "re-creation" in the true sense of the word, where plain sociability, play, and fun, with much joking and ribbing, are inseparably mingled with the work and help to keep everybody in his proper place. These activities, therefore, are positive expressions of some of the most fundamental values in the life of the community, social functions through which the participant is granted the integrity of individual identity as well as, at the same time, the security of belonging in a community where no one gives or takes orders.

In various subtle ways, these values were threatened by the invasion of the Economic Man with his ethos of progress, economic advancement, and contract relationships. And the issues that more than anything brought out in the open the different views, interests, and value orientations of the Tristan Islanders on the one hand and of the Company and the Administration on the other were the interrelated issues of property, money, and contract labor.

It will be recalled that the Tristan community was started as a communal enterprise, with all property held in common. As new settlers arrived, however, they were not given full property rights along with the original founders of the community. In fact, the principle of communal ownership was quickly abandoned, although common labor was still maintained for some time. This was formalized in the revised agreement drawn up by the settlers on December 10, 1821, in which William Glass was declared to be "at the head of the firm." The document states in part:

> We the undermention'd having enter'd into Copartnership on the Island of Tristan de Acunha, have voluntarily made the following agreement. (Viz)
> 1st That whatever profit may arise from the sale of Oil, Skins, &c shall be equally divided between all Hands.
> 2nd Every thing that arises from the produce of the Land, shall be equally divided in the like manner, as long as the People continue to Work at the same; it is at the same time to be understood that the whole of the Land, Stock, &c &c is the sole and joint property of Wm. Glass and John Nankevile. . . .

The wording of this document seems to imply a corporate ownership rather than a communal one, and a monopoly at that, but with communal usufruct. Soon, however, even this element of communism was given up, and by the 1850's, as we have seen, private ownership was fully established, each household being completely independent of the rest. Today the only reminder of an original communism is the fact that the pastures are held in common—which is indeed the usual pattern in European (and any other) peasant culture—but with the right for an individual to fence in his own plot of land for cultivation without any compensation to the community.

Private property is, of course, a dominant element also in the ethos of the Economic Man. However, in Western civilization this principle has an important limitation which is expressed in the concept of *ex-*

propriation as an exclusive right of government. This concept may, in fact, be a cultural remnant of the rights of kings to all landed property in a feudal society. Today it is a clear manifestation of the fact that in the Western system of values, Progress as a communal goal (that is, "for the common good") takes precedence even over such a sacred principle as that of private property.

When the social experiment on Tristan da Cunha was in the planning stage, the complete reorganization of the economy of the island was an intrinsic part of it and included the establishment of an agricultural industry under company auspices. This, obviously, was the rational thing to do for a real "uplift" of the Tristan economy. But it was equally obvious that it would require extensive expropriations. The peculiar conditions of landed property on Tristan, however, with which we must assume Mr. Lawrence, the mastermind of the project, was entirely familiar, may have given rise to hopes that such complete reorganization of the Tristan economy would indeed be possible without creating too much of an upheaval or involving the Company in high compensations to individual Islanders. The Tristan concept of landed property could be interpreted as saying that all land is essentially free and open to individual or corporate appropriation and use, and that all that had to be compensated for was the relatively small stock of cattle and sheep. Moreover, the Company could possibly claim that it would be acting according to island custom in appropriating the greater part of the pastures and only wanted to revert to the old principle of corporate rather than private ownership.

It is not known that this radical proposal was ever presented to the Islanders or that a serious attempt was made to implement it. It must have been realized by the planners that such a program would have been a most serious infringement of the Islanders' core values of individual integrity and independence and would inevitably have aroused the most energetic resistance, or at least intense resentment, on the part of the Islanders, who were fully aware of the possibility of expropriation should it be considered to be in the interest of the Company or the Administration. The outspoken Mary Swain was not the only one who used to warn the Islanders: "If you don't watch out, some day they will come and take your houses and potato patches away." It was not very likely that the Islanders would yield on this point, and the

Company gave up the idea of an agricultural industry, I suspect not only for economic reasons.

More subtle, and far less conspicuous on the surface of things, was the conflict of values that ensued from the introduction of money as a means of exchange. To all appearances the Tristan Islanders took to the use of money as a measure of material value with no difficulty at all. Not only did they readily accept the monetary values of imported goods as dictated to them by the Island Store; by direct analogy from the wages and other contracted payments that they received from the fishing industry, they soon also learned to put a cash price on some of their own products and services.

An interesting innovation connected with the introduction of money is concerned with the landing of stores and mail from ships. As long as the stores were bartered collectively from a ship or brought out as a charitable gift to the community, there was, of course, no question of anybody paying the Islanders in money or in kind for the strenuous work of bringing the stores ashore in their boats. And it entered nobody's mind that it should make any difference if the stores belonged to an arriving minister or other outside visitor. When the Norwegian expedition arrived at Tristan in December 1937, all the men of the island spent two full days landing our one hundred tons of provisions and equipment in their longboats, and an additional day bringing it up to the site of our camp with their donkeys and oxcarts. No one had mentioned a reward for the work, and they did not ask for one.

Today landing stores and mail from a ship is a job for which the Islanders expect to be paid, whether the stores are for the canteen, for the Administrator or the Company, or for a scientific expedition.

A few Islanders have picked up the "business" of selling fresh meat, vegetables, eggs, and fish to outsiders at the Station as a more or less steady source of income, specializing to some degree in growing vegetables or raising chickens and eggs for sale, and one man made the sale of beef his specialty, keeping a relatively large herd of some twenty head of cattle near the Settlement for this purpose and offering his beef for sale both at the Station and to the fishing ships. The prices were fixed at a shilling and sixpence per pound of beef and sixpence a pound for vegetables, regardless of kind.

Closely connected with the practical use of money as a medium of exchange is the concept of money as an abstract measure of material value. In more recent years the Islanders will regularly talk about a longboat as "costing" about two hundred pounds. The longboats are indeed objects of great pride to the Islanders, and putting a price tag on them may be an attempt to explain to an outsider (in a language that he is supposed to understand) how valuable they are. To an Islander, two hundred pounds is a sizable sum of money. That this is more than a manner of speech, however, is indicated by the fact that the Islanders charge extra for the use of a longboat in landing stores from a ship. Likewise, a man may talk about the value of his house in terms of how much money he has put into it, and again two hundred pounds is the figure most frequently quoted. In both cases the monetary value ascribed to the object simply equals the estimated actual purchasing cost of the materials used in making the object (not including time spent on the work, wear and tear of tools, etc.) and has nothing to do with an estimated or actual market price—a longboat has, in fact, never been bought or sold, and the only house that has ever been sold for money on the island since 1908 was recently transferred for a price of eighty pounds.

Once money is accepted as a medium of exchange as well as an abstract measure of value, the concept of money as a vehicle for the storage of material assets follows almost inevitably. Saving anything that could possibly be of use was an art that the Islanders had learned thoroughly during the period of isoation, and as money became available (and usable), it naturally was regarded as something to be "saved for a rainy day," a practice that was strongly suggested and encouraged by the establishment of a branch of the British Postal Savings Bank under the management of the Administrator. Of necessity, the amounts saved by the Islanders have been fairly modest, mainly because of the limited availability of money. It may be estimated, however, that the average Tristan family regularly keeps an account in the Postal Savings Bank at a level of about two hundred pounds, with a wide range of variation. In addition, nearly every household keeps a small amount of cash, sometimes as much as seventy to eighty pounds, tucked away in a chest drawer or in a cup in the cupboard.

With this ready acceptance of money in various applications, it is all the more remarkable that it is used almost exclusively in dealing with outsiders. This does not mean that money never passes from one hand to another among the Islanders. Money may have many different meanings, depending on how it is defined by its users. On a limited scale, money did enter the internal economy of the Tristan community, not primarily as a medium of exchange or as an objective measure of material value but as a useful commodity. In this sense it may be used in the ongoing exchange of goods and services within the Islanders' system of selective reciprocity, and with all the symbolic significance of a gift.

Two cases of this use of money on Tristan in recent years came to my attention. An old man, who was not gainfully employed, helped the husbands of two of his granddaughters in the potato digging. In return one of them took him to the pub and treated him to a couple of drinks; the other presented him with a ten-shilling note. In the other case an old man in full-time employment as a caretaker at the Station had his brother-in-law cultivate his potatoes, a job that is regularly done two or three times during the growing season, and gave him ten shillings in return. It was obvious from the manner in which the money was presented and accepted that in neither of these cases was the money note considered either by the giver or by the receiver as a "payment" or compensation for time spent or work done. In this kind of transaction money clearly represents a subjective symbolic value to the Islanders, quite apart from its objective nominal value, which alone makes it applicable as a medium of exchange in the Island Store.

The prevailing attitude of the Tristan Islanders toward money and their conception of its symbolic significance came out clearly in an interview I had with one of them in England during the summer of 1962. After discussing the blessings of the fishing industry—"that's where the people arn all their money was from the factory"—I raised the question whether the Islanders had started buying and selling between themselves. The answer came with emphasis and warm conviction:

No—we never come to *that* stage, and I don't see Tristan'll ever come to that stage for to buy and sell off one 'nother. Maybe generation after generation, in 'nother hunnert years, I can't say what'll happen then, but not yet of all. No, the people of Tristan, they's jus' like one family, and they live happy, and one help the h'other, and if I's out in my farm and doing my potatoes and someone's finish' his'n,

he'll come along an' give me a hand, and the next day he got something to do, I go an' give him a hand, so we all help one 'nother. On
Tristan, they's jus' like brothers 'n' sisters.

Whatever exaggerations may be implied in this statement about the
Tristan community being "like one family," it is clear that in the
thoughts of this Islander, money is something that does not properly
belong in the familial relationship between "brothers and sisters." The
statement indicates an explicit rejection of a pattern of conduct which
is regarded as opposed to, and incompatible with, the established pattern of selective personal relations, in which a Tristan Islander finds
his identity as well as his sense of belonging. What the Islander seems
to be saying is that money-making is fine but only to a point where it
does not interfere with certain nonmaterial values present in the Tristan way of life. His statement even indicates a surprisingly articulate
awareness of the irreconcilable contrast between a subjective reciprocity and an objective equivalence in human relations. The former is a
personal relationship, which is perpetuated and confirmed every time
it is expressed in the form of a gift, a service, or a return service. The
latter is an impersonal relationship, which is terminated by the act of
paying up the account and therefore, in fact, an explicit denial of personal reciprocity.

There is no doubt that in the value system of the Tristan community precedence was still given to personal reciprocity over objective
equivalence, even at the sacrifice of monetary gain. In this culture
there is not much room for the profit motive except in dealing with
outsiders. And without it, no rational division of labor could develop.
Again, the Company, with its well-intended social experiment, yielded
gracefully to necessity and gave up the plan of replacing the "irrational" and value-laden subsistence economy with a rational exchange
economy based on money and profit.

Finding a "committed" labor force is a perennial problem when industry tries to establish itself in a new territory. The problem has been
widely discussed by industrialists and industrial sociologists alike, and
the outcome of these discussions seems to be—although it is seldom
expressed quite as bluntly—that it is extremely hard to find a fully
committed labor force among people who are economically free and
independent. So the solution of the problem must be for industry to
seek out a population with a comparatively large section of disenfran-

chised people, or to create such a situation by undercutting independent economic activities, either through manipulations of wages and
prices or through monopolistic concessions granted by government.

However, that this is much more than a purely economic problem
was demonstrated clearly in the case of Tristan da Cunha. Before industry moved in, here was a whole population that, at least in the eyes
of the outside world, was in a state of economic destitution. Yet the issue of "labor commitment" in terms of a binding labor contract was
the stumbling block that broke Mr. Keytel's efforts during the first decade of this century and forced the Development Company to make
considerable concessions in the 1950's.

Economic factors were indeed involved, such as the limited scope of
the fishing industry, curbed by weather conditions and by limited investments, which meant that the fishing industry could only supplement but not supplant the subsistence economy of the island. For this
reason the fishing industry was unable to reduce the Islanders to a
total dependency on its wages. Even the "permanent staff" did not live
entirely "out of the canteen" as the Station people did. Besides, in
their frugality and in the absence of the "acquisition motive" of the
Economic Man, the Islanders had only a limited desire for economic
advancement, which further reduced their dependency on the Company in an economic respect.

Still, the economic advantages of a full commitment to the fishing
industry were obvious and well recognized by the Islanders. These advantages, however, were apparently outweighed by certain noneco-
nomic values that were felt to be at stake.

In the first place a labor contract implied working under a boss, and
this was something the Islanders were not used to and did not like.
They had great difficulty expressing it in words. Maybe they did not
want to seem oversensitive or arrogant, least of all in front of a micro-
phone and a tape recorder. It is obvious, however, that contract labor,
with its implication of subordination under a boss, was not considered
by the Islanders to be entirely compatible with the dignity and integrity of a free person. At least it was more pleasant to be on one's own.
Here is what one elderly Islander had to say about it:

I'm not use' to workin' under a boss—I mean, I don't mind workin'
under a boss when the boss can come 'n' tell you, oh, you made a good
job of that, I like it the way you done it or something, you know. But

when you's workin' under a boss here, you come along he may say to you, uh, look, it's a rotten job you made there, you know—well, you's workin' to please somebody else, not to please yourself. But on Tristan, I work to please myself. Well, I know, I's doin' a job, I do it to my own ability, I would say, and then if af'r I's finish' it, I stand off and I look, and then I thought to myself, I made a rotten job of that, I don't like it—all right, I'll leave it for a few days, and that come down I'll do it some other way—well, then I's doin' it because I don't like it. But if somebody *else* got to come along and tell you to do it, then you feel small. You see? Well, I mean, a man at my age, up to sixty, and you always use' to bein' your own boss, then all of a sudden you got to come underneath a boss—it's not the same thing.

It was obvious that the man had talked himself warm on a subject that was close to his gentle heart. Of course, his pride and independence was a value that could be bent a little on occasion, at least temporarily, to make a little money for "luxuries." Nevertheless, the implication of subordination associated with a labor contract was, no doubt, an important factor in the Islanders' refusal to let the fishing industry interfere with their subsistence economy and its freedom and independence. This is also why most of them preferred by far to work as independent fishermen for the Company, signing up on a day by day basis, rather than as wage earners under a time contract.

Time was another implication of the labor contract that caused confusion at first and then conflict when it was realized that even here essential core values were at stake. The Tristan Islanders fully accepted the notion that a labor contract was indeed a claim on their time. The idea was not at all unfamiliar to them, for in their own system of selective reciprocity they are constantly faced with obligations that put a claim on their time in preference to individual interests or inclinations. Through generations of practice these obligations have been arranged into a firmly established hierarchy, corresponding to the accepted hierarchy of values, determining which obligation takes precedence in case of a conflict. Thus, if an Islander owns cattle at Stony Beach in partnership with his brothers and they decide to go for meat, it is obvious that the painting of his front room or whatever work he may have planned for that day will have to be put off, for he is under an obligation to go along and help with the work. However, if his wife's cousin has a thatching on that day and has invited him to assist, his brothers will have to wait till some other day or go without him (still giving him his share of the meat), for a thatching may take precedence over a trip to Stony Beach, depending on the closeness of the respective relationships. The one activity that seems to take precedence over all others is the "fatting trip" to Nightingale in March. When that event comes up, everything else is dropped.

When contract labor entered the scene, the Tristan Islanders tried to fit it into their hierarchy of obligations. It was immediately clear that the labor contract would take precedence over individual interests and inclinations: you could not stay away from the job just because you felt like a day off or because you had some private work to do. But it was not recognized by the Islanders—in fact, they refused to accept the idea––that a labor contract should always take precedence over a thatching gang or a cooperative trip to Stony Beach. To them, the one obligation is as binding as the other, and the latter is infinitely more important to them because it is a personal obligation rather than a contractual one. When such events came up, therefore, they would simply not turn up for their contracted jobs, sacrificing their day's or week's pay, as the case might be. Or they might send a substitute, expecting him to be accepted by the employer.

The Company was flexible as usual. In fact, this was another reason for giving up the idea of relying entirely on Tristan labor. And since the Islanders were not under a permanent contract, there really was nothing the Company could do about it.

There were other, more subtle implications of the labor contract, some of which were only vaguely recognized by the Islanders. We have seen that practically every activity connected with the subsistence economy is tied in closely with a system of aid and services that is selective and reciprocal, and that it is within this system of selective reciprocity that the Tristan Islander finds his individual identity as a member of the community. Every piece of work that he performs, therefore, is a self-expression, a manifestation of his individuality as well as of his position within the web of social relations that make up the community. This applies whether he is working alone or in a group; for even when working alone, the product of his work becomes a part of his self as seen by others, a symbol of his status in a multifarious interpersonal relationship.

By contrast, contract labor is impersonal. It puts the worker in an impersonal relationship both to the product of his work and to the work process itself because, in contract labor, the work is not an expression of a personal reciprocal relationship. In the labor gang, the worker can not choose his co-workers as they have been chosen for him. He can not define his own role in accordance with established personal relationships as his role has been assigned to him by a boss. He is merely a number among other numbers. Contract labor, therefore, can never be a self-expression within the social context of the community. It is mere toil and drudgery, and a denial of personal integrity.

This is what Karl Marx, in his *Economic-Philosophical Manuscripts* of 1844, described as "alienation":

What constitutes the alienation of labor? First, that the work is *external* to the worker, that it is not a part of his nature; and that, consequently, he does not fulfill himself in his work but denies himself.

His work is not voluntary but imposed, *forced labor*. It is not the satisfaction of a need but only a *means* for satisfying other needs.

Finally, the external character of the work for the worker is shown by the fact that it is not his own work but work for someone else, that in work he does not belong to himself but to another person.

This may indeed be what the Tristan Islander tried to communicate when he said: ". . . when you's workin' under a boss . . . well, you's workin' to please somebody else, not to please yourself. But on Tristan [that is, in the subsistence economy], I work to please myself."

Symptoms of alienation in this sense may be seen in the Islanders' apparent indifference to the work they are doing under contract, especially as compared with their own subsistence work. On their own the Islanders are generally hard workers and usually take pride in being able to work fast as well as in doing a good job. Although time is of no particular concern, skill is of the essence, and every working activity may become an opportunity to "have a race," sometimes accentuated by small bets for a cigarette or a tot in the pub. The Tristan longboat, an Islander's most important instrument of genuine self-expression, is built for speed and beauty rather than for load capacity and safety, and whenever two or more longboats go together, there is a race. But this striving for a show of perfection and skill is not limited to the boat work. Whatever an Islander does, he likes to do it well, and the most menial task may be regarded as a challenge. Although the Islanders seldom partake in competitive sports or engage in contest for its own sake, the most trifling job may be turned into a match, whether it is fishing, walking in the mountain, carrying heavy loads, or digging potatoes.

None of this is present in contract labor, and complete indifference to the Company and its efforts was often shown. In this community, where theft was rare and nobody ever locked a door, pilfering from the Company stores became a sport and something to brag about. One Islander told me—in fact, he was boasting—that during the brief operation of the canning factory, before the installation of the freezing plant, he used to be in charge of the boilers, and if the fish were slow coming in, he would keep the steam pressure low so as to stretch the working hours for the women on the canning line. There is ample evidence that to the Islanders, work under contract had become a commodity, a means to an end that is external to the process of work itself as well as to its product. This, according to Marx, is also a part of the alienation process. And as the end is money, work becomes a necessary commodity to the worker to the extent that money is necessary. Herein lies, in fact, the only value of contract labor as far as the worker is concerned.

After the establishment of a fishing industry on Tristan, money had indeed become a necessity, but not a crucial one. It was still possible for a Tristan family to make a living without having to depend on contract labor as a source of cash income. On the other hand the increased living standards that the fishing industry brought had changed the lives of the Islanders and had given them a new scale of values as well as a new concept of what it meant to "make a living." This is what a disillusioned old Islander was referring to when he said: "The island will never be the same, it's too far gone now."

The old and the new attitudes were directly confronted in a conversation I had with an island couple. The husband was complaining about having been without a job for several months: "How can you make a living with no money?" And the wife corrected him: "We can make a living without money; but what for a few luxuries?" The question was indeed whether the new scale of values had undermined the old value system of the Tristan community and thereby its whole way of life. That question was soon to be put to a crucial test.

11   *Death of an Island?*

The first warning of disaster came on the 6th of August, 1961. It was a Sunday evening, a time for rest and for quiet visits with neighbors, friends, and relatives, with soft and lazy small talk over a cup of tea. In the houses people were huddling around the open hearth, which offered a friendly escape from the misty chill of the late winter, and surely there was talk about the weather. For on Tristan, the weather is not just a conversation piece resorted to when there is nothing else to talk about. It is a vital concern because, even now, with the fishing industry and all, it means the difference between "fat" and "hungry" times. And that winter of 1961 had been the worst they had had for a lifetime. For weeks on end the beach had been a thundering roar of froth and spray, turning the little village into a landlocked strip of wind-whipped ground under the fog-shrouded mountain. The boats were lashed down, the factory idle, and earnings had dropped to the point where the fishermen had to dip heavily into their savings. So it was surely a time for old people to reminisce—about the time when nearly all the boats were lost on the beach, crushed by the mighty waves, about the stormy winter long ago when more than half the cattle perished, or about many a year when potatoes were dear because hail and wind had cut down the crop. And in those days there were no savings to dip into.

The young people would surely listen to the stories in awe and amazement. Some of them could hardly remember the time when the Tristans were all by themselves, when the most exciting event was the arrival of the "big mail" with packages and gifts from the many friends of the Islanders in a faraway Outside World. "That was before the soldiers came," the old ones would explain. In spite of hardships and hungry times, those were happy days, but to the young people as distant as a stone age. Perhaps, as they listened to the ruminations of the oldsters, they would feel a warm glow of pride in belonging to a people who had weathered many a storm before and survived many a frugal winter. And deep silence would fall over the group, the sort of calm, soothing silence that has always been a large component of Tristan conversation and could last for long, endless minutes, broken only by the tick of a clock somewhere in the room, the faint click of rapidly moving knitting needles, and an occasional clang from a teacup.

Suddenly the ground trembled. Windows rattled, crockery fell from the shelves, and amidst it all a distant rumble rose and fell, then faded away. A different kind of silence fell over the group, tense, horror-stricken, as the knitting needles stopped and everybody froze in motionless fear. This was something new and terrifying. Never as long as people had lived on Tristan had anything like this happened before. Even the old people had never experienced anything like it.

Finally the spell was broken by an almost whispered "What was that!" And everybody rushed out only to find that the whole village was in a turmoil. Everywhere, people were coming out of their houses in great agitation, everybody shouting the same fearful question: "What was that?"

Some speculated that it might have been the shock of an atomic bomb. Three years earlier the United States had exploded an experimental nuclear device in the stratosphere above a point only sixty miles south of Tristan. Although no one on Tristan was aware of the experiment at the time and the Islanders learned about it only two years later, they knew that things like that were taking place. Others thought that a volcano might have erupted on the ocean floor nearby. No one dreamed of the prospect that the village itself was, in fact, sitting on the very top of a nascent volcano.

The following day, Monday, was quiet. But new tremors followed Tuesday and Wednesday, and in the early morning of Thursday, August 10, six tremors were felt in rapid succession. The frightening impact was heightened by a violent thunderstorm with hail and whipping rain, which accompanied the tremors.

Urgent radio messages were sent to Cape Town and London, but the replies were reassuring. The seismograph at the Magnetic Observatory in Hermanus, South Africa, had recorded only one tremor on Tuesday, August 8, and that one appeared to be further away than

Tristan da Cunha. From London came the message that the tremors probably were the effect of a slight settling of the earth's crust along a possible fault line—nothing to worry about.

But the tremors and shocks continued, and by the end of August they were a daily occurrence, with two or three jolts every day. One day twenty-four tremors were counted in less than twenty-four hours, some of them very heavy. On Sunday, September 17, while the congregation was gathered in the church for evensong, there was another quake, the heaviest yet. Mr. Peter Wheeler, who was serving as administrator of Tristan at the time, described it: "Suddenly the walls heaved, the floor trembled, and for a sickening second the roof threatened to cave in."

The previous day the fishing vessel *Tristania* had arrived from Cape Town to start another season of fisheries in the surrounding waters. The arrival of the fishing ships is always a happy event on Tristan, for it marks the end of a long, stormy winter. This time they were especially welcome, for it had been a hard winter, and no ship had touched at the island for five months. As usual on the day of arrival, Captain Scott, the master of the *Tristania,* and some of the other officers came ashore to greet their friends at the Station as well as in the Village—and Captain Scott, a boisterous sea dog whose stentorian voice and rough manners never quite managed to cover up the kindness of a heart as big as his enormous fist, had many good friends among the Tristan Islanders. He had read about the tremors in the Cape Town newspapers but, like most people outside the island, did not consider them too serious. He had even brought a new factory manager and his family as passengers in the *Tristania*. But the severity of the shock that Sunday afternoon had him worried.

It was well known to everybody on Tristan that the whole island is a product of volcanic activity. The evidence is obvious, even to the untrained eye, and present everywhere: the conical shape of the island itself with a big crater on top, and numerous smaller cones scattered over the hillside and along the beaches, most of them with craters. It was also evident from the sizes and shapes of the craters that some of the eruptions had come in the form of violent explosions. Not far from the Settlement are the two familiar landmarks, the Hillpiece and Burnt Hill, rising some 300 feet above the surrounding ground, each with a crater so deep that the bottom of it is on a level with the outside foot of the hill. But the lush vegetation everywhere, the deep soil, and a few peaceful crater lakes, including the ice-cold lake in the main crater, bear evidence that all this happened thousands of years ago. Only on the south side of the island, near Stony Beach, is an ugly, craggy heap of huge lava blocks obviously spewed from a gaping crater still visible to anyone who cares to climb the rugged sides of the hill, where so far only lichens and mosses have found a foothold. Stony Hill is its well-deserved name. Even this ugly boil in the landscape, how-ever, had been shaped hundreds of years in the past. No eruption was recorded or known to have taken place throughout the more than 450 years since the island was discovered. To all appearances Tristan da Cunha was an extinct volcano.

But the situation on Tristan in September 1961 gave good reason for worry. And the Administrator was not about to sit down and let the geologists in London decide whether he and his people were in danger. By sending out small parties of observers to various parts of the island as well as, with Captain Scott's help, to Nightingale, it was indeed found that the disturbance was concentrated in the area of the Settlement. No tremors were felt on Nightingale at all, and even a se-vere one—the heaviest so far, where "ornaments tumbled from mantel-pieces, crockery rattled in cupboards, and there was a pronounced thump followed by a prolonged shudder"—passed unnoticed at Stony Beach on the other side of the island. This was, as Mr. Wheeler ob-served, "at once disconcerting and encouraging" because, even though the village was in the apex of the disturbance, refuge could be found if necessary on Nightingale or even on the other side of the main island itself.

Comforted by this observation and by new assurances from London that the tremors were not believed to be due to volcanic activity, the Islanders settled down to accept the daily jolts as part of life. They went about their business as usual and, as it was the time for planting potatoes, that is what they did. In the meantime the other fishing ves-sel, the *Frances Repetto,* had also arrived, and the two ships took up their usual operations, fishing around the islands.

The "shakes" seemed to decrease in frequency, and occasionally as much as two days might pass without a vibration. But then they came with double force, loosening rocks and boulders in the perpendicular hillside behind the village, causing them to come down with a loud rumble in a cloud of dust, scattering frightened sheep grazing under the precarious cliffs. One cow was killed by falling rocks not far from the houses, and the water supply to the factory was cut off when a surface pipeline was broken. To keep the factory going, an emergency pipe was run from the main water supply of the village, but soon that was destroyed, too, leaving the Islanders once more to fetch their water from the Big Waterin', which continued to run fresh and cool by the village.

In the early morning of October 8, two months after the first tremor, another heavy shock jolted the village. Directly behind the Settlement, part of the cliff face came down with a thundering roar, leaving a big, ugly scar a hundred feet wide in its entire length from top to bottom. In the eastern part of the village cracks appeared in the walls, and doors jammed. On the ground outside, crack lines could be seen across cart tracks and footpaths, where the grass had been worn away. But the houses in the western part remained undamaged.

Late that night most of the Islanders living in the eastern part of the village decided that their houses were unsafe. Bundling up their children and taking with them what bedding and warm clothes they could carry, they moved in with relatives and friends in the western part, making their beds on the floors wherever they could find a space.

But strange things happened. The next morning, when some of the men went back to inspect their houses, they found that the doors opened and closed easily, most of the cracks in the ground had closed up, and everything seemed to have returned to normal except, of course, that the water supply was shut off in the whole village. Some of the families started to move back to their homes, as if in a stubborn belief that nothing serious could really happen to their village.

That afternoon, however, new and bigger cracks developed in the grassy slopes east of the village, only some two hundred yards from the nearest house. The biggest fissure soon developed into a crevice about ten feet deep, in which a bleating sheep was trapped, trying frantically to climb the steep sides of loose dirt. Then the bottom of the crevice was pushed up slowly, and as it reached ground level, the sheep jumped out and continued grazing as if nothing had happened.

This was indeed the beginning of an eruption. Soon the eastern bank of the newly formed crevice started to rise—five feet, ten feet into the air, forming a vertical wall of loose dirt and stones. Then the wall crumbled, and the rising ground was shaped into a "bubble" that continued to grow at a rate of five feet an hour or more. By dusk it had reached a height of about thirty feet above the surrounding ground.

The alarm was struck. The old shell case left by the Royal Navy, which served as a village gong, was sounded, and the men gathered in the Village Hall to discuss plans for an evacuation of the village. The Naval Station at Simonstown was summoned by radio, and the two fishing vessels were alerted for a standby.

An immediate course of action was quickly agreed upon. The plan called for the embarkation of the whole population of 264 Islanders and 28 expatriates in the *Tristania* and the *Frances Repetto*. They would then be transferred to Nightingale, where about forty wooden huts, some of them with fireplaces, would offer cramped but adequate shelter while waiting for assistance. However, it was getting late in the day—too late, in fact, to get everybody safely ashore on Nightingale before dark. And as the two small fishing ships could not possibly accommodate 292 passengers overnight, it was decided to seek temporary refuge at the Potato Patches, some three or four miles west of the village. In the drizzling rain and bitter cold of the waning day, with bundles and suitcases and rucksacks, with babes in arms and little children trailing along holding on for their lives to their mothers' skirts, slowly and sadly the people made their way over the rugged road in the falling dusk.

Old Mary Swain, in colorful Tristan vernacular, gave a vivid description of the dramatic events of those fearful days and nights when she was interviewed a month later by Mr. René Cutforth, of the BBC. When asked what happened to her on that fateful night, she said:

Oh, gosh, I can't tell you that! It was terrible. My son came and took me to the other side the line—the west of the line, you know—and he said, "Mother, you mus' come to the wes' line," he said, "because Mr. Wheeler said no one's to be to the eas' line."

"Nonsense, I'm not leavin' my home," I said, "I'm goin' to bed."

So he said, "No, Mother, you mus'n't. You mus' come," he say, "haf't'go'n' stay with me for the night."

So all night through we hear bum's and boulders and boulders coming down—I thought 'alf of the mountain was comin'!—So I slept on.

In the morning, I say to'm, my son Willie, "Mother's goin' down cookin' ou's breakfas' at our own house 'n'my lunch."

He said, "You bes' not, you's disobeyin' oders."

"Oh, I can't 'elp it," I say, "I'd rather be in the old house, I's use' to grufftness [?]."

So, my husband, you see, when 'e got 'is—finish' 'is lunch, he said 'e felt a bit weary, so he say he's goin' to bed.

I said, "You bes' not," I say, "you mus' remember you're on the east o' the line," I say, "I'm goin' up to Willie's."

An' when I said I'm goin' up to Willie's, he said:

"Well, that's alright."

I said, "Well, I'll promise you 'f anything happen terrible, I'll rush to you."

So I went up Willie's, and I went to bed, layin' down that much, you know, you felt *so* weary after all those bum's an' bruises, 's what I use' to call it. And he come 'nto the bedroom, 'e said:

"Mom, you bes' get up."

I said, "Why, sony?"

He said, "Mom, you bes' get up," 'e say, "the h'earth is opening."

"Oh, God," I say, "no, my boy!"

"Yes," he said.

I said, "Where is Daddy?"

He say he send one of the children down to wake Daddy up. "No, fear," I say, "I mus' rush myself."

So I rush' to my house, I said to'im:

"Fred," I say, "Fred, jump up quick," I say, "the earth is opening!"

"Huh?"

I said, "Jump up quick, the earth is opening!"

So 'e jump' out o' bed 'n' rush' to the—where we keep potatoes 'n' got 'is trade bag 'n' came in. An' when he came in, I'd to stuff in a whole lot o' rubbish, 's what I thought, into this sack 'n' sayin' to myself, this is nonsense, takin' all this stuff with me, I said, jus' might's well leave it because I can't carry it. Well, 'fore we got so far, the dong hit. Mr. Wheeler's want them in the Hall for to tell them what to do.

He rush' back, he say only take a little bit belongings, he say, because Mr. Wheeler say jus' take a bit belong's. So, I had a quantity, my [sewing] machine, you know, sack on my back, an'—the bes' one was, I had a—I jus' buy a pair o' shoes out o' the canteen for ma husb'n for a Chris'mas present. When I got so far up on the grass, to my astonishment, I had the box an' not the shoes, the shoes was dropped out on the grass. So, gosh, I said, I gota'ave to do it, I gota rush back 'n' get those shoes, I can't 'elp it. My life or the shoes. So I rush' back for the shoes 'n' I picked one up on the grass here 'n' 'nother one 'bout three or four fathoms away from it. So I picked that up an' stuck it in my arm 'n' I rush' towards Willie's again. Then, from there, I said my machine's on the grass an' also my clothing, I mus' rush back 'n' get that. So I rush' back for to got that. By the time I got to my house—'course it's quite a distance—I couldn't fetch it, I w's too 'xhausted, I couldn't fetch it, I 'ad to left it on the grass again. So Willie sent 'is two sons, Peter 'n' David, to get it for me.

So, by the time we got up to Willie's, the dong hit again:

"Get the donkeys 'n' go for the Patches!"

So we jus' 'ad to put on what we could on the donkeys 'n' carry what we could. I know what *I* had on my back—I 'ad a rifle, a big h'overcoat, an' a mac. I 'ad 'nother sack wi' some clothes in, I couldn't do that, I 'ad to give that to a boy to took for me. I got so far, I w's so 'xhausted I 'ad to lay on the grass again, 'ad another rest.

Freddie w's much tireder what I was, so he couldn't do no more. Then I 'ad to got a torch 'n' show him along the road, an' it w's jus' puddles 'n' ponds 'n' raining an' cold an' wet. So we got to the hut. When we got to the hut 'bout the Potato Patches, we all w's crowded together like sardines in a tin, 't *was* 's sardines, that's'e truth, in a tin, cold, miserable, no drink, no supper, no nothin'.

Fred and Mary Swain, both in their sixties at that time, were indeed privileged because of their age to sleep in one of the few huts out there by the Patches. Not everybody was that lucky. Most of them had to find a place to rest their tired bones as best they could: in an empty barrel, in a ditch, huddled against the low stone walls that served as fence and property markers around each potato patch, or wherever they could find shelter against the chilling wind. A couple of tents were reserved for the infirm and the sick. The night was bitterly cold.

Little by little the group dozed off. Seldom has a slumber so deep descended on any group of exhausted human beings, unless they were children in their blessed nightly oblivion. For only three miles away, a volcano erupted with fury. And they slept through it all.

Offshore, the *Tristania* and the *Frances Repetto* were on the alert. About two o'clock that morning they observed a thick cloud of smoke rising from the swollen boil under eerie illumination from a flickering glow in its gaping mouth. Then the volcano erupted. Huge rocks and boulders flew into the air, and soon after, red hot lava was flowing freely.

Captain Scott tried to rouse the people on shore by radio to alert them to what was happening near the Settlement, blocked from their view by the Hillpiece and Burnt Hill. No response. Then he fired rockets. Still no response. It was dawn before radio contact was finally made and the weary and drowsy Islanders learned that the "bubble" had blown its top. Mary Swain was surely not the only one who thought, "Well, that's the end of our island."

Preparations for evacuation started immediately. It was decided to bring the people out to the ships from Boat Harbour, a beach right under the Hillpiece, which was used occasionally by the Islanders when a northeasterly swell made the two Settlement beaches too rough for boat work. Some of the men returned to the Settlement to get the boats. As they came over the rise where the mighty Goatridge pushes its craggy mass into the grassy slopes of the plain, the Settlement came into view, and behind it a new, ugly cone of crumbling rocks and boulders, about two hundred feet high by this time. Smoke belched forth, and even now, in the growing daylight, the lava flow and hot cinders emitted from the crater had a distinct glow. There was a stench of sulphur in the air.

To get to the Boathouse on top of the bank, where the longboats were lashed down, keels up, the men had to walk through the desolate village to within two hundred yards of the fiery hill. With anxious glances at the rumbling, belching, spewing monster behind them, the men unlashed the boats, turned them over on their keels, and dragged them down the steep road to Little Beach. In a short time four longboats were launched and were being rowed down toward Boat Harbour with rapid strokes, the men standing up in the boats, pushing the oars as they were wont to do when speed was of importance.

Boat Harbour hardly deserves its name. It is an open beach like the rest of them around Tristan, only slightly retracted to form a shallow bay. The slope is rather flat, making for a comparatively wide surf-line, and just outside the breakers are a few submerged rocks, or "blinders" as the Islanders call them, which take some fancy maneuvering and exact timing to get by. But when the swell is from the right direction, the bay offers fair shelter.

This time, however, the swell was from the wrong direction. For endless minutes the four boats were lying in wait, bobbing on the rising swell, the oarsmen ready, all eyes intently watching the surf breaking over the blinders and onto the beach ahead, where old women and children were being helped down the precariously steep bank by sons and grandsons, husbands and fathers. First in line for a landing was the *Longboat* with Lawrence Lavarello, Gaetano's youngest son, at the helm. Lawrence, more than any of his brothers, had inherited his father's passionate love for boats. He was now the proud coxswain of the proudest Tristan-built craft ever to cross the waves, the *Longboat,* now an impressive thirty feet long. Here, in front of this raging beach, he was faced with a challenge that he could not turn down.

Finally, Lawrence and his crew made the dash. With the whole community watching in breathless suspense, they surfed their boat safely to the beach, and the first boatload of refugees from Tristan da Cunha was taken aboard. Among his passengers on this trip, Lawrence had his mother, Jane Lavarello, eighty-five years old and the oldest inhabitant of the island. She is a granddaughter of Corporal Glass and presently the only survivor of that generation.

One more boatload of refugees was conveyed from Boat Harbour to the fishing ships waiting offshore. But the risk was too great, and the cautious Islanders decided that the rest would have to walk back to the Settlement and be taken off from Little Beach, where the sea was calmer and no rocks or blinders were impeding the approach of the boats. So the weary Islanders climbed back up the steep embankment, gathered their sacks and bundles once more, and started the long trek back the same road they had struggled only a few hours before. Perhaps for the last time they trotted the familiar path through the Valley, across Little Sandy Gulch, past Knockfolly Ridge and Bugsby Hole to a place called Straight Bushes—peculiar names given to these places and landmarks by the old-timers long ago, but as familiar to the weary wanderers as the name of a relative or friend. Approaching Jenny's Waterin' and Hottentot Gulch, which normally would greet them with a friendly "almost home," these magnificently calm and God-fearing people showed the first signs of real fright at the sight of the new, as yet unnamed, cone-shaped hill rising directly behind the village, thick smoke wallowing from its top, and deadly lava pouring down its sides. This was a stranger in the landscape, fearsome, hostile, an intruder in their peaceful lives. This was the monster that was now driving them from their homes. It was so dreadfully close, and having to walk straight against it to get through the village and onto the beach, where the boats were already waiting, was more than some of them could take. A group of women broke away from the rest and hurriedly made for Hottentot Point and the beach below, from where they had to negotiate a rugged, narrow shoreline to get to Little Beach and the boats, but where the high embankment hid the ugly sight from their view, giving them the kind of imagined security that the ostrich is supposed to seek when he buries his head in the sand.

With four longboats shuttling back and forth, the embarkation was soon completed. In the early afternoon the two fishing ships, with the entire population of Tristan da Cunha jammed on board, weighed anchor and steamed toward Nightingale, bringing the four longboats along.

In the meantime, in response to the distress signals from Tristan received the previous day, the frigate H.M.S. *Leopard* was already on her way at full speed with relief supplies. She was expected to cover the fifteen hundred miles from Simonstown in three days and should arrive the following Friday. Another ship, the Dutch Royal Interocean Lines' M.V. *Tjisadane,* was approaching Tristan from the west. She was bound for Cape Town from Rio de Janeiro and was scheduled by previous arrangement to call at Tristan to pick up a retiring British nurse and two Tristan girls who were going to England to receive training as nurses. Now the captain was informed by radio about the evacuation, and the ship was directed to Nightingale, where she was expected to arrive the following day.

With these encouraging prospects, plans were made for the next steps to be taken. Because of the Islanders' deferential attitude to the authority of the Administrator, the burden of decision fell entirely on him. But young Mr. Wheeler had not appeared to be an authoritative person. He had been one who would listen to advice and suggestions, and the Islanders seemed to feel confident in his presence, which was not true with some other Administrators they had had. Besides, at this stage the Islanders were remarkably calm, and they did indeed have a few suggestions to make.

For one thing, although they realized that it would take some time before they could return to normal life, the Islanders were not about to abandon their island, at least not yet. No one, of course, knew how much damage there would be from the volcano, or whether the island would explode and disintegrate altogether. But until this happened, they were not going to give up hope. And they were concerned about their cattle and sheep and other property that they had left behind. In particular, they were worried about their dogs, fearing they would run wild, form packs, and start killing sheep and calves. In fact, some had suggested that they should destroy the dogs before they left the island but were persuaded there was no time for that. Now they were anxious that a small hunting party should, if at all possible, return to the island at an early opportunity and kill the dogs. For this purpose, many of the men had taken along their precious rifles, which ordinarily were used to hunt wild cattle at Stony Beach.

So it was decided that a small party of, say, six volunteers should remain on Nightingale to watch the course of the eruption and, if possible, return to Tristan in a longboat to take care of the stock and other property for the whole community. The rest would embark either in the *Tjisadane* or in the *Leopard* and proceed to Cape Town, where permits to enter and other assistance had already been offered.

By nightfall everybody was safely landed on Nightingale and settled in for a relatively comfortable night to the wailing music of petrels and nightbirds.

But while the Islanders were slumbering peacefully in their huts, thankful to be rescued, with worries about their future but no despair, confident that some day soon they would be able to return to their homes, a different fate was planned for them by forces beyond their control and comprehension. It appears that some people in the Colonial Office were never quite able to let go of their favorite notion with regard to Tristan da Cunha, although the idea had been dormant for many years. The question of total evacuation had not been raised since 1939, when shortly after the island was made a "dependency" of Saint Helena, such a move was discussed briefly until the idea was eclipsed by the war.

It was ironic that the question of total and permanent evacuation should be revived again at this time. Since the establishment of a fishing industry on the island, the community had prospered as never before in its entire history. Shortly before the eruption Sir Douglas Gane's Tristan da Cunha Fund had started liquidation procedures; Sir Irving Gane, who had taken over the management of the Fund after his father's death, issued what he described as a "Final Report," noting that the Islanders were "no longer in need of charitable support." Some influential people in the Colonial Office, however, seemed unable to forget that for some time in the past the Tristan community had been what they were pleased to call a "nuisance" to them, with distress reports and relief expeditions, notwithstanding the fact that most of the actions taken by the authorities in behalf of the community had been based on reports by outsiders, which in the end turned out to be greatly exaggerated presentations of the conditions on the island. And now, with the whole population forced off the island by a volcanic eruption, they saw it as "a godsend opportunity to get rid of a problem," to quote a source close to Whitehall and Great Smith Street.

It is also ironic that one of the main arguments for total evacuation and liquidation of the Tristan community should be the cost of maintaining an administration that the authorities had imposed upon the Islanders against their known wishes. Those costs were largely covered by revenue from taxes levied on the Tristan da Cunha Development Company and from postage stamps, which now had been introduced and soon became philatelic collectors' items, sold in sheets to dealers all over the world directly from the Crown Agents, who produced them. But there it was, "a godsend opportunity to get rid of a problem."

While the Islanders and most of the expatriates were landed on Nightingale, the Administrator had stayed on board the *Tristania*, whose radio provided uninterrupted contact with authorities in Cape Town and Pretoria as well as in London. It must have been during that night that the fateful decision was made. All through the night telegrams were exchanged between the Administrator and the authorities in London, and the concluding message from London is reported to have said: "Use your own judgment." When the *Tjisadane* arrived early next morning, the Administrator ordered *all* the Islanders on board that ship, including the six volunteers who had planned to stay behind on Nightingale. They were also ordered to surrender their rifles, which were to be deposited with the police in Cape Town. Obviously, there had been a change of plans. But as usual when they received an order from an Administrator, the Islanders obeyed without a question—as one of them explained later, when asked why some of them did not stay on Nightingale after all: "Well, you see, Mr. Wheeler say 'e think everybody should leave and go, so—that's all there was to it."

The Islanders had not the faintest idea what was happening to them, nor did they seem to feel any great anxiety on that account. They were used to not being able to understand the reasons for the actions and provisions of the administration; those were as inscrutable as the ways of God in His mercy. And as nothing could shake their faith in God's ultimate wisdom and benevolent providence, so they never for a moment doubted the ultimate benevolence and wisdom of the Crown and the colonial administration. That day in 1961 they were a living confirmation of what Mr. Hammond Tooke had observed in 1904, when he wrote: ". . . but they must have lost the instincts of suspicion and circumspection, which ultimately, in less favoured countries, are necessary in order to carry on successfully the struggle for existence."

So the Islanders embarked in the *Tjisadane*, blissfully ignorant of the fact that, on that day, the death sentence was spoken on their way of life—a way of life which was dearer to them than life itself.

12   Out of the Past

When the *Tjisadane* docked in Cape Town five days later, it was like a meeting of two worlds. How weird must not our civilization have appeared to these unspoiled mariners so suddenly torn from their modest homes in the ocean, where their lives had been ruled, blessed, and cursed by nothing but the three primeval elements, Earth, Air, and Water, until the fourth element, Fire, drove them off. Now they saw for the first time a place where Man seemed to have conquered the elements and put them in his service. Even the mighty force of the ocean, which the Islanders knew so well, had been halted and tamed by strong, man-made jetties and piers offering safe anchorages and secure berths for the most splendid ships. Nature herself appeared to have retreated to the surrounding hillsides and beyond, yielding to a sprawling city with smooth paved streets and magnificent structures, and houses and houses as far as the eye could reach. It did not strike them with horror. They found it beautiful, and as they lined the railing, gazing in amazement at all this magnificent splendor from the relative safety of the half familiar ship, there was only one simple word that could express their thoughts: "It's lovely."

Yet it was strange, inconceivable, and bizarre—the hustle and bustle of a busy dock, with towering cranes heaving and swinging, people moving in all directions, and in the streets beyond, a rumbling traffic of motorcars and trucks and buses coming, it seemed, from everywhere and going nowhere, just moving along in an endless, aimless rush. A thousand unfamiliar sounds and noises, clanks and squeals and rumbles and roars, filled the air and penetrated their hearts with an undetermined anxiety, and perhaps for the first time in their lives did these independent, rugged individualists feel a deep, intense, bewildered need for each other. "All we ask," they said, "is that we are kept together."

The city of Cape Town had prepared a splendid reception for her involuntary guests, and assistance was generously offered. At the first report of disaster on the island, extra staff had been put on duty in the Cape Town Radio Station at Kommetje, keeping a twenty-four-hour vigil during the emergency. The South African Government, through Senator Jan de Klerk, Minister of the Interior, offered "any necessary assistance," including temporary permits to enter South Africa, and the Mayor of Cape Town was authorized by the City Council "to take any steps necessary" to ensure that the Islanders would have their needs met when they arrived in the city. At Red Cross House, generous gifts of clothing, much of it brand-new, were coming in at such a rate that an announcement had to be made asking the public not to bring more. African Consolidated Theatres gave a special celebrity show, all expenses covered, inviting actors and performers of the town to donate their services, the entire proceeds to be for the benefit of the Islanders.

Additional assistance arrived from outside South Africa. The people of Saint Helena contributed to a fund established to aid the Tristan Islanders. The Society for the Propagation of the Gospel, from their headquarters in London, cabled the Anglican Archbishop of Cape Town, Dr. Joost de Blank, placing £1,000 at his disposal, half of which was a contribution from the British Council of Churches.

On the whole, it looked as if the city of Cape Town, with generous help from outside, was prepared to take the Tristan Islanders to her heart for as long as it would take before they could return to their homes. But the authorities had other plans.

Even while the *Tjisadane* was still at sea heading for Cape Town with her precious cargo of refugees from that disaster-stricken island, a representative from the British Embassy in Pretoria flew to Cape Town to make arrangements for the Islanders' immediate transportation to England. The day after their arrival, the trusting refugees, still unaware that this was intended to be a one-way journey, were transferred in buses, with the few precious belongings they had managed to take along in knapsacks and bundles, from the *Tjisadane* to the *Stirling Castle*, which had just arrived from Durban on her way to Southampton. And on Friday, October 20, after four exciting days in Cape Town, and only ten days away from the straw-thatched stone cottages which had been their homes, the 264 Tristan Islanders sailed for

England to the cheers of 1,200 Capetonians who had braved a chilling drizzle to wave good-bye to their newly won friends.

It is a long voyage from Cape Town to Southampton. And in the monotonous tranquility of the lonely ship, away from the hustle and bustle of the busy city and the heartwarming sympathy of friends and strangers, the full horror of what had happened descended upon the weary Islanders. It was here that Johnny Green's spirit died.

I remember Johnny well. I believe he could be described as a typical Tristan Islander—quiet, kind, and warmhearted, always willing to help another fellow, but in the unobtrusive way that the Islanders have cultivated to refinement, giving you a feeling that you are doing them a favor by allowing them to help. Johnny's face was full of freckles, and a mocking grin was always lurking in the corner of his eye, ready to burst into a broad, delightful smile at the fun of being alive. It is perhaps revealing of his character that his favorite song should be Harry Clifton's humorous "Sweet Pretty Polly Perkins from Paddington Green" with the self-effacing opening line: "I'm a poor broken-hearted milkman." I do not know where he picked it up, but he sang it often and always delighted his audience with the way he drew out the first two notes of the refrain in facetious exaggeration, then hurried up to get a few extra syllables in:

> She-e-e wa-a-as beautiful as a butterfly
> and proud as a queen,
> She was sweet pretty Polly Parkins
> from Paddington Green.

Johnny was a young man of forty when I first met him in 1938. He had a fairly large family, even by Tristan standards. His oldest, and only daughter, Kathleen, was just at the courting age. She looked like her mother, serene and shy, beautiful in her way, with the warm hue of her oval face and a shade of a demure smile on her sensitive lips. She was like a second mother to her five freckled brothers—Douglas and "Harbet," who were just then thinking of how to become men; Alan, always with a happy smile on his face; Dennis, the obvious leader of a gang of little rascals who used to bring plants and flowers and berries and rocks and more flowers to our camp for a piece of chocolate; and little Harold, who at four could not say 'k' but quite undauntedly offered the guest "a tup o' toffee."

They were all married by now. Only Harold, the youngest, stayed at home with his wife Amy, his son Richard, and little Pamela, who was the one of all the grandchildren who looked most like her granddad, with freckles across her obstinate little nose, the same mocking grin lurking in the corner of her eye, and her mouth tightly shut as if she were holding back a giggle all the time. But all of them remained very close, as one great big family, and every Sunday afternoon, as sure as sunrise and sunset, they used to gather for a cup of tea at the house that Johnny himself had built just below his father's old house and next to his brother Alfred. But now—what would happen to it all?

The thought of his home filled Johnny's heart with worries and sadness over lost happiness. And he wept—some say he wept all the way from Cape Town to Southampton, fourteen long days and nights. Soon after they arrived in England, he died.

The Tristan Islanders were indeed facing an uncertain future when they stepped ashore in Southampton on the 3rd of November, 1961. The British Colonial Office had announced that the refugees "would be allowed to decide their own future," which was a generous gesture since Tristan da Cunha had been abandoned without giving the Islanders a chance to express their opinion. Their desire to stay together remained strong; in fact, they did not seem to care much where they were settled as long as they were not split up. And the authorities did everything in their power to meet this demand. The problem was to find a place where a community of 260 people could make a living without risking that the younger ones would seek their fortune elsewhere, leaving a community of old and infirm unable to fend for themselves. The Shetland Islands had been suggested as a place where the Tristan Islanders would be in familiar surroundings; the Chairman of the Council of Social Service for the Shetland Islands had, in fact, cabled the Colonial Office, inviting the Islanders to come. Similar offers and suggestions came from other parts of the United Kingdom as well as from abroad.

For the time being, until the question of resettlement could be solved, the Islanders were taken to Pendell Camp, one of several disused army camps in Surrey. One official described it as "an ideal place for refugees . . . . They will have everything they need—plus privacy." Christopher Brasher, of the *Observer*, probably came closer to the truth when he said: "Pendell Camp is a desolate place in which to wake up into a new world." The Islanders had a roof over their heads, but otherwise very little—and least of all privacy. Their sleeping quarters were in large barracks, where each family tried to provide a little privacy for itself by draping whatever blankets and clothing they could spare over clotheslines. And the heating apparently left something to be desired. One Islander told me that they often found ice on the drinking water in the morning. But then this was the coldest, snowiest winter that England had seen for many years.

There was no lack of goodwill and charity on the part of the English. Actively engaged in the efforts to help the Islanders adjust to British life were a number of voluntary charitable organizations—the British Red Cross, Saint John Ambulance Brigade, and foremost among them, Women's Voluntary Services, which the Islanders soon learned to know as the W.V.S. without knowing what the letters stood for. Even before the Islanders arrived, the women of the W.V.S. had been working hard preparing the quarters at Pendell Camp, cleaning the facilities, furnishing curtains, rugs, and flowers. And they continued to be of valuable and heartwarming service as long as the Islanders remained in England.

Financial aid came from a variety of sources. Immediately upon hearing about the plight of the Tristan Islanders, Sir Irving Gane had reopened the Tristan da Cunha Fund, and contributions poured in from every corner of the United Kingdom and from abroad, from girls' schools and boys' clubs, from hospitals and churches, and from every conceivable voluntary society, whether its primary purpose was Scottish dancing or carol singing. The BBC arranged an appeal on television by Mr. Wheeler, the Tristan Administrator, which in a few days brought the handsome sum of more than £7,500 in contributions. Newspapers, banks, and insurance companies made substantial donations. In the end Sir Irving found himself with assets amounting to almost £20,000.

The authorities were busy trying in various ways to help the Islanders in the transition from one world to another. Since the official intention was that this was going to be a permanent transition, one of their first concerns, naturally, was to introduce the Islanders to the economic system of twentieth-century England, in particular to get them acquainted with the job market. From the fishing industry on Tristan the Islanders knew about wage labor and labor contracts, although they did not like them and preferred to make their living independently. They were also familiar with the British money system. But they were completely lost when it came to finding a job in a completely industrialized society. The initial job hunting, therefore, fell on the Administrator, Mr. Wheeler, who remained in charge of the community, at least for the time being. And in this he was quite successful. Within a week some of the refugees had jobs, two of them in a feed factory near the camp, others in a brick factory or on a nearby golf course. One bright girl even found employment as a store clerk. And before long nearly all Tristan Islanders able to work, including women, were gainfully employed.

But there were other problems for the authorities to deal with. One of them was health. It was readily recognized that this population, having lived for so long under the protection of relative isolation, would be extremely vulnerable to the infectious diseases of modern civilization, and every possible precaution had been taken when the Islanders reached Cape Town and again when they arrived in Pendell Camp, with all sorts of inoculations. The medical Research Council in London assigned a team of doctors and scientists to study the physiological and pathological effects of civilization upon these people, and to give them every possible medical care and attention. The team included a medical anthropologist, Dr. J. B. Loudon, and a social psychiatrist, Dr. Kenneth Rawnsley, besides specialists in bacteriology, nutrition, and chest diseases.

Yet the Islanders' first winter in England was a perpetual fight against colds and bronchial infections, to which they seemed to be particularly susceptible. Johnny Green was only the first of the Islanders to succumb. Before two months passed, three more Islanders had died, all of them from pneumonia. Several others were seriously ill with pneumonia and bronchitis, and all of them had one or more bouts with influenza, coughs, and colds.

The Tristan Islanders had their own diagnosis of the situation. They were convinced—in fact, they knew from long experience—that mental depression and "worries" were the surest producers of illness and pain. And worries they had in full measure—about their jobs, about money, about their future, but most of all about their homes back on Tristan. Would they ever be able to return to the only way of life they knew? Would they ever again gather the family for a quiet cup of tea on Sunday afternoons? Or go to a dance in the Village Hall, all spruced up, to celebrate some happy event? Or see the boats return from Nightingale, with all the ribbing and teasing and merriment on the beach? This was all they were thinking about. This was all they were talking about. And not a day passed in that miserable army camp in Surrey unless somebody—man or woman—broke down in tears.

The medical team was not unaware of the ill effects of the mental state that the Islanders were in. Influential forces in the Colonial Office had suggested that the community be broken up and the people spread out in different locations in order to speed up the process of assimilation and, at the same time, to make it easier to find work for all. This was strongly opposed by the medical men, particularly by the social scientists on the team, who predicted that if an attempt were made to break up the group, the people would rapidly deteriorate both mentally and physically. And the scheme was dropped.

For the same reason it was not yet considered an opportune time to let the cat out of the bag concerning the future of the Islanders. The fact that the Government never intended to return the Islanders to Tristan was kept strictly secret both from the Islanders themselves and from the general public. The hope was apparently that when the Islanders were settled in more comfortable quarters, they would in time learn to enjoy the blessings of modern civilization and forget about their poverty-stricken life on a bleak island in the middle of the ocean.

In the meantime the search for a suitable place for resettlement went on. Finally, toward the end of January, the Islanders were again on the move. They were herded like sheep into large buses and driven through the gently rolling, snow-covered meadows of Surrey and Hampshire, down along the western shore of Southampton Water, through Hythe and Fawley to a place called Calshot. Here, at the end of the road and separated from it by a white-painted picket fence, were several rows of gray stucco houses, two stories high, each with a little front yard surrounded by a hedge. These were the new homes of the homeless refugees. The place was soon to be known as Tristan Close.

The Close was part of a Royal Air Force Married Quarters Settlement near the former RAF station at the mouth of Southampton Water. Only a few houses across the road were still occupied by RAF personnel. The others were empty. There were about fifty of them, not quite enough to give each Tristan family separate quarters. But by putting elderly couples in with one of their married children, an arrangement that the Islanders were familiar with from their own community on Tristan, it worked out to give fairly adequate housing for everyone. Here the Islanders could stay together in a community that was clearly separated from its surroundings. They would even have their own chapel, community hall, and post office, and a country store was located conveniently across the road. The site also satisfied the hopes of the authorities, who would like to see a rapid assimilation of the Tristan community into modern British society rather than "trying to recreate Tristan in Britain." In nearby Fawley, only two miles away, a huge oil refinery was spewing its black and yellow smoke and flashing its flares from a forest of smokestacks and flues. Several smaller industries were operating in other towns of the area. Besides, Totton and Southampton were within easy reach by bus. All this would offer ample opportunity for jobs as well as for schools and shopping. At the same time the shock of the sudden transition to a totally industrialized society might be lessened by the rustic, almost idyllic surroundings (in any direction away from the oil refinery), where the famous ponies of the New Forest, to no surprise of the Islanders, had the freedom of the roads.

As a farewell gift from the Government—for it was now the intention that the new settlers should be on their own—the houses were fully furnished. The W.V.S. women were again on hand to make the houses ready with curtains and flowers. Curtain material was provided by the Tristan da Cunha Fund, which also furnished rugs and carpets, bedspreads and quilts, food supply for the first few days for every household, and as a timely reminder that the Islanders were now settling in a modern, civilized society, an alarm clock for each household. So everything was set for the Islanders to join the rat race.

For anyone who has grown up in our modern civilization it is hard to imagine what it takes to learn it almost from scratch—not only the big things, like the unfamiliar sights and sounds, most of which one must learn to ignore, or the intricate bureaucratic machinery of modern government and organization, which most people never learn anyway, but tiny little things of everyday affairs, like how to use a telephone or ring a doorbell. Some of the Tristan Islanders learned it the hard way. One young girl had gone to see the chaplain. Noting that her modest knock on the door received no answer, a friendly stranger passing by showed her the little button on the side of the door and told her to press it. The girl looked at the button, then at the stranger, who nodded encouragingly and went on his way. For a couple of minutes the girl was just standing there. Finally, after having inspected the little button carefully, then her thumb, she mustered enough courage to do as she was told. Unfortunately, the friendly stranger had forgotten to tell her to release the button after the appropriate time, and the girl pressed—and pressed—and pressed, until the door flew open, and an irate padre appeared in the doorway, asking what this was all about. The frightened girl stepped back into thin air and almost fell down the steps.

It took some time before the Islanders learned not to knock on the door or remove their hats when they entered a store. And it was most difficult to get used to not being greeted with a friendly hello by strangers they met in the streets or on the road. Perhaps some of them noticed with astonishment that our civilization has more "don't"s than "do"s among its codes. Most confusing were the many "don't"s of the traffic signs and learning which of them applied to pedestrians and which applied only to motor vehicles. One minor problem was the delay the Islanders caused in the delivery of milk, bread, and meat in the area because every delivery man who came to a Tristan house was invited in for a cup of tea.

But there were more serious things to learn, such as not to trust a stranger. This was so contrary to their own experience and concept of human decency that some of them never learned it. One day in early August, after fully nine months of "civilized" living, young Stella Glass and her mother-in-law went to Southampton shopping. They had bought a big sack of potatoes and were dragging it along toward the bus stop. On the way they stopped at a clothing store to buy a head scarf, and not wanting to drag the dirty sack of potatoes into the nice store, they left it outside. When they came out, the sack was gone. Thinking that some friendly person might have found it and taken care of it, they went back to the place where they had bought it and asked if somebody had turned in a sack of potatoes. That the sack had actually been stolen seemed to be beyond their comprehension. In the end, of course, they had to return home without the potatoes.

When Joseph, Stella's husband, heard the story, he explained knowingly: "Well, next time it happen, you find a telephone, put your finger in the 9 and turn," demonstrating the motion with his hand, "then you put your finger in the 9 again and turn," repeating the demonstration, "and then the third time, you put your finger in the 9 again and turn," demonstrating again—999 being the standard emergency call in all British cities and towns.

Timidly, Uncle Gordon suggested that another solution, perhaps, was not to leave the potatoes unguarded.

Crime was such an unbelievable thing that it was hard to realize that it actually occurred. Stella Glass was not the only one who had difficulty getting this into her pretty little head. And violent crime was even more unbelievable. Once, however, it struck pretty close to home. It was shortly after the Islanders had moved to Calshot. Big Gordon Glass, who was now sixty-two years old, and who had lost his right arm in a factory accident on Tristan, had obtained a job as a night watchman at a port installation near the Close. One night he was mugged by a group of young hoodlums, who demanded his money. When not a penny was found in his pockets, they took his prize possession, a watch handed down from his father, smashed it on the cement, and ground it out under their heels; then they beat him up and left him lying there, bruised and bleeding. For some time after this the Islanders did not dare go out after dark, and when they read in the newspapers about a murder or robbery, be it in Southampton or London or distant Glasgow, they sat in their houses behind locked doors, too frightened to open for anybody.

There were a few scuffles with teen-age hoodlums and "teddy-boys," who used to come down from Hythe and other nearby towns, especially on Saturday nights, to break up the dance parties that the young Tristaners tried to arrange in their own community hall. These confrontations diminished when the Islanders reluctantly took up the challenge and learned to fight back. But having to fight to defend their territory made a deep impression on some of them and confirmed the general distrust in outsiders which was now developing to the point where the Islanders were unwilling to mingle extensively with anybody except their own people.

The importance of these early experiences can hardly be overestimated. They surely convinced the Islanders, if they did not know it already, that their own way of life, with its freedom and independence, its tranquility and peace, and with its absence of violence and crime, was not only different and unique, but better than that of the Outside World with all its glamour.

Accent was given to the Islanders' uniqueness by the fact that they remained in the spotlight all the time. Press, radio, and television trained their microphones and cameras on them in a continuing barrage of interviews and reports, and the medical and social scientists in charge of the community and its welfare complained that the Islanders could hardly take a step without the newspapers having something to say about it. The newspapers, in return, reported indignantly that life was being made "impossible" for the Tristan Islanders by the nosy prodding of the scientists, including "a Norwegian professor from an American university, who spent four months on Tristan in 1938." Wherever the Islanders went, and wherever they got in touch with the English, whether at work, in shops and stores, or in the few social contacts that they had, they were inevitably cast in the role of being "Tristans," impressing people with their dignity and good manners, and politely answering questions about life on Tristan. Even when frequenting the pub in Fawley, as some of them did, especially on Friday nights, they could not escape being recognized as Tristaners and being treated as special guests both by the innkeeper and by other patrons.

With all this going on, the Islanders were not given much of a chance to forget their identity, even if they had wanted to do so. There is every indication, moreover, that they accepted their assigned role with pride if not always with pleasure. In fact, they were rather annoyed sometimes at the prevailing image, often reinforced by the press, of the Tristaners as a rather "primitive" bunch, naïve and ignorant, with "interesting" customs and a "peculiar" speech. Of course, the journalists often took liberties in their reports, and their imitations of the Tristan speech were invariably exaggerated and for the most part far off the mark. They were sometimes condescending, even downright rude and insulting in what they wrote, as if they did not expect their subjects to read the reports, or did not care if they did. And in an understandable effort to bring out a good "human interest" story of "the peasant coming to town," some of them overstressed the Islanders' ignorance and naïveté.

The Islanders read every piece about themselves that came into

their hands and snorted: "It's all lies!" And it became a matter of
pride to show the "h'English" that the "Trisst'ns" were just as civilized
as anybody else and definitely more so than the hoodlums, the rob-
bers, and the murderers who were given such big spreads in the newspapers. Indeed, the self-esteem of the Tristan Islanders had come a
long way from the diffident humility of the nineteen-twenties and thirties.

It was particularly in dress and speech that the Tristan Islanders
stood out conspicuouly among the English. And with all the fuss made
about it in the press, the Islanders became sensitive in this respect.
They did not come entirely unprepared, however. For almost twenty
years they had at least had some contact with the Outside World
through the Station and its changing population. And they had received some measure of formal education through the school on Tristan, particularly in Standard English, resulting in some adaptation of
their local dialect, especially when talking to outsiders. But the social
distance between Village and Station, maintained as much by the Islanders as by the Station people, had apparently prevented a strong influence on the Islanders' dress. The only difference from 1938 I could
notice when I saw them in England in 1962 was that the women's
skirts had become a little shorter. And I heard of only one girl, an extremely independent granddaughter of Bob Glass, who had dared exchange her woolen stockings for nylon hose, risking the critical judgment of her kin that she was trying to put herself on a level with the
Station people.

But now, noting that the same type of dress was worn by "important" and "unimportant" people alike, there was a rather quick change
of attitude. Some of the younger women, especially, soon adopted the
modern taste and style, although some of their elders frowned upon
the indecency of knee-length skirts, nylons, and low necks. Before long
even lipstick and nail polish became fairly common, and more and
more women had their hair cut short and even learned to use the
beauty parlor.

In some other respects, also, there was an amazingly quick adaptation to the forms and symbols of modern civilization. In their homes
the Islanders readily took to electric cooking, acquired radios and television sets, and after some initial confusion even learned to buy on the
installment plan, or "hire purchase," as the British call it. They rap-

idly became familiar with modern means of transportation and learned to find their way around Southampton and London on their own. Many of the younger men bought themselves motorcycles and scooters, some of them brightly painted in red and white, or blue and white, with helmet and jacket in matching colors. And the teen-age boys rode around on shiny bicycles, all equipped with the proper attachments.

Likewise in their work, the Islanders appeared to have no difficulty adapting themselves to any kind of job. They worked in garages and service stations, in various kinds of factories, where they quickly learned to work on the assembly line, in road construction and street cleaning, or at a large yacht club near Lymington. Whatever the job was, they seemed to take pride in being at least just as good at it as their English coworkers. Most of them were eager to learn, and some of the men became fairly skilled mechanics.

An interesting little piece of adaptation was made by one Islander, who soon discovered that, with seven or eight children in the house, his unemployment compensation when out of work exceeded the wages he could earn working—so he quit working altogether.

With all this marvelous adjustment to the most conspicuous patterns of modern civilization, the authorities may have felt confident that the evacuation of Tristan da Cunha had been a success, and that the time had come to withdraw any patronizing supervision of the community at Calshot. In early February 1962, in answer to a question in the House of Commons, Mr. Maudling, the Colonial Secretary, said that he "doubted whether Tristan da Cunha would ever be safe for permanent settlement again." Following that statement, a Member of Parliament suggested that Tristan would be a suitable site for nuclear tests since the island had been "abandoned by its inhabitants."

In April of that year, the Administrator and the Chaplain were removed from Calshot as their terms of appointment expired, and the Colonial Office closed its files on Tristan da Cunha.

13   *Let My People Go!*

The Tristan Islanders had not at all abandoned their island. In the noise and rush of a busy world, amid jobs and bus rides, under the hair dryers, or half asleep in front of a television set, they dreamt of nothing but their homes far away, waiting, wondering when the Government would finally send them back. Nothing else seemed to attract their lasting attention or interest, and worry about their homes on Tristan continued to take its toll in illness and colds.

Tristan Close was almost like a ghost town. The straight rows of gray gables stood there austerely, as if guarding a secret. The streets were empty. On a warm day, an old woman would sit on a wooden box in front of her house sunning herself, her head bowed as if half asleep, and her head-scarf pulled forward to shade her face. A few children played quietly in a sandpile.

In the evening, when the buses arrived with people returning from work, the Close came to life, but only for a moment, as a steady stream of men and women moved down the streets. At a rapid pace, and without much talk, they went to their respective houses, as if in a hurry to get inside to the sheltered security of their homes, away from this cold and cruel world where people did not even say hello. And again the streets were empty, without a sound. In the houses people sat behind drawn curtains, often behind locked doors, waiting for news. Trunks and boxes were stubbornly kept in readiness, partly packed for the voyage home. But in the deep of many a heart, hopes were fading that such a voyage would ever take place.

This is how I found the Tristan community in Calshot when I came for a visit in June of 1962. My first call was on Fred and Mary Swain, in whose house on Tristan I had spent so many a pleasant evening in 1938, and to whom I owe so much of what I know about life on Tristan. Fred was "retired" now and was living on the "pension" that the British social security system generously offers to all British subjects living in the United Kingdom. Fred and Mary were staying with their son Willie—all their six children were married by now—and they were regularly performing the eternal job of grandparents, taking care of their grandchildren while the parents were at work.

The joy of meeting again was great but subdued. It made me feel as if I were entering a sickroom with death lurking in the corner, where helpless humans are awkwardly trying to face the ultimate reality but dare not speak about it. Voices were lowered, and faint smiles flickered on faces tired from worries and wakeful nights.

After the prescribed pot of tea, which I shared with Willie since he had just come home from work, Fred offered to take me around to see the people I knew from twenty-four years before. We wandered through the empty streets of the Close. But Fred seemed to be walking around in a strange town. He did not even know where Chief was staying, although he lived straight across the street from Fred and Mary. We had to ask some children playing in a yard.

Wherever we went, there was recognition and reminiscence—about life on Tristan "before the soldiers came," about the old-timers now gone, but particularly about the boat trips we had had together around the beaches. And faces lit up in smiles as minds wandered dreamily back to happier days. The Islanders amazed me by remembering each one of those trips so well: who went along, what we were doing, what happened on this or that trip, little details that I had long since forgotten. Yet they must have made hundreds of similar trips since then. I was often corrected: "No, that was on the trip when we took the *Lorna* to Sandy Point for apples, it was . . . ."—then came the list of those who went, slowly, maybe, and with some strain to include everybody, as if it were a matter of life and death not to leave out a single name.

One trip, especially, seemed to be remembered with joy by everyone who had taken part in it. That was the big apple trip to Stony Beach in March 1938, with the *Lorna* and the *Longboat* and thirty-two hands altogether. It was indeed a memorable trip. Some of the old hands went along: Henry Green, Jane Lavarello, and last but not least, Frances Repetto, who did not often go on boat trips—she used to get seasick. On this trip, too, she had a touch of it, and as soon as she was put ashore at Stony Beach, she performed a grotesque dance of joy at being again on firm ground. She had not been to Stony Beach since she was a girl of fourteen. That was back in 1890, when old Peter Green and Captain Hagan were still living. In those distant days there were no cattle at Stony Beach, the whole slope up to Stonybeach Gulch had been covered with tall tussock grass, and Frances expressed amazement to see it all gone. She admired the mollies circling with motionless wings in the updraft along the hillside, and she laughed at the penguins with their clumsy and hot-tempered antics, which made their "eyebrows" of bright yellow tassels bristle with excitement. We were wind-locked in the dead lee of the island and spent four leisurely days in the most beautiful weather, hiking for birds and berries, with songs around a blazing bonfire at night. And Frances Repetto was the center of it all, affecting all of us with her girlish, innocent joy.

One of the first visits Fred and I made that day in Calshot was, of course, to Sidney and Alice Glass. Alice is Fred's daughter, and apparently she used to be Frances Repetto's favorite granddaughter. She was picked by her grandmother to serve as a cook and general housekeeper for the Norwegian expedition, and in true Tristan fashion she offered her services with no other compensation than the meals she prepared. She and Sidney were "courtin' " at that time. I am sure that few scientific expeditions have had a field laboratory kept as spotlessly clean as ours was. The floor was scrubbed every day. And once, when all of us had taken off for a trip to the Peak and were gone all day, Alice had decorated all the shelves with newspaper neatly cut in tongues hanging over the edges, just as they used to have it in their homes. One can imagine what a job it must have been to remove all those hundreds of bottles and containers that our medical men used for their tests and bacteriological cultures, and for several days after that, utter confusion reigned in the lab as the two medics hunted frantically for ingredients that had been misplaced. But it was done out of a good heart.

Alice was full of fun and mischief, a big tease, and a constant source of merriment and laughter. One day she laughed her head off because I had asked her about the growing of vegetables on Tristan, completely ignorant of the fact that what the Islanders grew in their gardens was called "wegeables." She used to sing and lilt all day at her work; in fact, she was the one who gave me many of the old songs I collected on Tristan. Her favorite, though, was Weatherly's heart-rending "Danny Boy," which she had picked up from an old, badly scratched phonograph record.

It was a different Alice that I met that day in Calshot. She seemed shy and reserved, and she engaged in a rather constrained conversation about her three daughters, the oldest of whom was soon to be married. She did not at all look well, and I knew the reason when she gazed at me with the eyes of a frightened doe and asked me with trembling voice: "They can't keep us here?—Can they?" There was a deep, helpless fear in the expression of her face, yet mingled with desperate hope, reminding me of what I so often had seen on the faces of my co-prisoners in a Nazi concentration camp.

It was just about this time that the Tristan Islanders started to get an inkling of what was in store for them. There had been news from Tristan in the papers—good news, the Islanders thought: The volcano had subsided, the village was undamaged, and the cattle were thriving. But there was not a word of encouragement from the Government.

In the meantime, on Tristan, the *Leopard* had arrived on the scene three days after the evacuation and had succeeded in landing a shore party to salvage some of the Islanders' personal belongings. These were later sent to Calshot and returned to their owners. The *Leopard* crew also reported having destroyed the dogs. Captain Scott of the *Tristania* had been busy trying to save movable equipment from the factory on Big Beach, had towed away a string of fishing dinghies, but soon had to abandon any further rescue work. By October 27, seventeen days after the eruption, the factory was buried under a rumbling mass of hot lava blocks, which continued to push on into the sea, bringing the seawater to a sizzling boil and sending up clouds of steam. Thirty thousand gallons of diesel fuel exploded with a roar.

In January, an expedition had been sent out by the Royal Society, the venerable British academy of science founded in 1662 "for improving natural knowledge." The purpose of the expedition was to observe the progress of the eruption, to establish its causes if possible, and to study its effect on the flora and fauna of the island. The expedition included two young Islanders, Joseph Glass and Adam Swain, who were to serve as guides. A former agricultural officer of Tristan, Dennis Simpson, also went along to investigate the condition of the domestic animals left on the island.

The expedition was landed on Tristan from the S.A.S. *Transvaal* on

January 30 and remained on the island until about March 20, when it
was picked up by H.M.S. *Protector*. During this time it was observed
that the eruption was subsiding. The emission of lava had stopped altogether, although sulphurous vapor and smoke still rose from the
cone. At night, a red glow was still visible from the central crater and
from cracks in the congealed lava mass, but by the end of February
even this phenomenon had ceased. The lava now covered both Big
Beach and Little Beach and was protruding about five hundred yards
beyond the former shoreline. But the village had been spared. Only
the most easterly house, the one belonging to Dennis Green, was burnt
to the ground, leaving nothing but the charred stone walls. Shortly
after the arrival of the Royal Society expedition, the engineer of the
Transvaal had got the generators at the Station started, and the expedition settled down very comfortably in the administrator's quarters.

The cattle were found grazing peacefully at the foot of the new volcano, seemingly unaffected by the convulsions of the past few months.
The sheep, however, had been drastically reduced in number, from
more than seven hundred to less than fifty. And while the chickens
were apparently unmolested, there was no trace of the more than fifty
geese that had been left in the village.

The full report of the expedition's findings was not published immediately. Apparently, the Government feared that a public report on
the generally good condition of the island would arouse hopes among
the Tristan Islanders that they might be able to return to their homes.
In fact, even before the expedition left England, the Royal Society had
been pledged to silence concerning the question of the possibility of a
resettlement and had issued a public statement saying that the expedition would be concerned entirely with the scientific causes and effects
of the eruption:

The expedition is purely of a scientific nature and is not concerned
in any way with questions of a sociological nature relating to possible
resettlement. That is a matter for the Colonial Office and other appropriate authorities to decide, and it is emphasized that the members of
the expedition are neither qualified to express an opinion on the matter, nor are they interested in the possibilities of resettlement.

In the preliminary reports to the press, the blame for the disappearance of the sheep and geese was put on abandoned dogs turned killers,

although the dogs had already been reported killed by the crew of the *Leopard,* and it seemed a little peculiar that hungry dogs should be so particular about their poultry fare that they would kill the last goose before they switched to chickens. Now, for the second time, the dogs were reported destroyed.

Kept entirely from the public was the fact that the abandoned houses had been looted, supposedly by seamen from passing ships. Reports of this must have come to the attention of authorities at an earlier stage, for when the *Transvaal* brought the Royal Society expedition to Tristan, she also carried two South African detectives sent out to investigate. Press correspondents on board the *Transvaal* had been requested "on security grounds" not to disclose the presence of the detectives, and no official report of their findings was ever published. But the evidence was obvious. The houses had been broken into and ransacked. Household goods, such as cooking utensils, furniture, and even sewing machines, were found on the grass around the village as if dropped by a prowler at the sight of something better. This is probably also how the sheep and geese disappeared.

Some persons close to the Colonial Office had thought it was a great mistake to send two Islanders as guides for the Royal Society expedition. And if the purpose of all the secrecy, both about the looting and about the true condition of the island, was to keep the news from the Islanders, the efforts were, of course, in vain. They had firsthand reports from Joseph and Adam. Naturally, they were terribly upset by the news about the housebreakings and lootings. But to them, it was only an additional incentive to get back to their homes "before they all go to 'rack 'n' ruin." There was no doubt in their minds, on the basis of what Joseph and Adam had told them, that "the island is fit," and many of them saw God's finger in the fact that their homes had been spared from the terrible volcano. True, the landing beaches had been destroyed; but at Garden Gate, just below the Village, a new beach had taken shape from debris that had been broken from the edge of the new lava field, then piled up and ground smooth by the surf. And behind the new Garden Gate Beach, as it was immediately named, between it and the former shoreline, a lagoon had been formed, which gave rise to excited hopes of turning it into a small boat harbor. It was a dream come true! And as the reports were pondered and discussed, elaborated and embellished, more and more Islanders became convinced that the volcano had improved their island rather than destroyed it.

It had been with great expectations, therefore, that the Islanders had gathered in the chapel at Calshot for a meeting called by Mr. Wheeler in April 1962. The little chapel was packed with people, and men were standing at the rear wall. Present also were the Reverend C. J. Jewell, the minister of Tristan, and Dr. Ian Gass, the leader of the Royal Society expedition.

The purpose of the meeting, as far as the administration was concerned, was apparently to present the results of the expedition to the Islanders in such a way that it emphasized the danger of new and more violent eruptions. The hope may have been that the Islanders would draw the conclusion on their own that an immediate return to the island would be unsafe. Dr. Gass was invited to speak on volcanoes in general and the one on Tristan in particular. Most certainly he was briefed on the delicacy of the situation. The administration was trying to avoid raising vain hopes of return to Tristan but, at the same time, did not want to slam the door in the faces of the Islanders. Accordingly, Dr. Gass stressed the unpredictable nature of a volcano—"it's like a woman, you never know what she will do next."

Although that remark drew a laugh, the atmosphere at the meeting was tense. The Islanders, of course, were not too interested in a lecture about volcanoes. They wanted to know about the houses, the cattle, the boats, the beaches. To them the question of return was no more a problem; they only wanted to know when, and the sooner the better. After Dr. Gass had finished his little speech, he invited questions, emphasizing that he was an expert on volcanoes, and suggesting that other questions be directed to Adam and Joseph. Unavoidably, the question of return came up immediately.

It was then that the dagger was tossed. In this situation, Mr. Wheeler had no choice but to try to explain the position of the Colonial Office as gently as possible. He pointed out that the question of return rested neither with him nor with Dr. Gass, nor even with the Tristan Islanders themselves, but solely with the Colonial Office and the Secretary of State for the Colonies. He also declared that whether the Islanders would ever return to Tristan or not was still "an open question." He pointed to the responsibility of the Government and said it would not be fair to expose the children of the community to the risk of renewed volcanic activity.

The Islanders' reaction was strong and immediate. Until then, their attitude had continued to be one of unquestioning deference to the authority of the Crown. Their conviction remained that the Colonial Secretary had not only the authority and power but even the right to determine their fate at will, even if his decision should be that they could not return to their island. The firm belief that such a decision would not be taken without compelling reasons rested solely on their solid faith in the ultimate benevolence of the Colonial Administration. It was this faith that was now being shaken, jarred to the roots, with an impact as great as that of the "shakes" which had rattled their homes and made the very ground under their feet sway and tremble before the eruption. For they saw no compelling reason for not returning to their island at the earliest opportunity, and for the first time the seed of a horrible thought was taking root among them.

Mr. Wheeler's remark brought a loud rumble of disapproval. The tension rose to a pitch, and soon the meeting got out of order and control. The Administrator left with Dr. Gass. The Chaplain, who tried to calm the Islanders down, was angrily rebuked by shouts from the group for not having prayed for the safety of the island; a shrill voice was heard above the rest: "A wolf leading his flock!" It was no less than a revolt, as yet unorganized and without leaders, but still a revolt against an authority which had till then been regarded as absolute, and whose benevolence had never before been questioned.

The horrible thought that they had been deceived, betrayed, and abandoned by their protectors had come slowly to the trusting Islanders. It had first appeared as a fleeting suspicion rapidly dismissed as inconceivable. But there had been many disquieting signs that had not escaped the supersensitive minds of the refugees: the attempted suppression of the news about the looting on Tristan; the one-sided and exaggerated emphasis on the destruction of the old landing beaches, with no mention of the new Garden Gate Beach in the official statements (the Islanders got that information from Joseph and Adam); the often repeated statement about the danger of new eruptions; the failure of the Chaplain to pray for the Islanders' return; the withdrawal of the Administrator and the Chaplain from Calshot with no replacements. There were other signs as well: statements by high and not-so-high officials to the press, which were interpreted and perhaps misinterpreted; rumors that Tristan was going to be used for nuclear tests; and never a word of hope and encouragement from the authorities. Now, with Mr. Wheeler's remark at the fateful April meeting that the return of the Islanders was an "open question," which could conceivably be answered in the negative, suddenly the clues fell into place like the pieces of a grim picture puzzle. Suspicion grew into a fearful certainty that there were mighty forces trying to prevent the Islanders from returning to Tristan, and that unless some drastic action were taken, they would indeed never see their homes again.

It was in this situation that Chief Willie Repetto, now a man of sixty, reluctantly rose to assume the responsibilities of his title. Still single, he was staying in the house of his younger brother Johnny and his wife Margaret, where the walls of the living room were adorned with Chief's framed diploma of membership in the Order of the British Empire and other honors that he had received as the Chief Man of Tristan da Cunha. That living room now became the natural gathering place for a group of Islanders who drifted in after supper each evening to ponder the situation. It was a select but not firmly circumscribed group. Membership in it was a matter of degree. The core of the group was composed of men and women who were close to Chief by kinship or friendship. There were, in the first place, his brothers Joe and Johnny, and his sister Martha Rogers, who had taken over the position as "Head of the Women" after her mother, Frances Repetto. And there were other members of the Repetto set. But the group was not limited to them, and there was a shifting fringe membership of more or less steady visitors, who moved in and out freely. Some of them came occasionally just to hear the latest news and left after a while without having uttered a word. Others attended regularly and became involved in the discussions, examining newspapers and other bits of information from whatever source they could be obtained. The sessions were tense with an anxiety that charged even the inevitable long pauses of a Tristan conversation with emotion, causing the women in the nearby kitchen to lower their voices to a whisper.

It was this informal group of Islanders who in May or June 1962, painstakingly composed a letter to the Colonial Office, in which they declared that they wanted to go home and asked that arrangements be made at the earliest convenience. In response to this letter, a group of Islanders was invited up to the Colonial Office in London to talk to Mr. Gordon Whitefield, who was in charge of the Tristan office, now in the process of winding up its business. But his reply was evasive. All that the Islanders were told was that the decision regarding their petition rested at a higher level of administration, and at that level the island was still considered dangerous. In fact, the Islanders found themselves entangled in a typical bureaucratic snare, with no one to argue with because they were consistently prevented from reaching the level of administration where decisions were said to be made. This situation is not unfamiliar to most of us who have had to deal with a bureaucracy, be it in government, business, or academic life, and it is hard for anybody to break through or circumvent. For the Islanders, completely ignorant of the intricate channels and pitfalls of a bureaucratic machinery, it was utter frustration. This is what Arthur Repetto, Chief's brother, tried to explain to me in a taped interview I helped to make for the University College in London for dialect studies:

We'ave no one to represent us now at all. See, 's only the Chief, an' he don't know the rules and regulations, you know, he's jus' the same 's myself. We ain't been brought up—on Trist'n, you see, we's—don't know the rules and the regulations, an' we don't know your way to go to certain people and—to the Trist'n people, they's jus' like they's stuck in one small group here an' around, and they don't know nothing. But if they was born and bred here, some of the people, and then they would know around the country, and then they could go to people and see 'bout 'ranging things, you see, but 's no one here what know anything about it.

In this desperate situation the Tristan Islanders pleaded for help and advice wherever they thought they could get it, and every outsider visiting Tristan Close became a potential savior, whether he happened to be a journalist, a brush salesman, or a social anthropologist. Martha Rogers was expressing the general feeling of helpless frustration when she exclaimed: "Oh, had my mother been alive, this wouldn't have happened!"

In the meantime Chief had grown in his new and unfamiliar role. It was obvious that his gentle patience with the Colonial Office, like that of the rest of the Islanders, was wearing thin, and he became more and more outspoken. He was beginning to resemble a Moses defying the power of the mighty Pharaoh with his ever-increasing demand: "Let my People go!"

His demand carried over land and sea to every part of the world. It echoed loudly in the press, not only in England but also abroad, with news reports, feature stories, and editorial comments under blasting headlines; and it caused rumblings in the British Parliament, with pointed questions directed to the Colonial Secretary by friends of the Islanders among the members.

In the early part of July another letter was sent to the Colonial Office. This time the Islanders did not ask for permission to go home. They declared that they were going, and if no assistance were available from the Colonial Office, they would go on their own. They presented a well-developed plan, which called for an advance party of twelve men to proceed to Tristan at the earliest opportunity, six of them to work on the island, doing the necessary repair jobs on houses and water lines and planting a new crop of potatoes, the rest to work as fishermen in the *Tristania,* which would be going out for the "big season" in September. The letter emphasized the urgency of the situation and the importance of having the soil prepared and the new crop of potatoes planted by the end of September. Knowing that the ice patrol vessel, H.M.S. *Protector,* was scheduled to sail from Britain about that time on her annual tour of the Antarctic, the Islanders asked that a passage for the twelve men be provided in that ship either to Cape Town or directly to Tristan. The rest of the Islanders would then follow during the southern summer, preferably in January or February, when weather conditions were usually good and the chances of landing the women and children without delay or mishap were at a maximum. Compensation for lost wages, as well as travel expenses if necessary, for the six men of the advance land party would be levied on each and all of the wage earners remaining in Calshot. The fishermen would take care of their own expenses as they would be making money. The letter was signed by all the men.

Even this letter, apparently, received no direct reply from the Colonial Office. Although it was widely publicized in the press, a Colonial Office spokesman even denied any knowledge of a petition from the Islanders. Instead, it was announced to the press, which at this time was the most important communication link between the Islanders and the authorities, that the government was going to "have another look" at the development of the eruption on Tristan and was planning to send another scientific expedition to the island in September or October. The expedition was to go in the *Protector,* and it was declared that no decision concerning the return of the Islanders could be made until the experts had presented their views.

All along, the Colonial Office had been trying to gain time, obviously in the hope that if the Islanders were only given enough time to adjust to their new environment, they would settle down, and all problems would be solved. The announcement of another scientific expedition to Tristan at this time may have been another attempt to delay action. Considerable pressure was now being exerted upon the Colonial Office, not only by the Islanders but also, and more effectively, by the press and by questions raised in the House of Commons. The Islanders' declaration of their intention to go on their own, of which the press was promptly informed, had forced the hand of the authorities. If the Islanders were to carry through their intention, the control of the situation would slip out of the hands of the Colonial Office. Some action had become necessary to lessen the pressure of public opinion as well as, if possible, to ward off the Islanders' plan to go on their own. At the same time, the insistence on "further investigation," with expert reports and deliberations in committee, would obviously take time and could, in combination with weather conditions at Tristan da Cunha, possibly delay action for another year.

Clearly, this was not a response to the Islanders' satisfaction, especially since they were told by a Colonial Office spokesman that the new scientific expedition would not take along any Islanders as guides. They were incensed at the idea, both because they were being excluded from taking part in decisions concerning their own lives and because they knew themselves to be better judges of conditions on the island, and of their own ability to survive under them, than the high gentlemen in the Colonial Office, who "know nothing about the island." When Martha Rogers read in a newspaper that the authorities still considered the island highly dangerous, she snorted: "Dangerous! What do they know about the island! There is no one what know if that island is going to blow up again except the One above. Dangerous! They might as well tell the men not to go to Nightingale because the boats may not return. Everything is a risk!"

Others chimed in that the island could hardly be more dangerous than England, with all the traffic accidents and murders.

The Tristan Islanders had one good friend in Allan Crawford, the Honorary Welfare Officer for Tristan da Cunha in Cape Town. He had been to Tristan several times as a surveyor and meteorologist, and out of these associations with the Islanders grew not only a warm friendship but a deep commitment to the welfare of the Tristan people. His many services to the island and its community received official recognition when, in 1955, on the recommendation of the Administrator of Tristan da Cunha, the Secretary of State for the Colonies officially appointed him Honorary Welfare Officer for Tristan da Cunha.

Although far removed from the unhappy community in Calshot, Mr. Crawford was not ignorant of the plight of his wards, for letters were pouring in from all his Tristan friends—and that included the greater part of the community—pleading for help and advice. Already in April, acting in his capacity as officially appointed Welfare Officer, he had given the Islanders his full support, informing the Colonial Office that, according to his own observations when acting as deputy leader of the Royal Society expedition, it was feasible and apparently safe for the Islanders to return to Tristan. He had acted as the intermediary between the Islanders and the Tristan da Cunha Development Company in obtaining an offer of free passage for twelve men from Cape Town to Tristan, and his advice obviously played a prominent part in formulating the plan that the Islanders were now embarking upon, attempting to find their way back to Tristan on their own if the Colonial Office refused to assist. He now supported the Islanders' latest request for a passage in the *Protector* by cabling the Colonial Office, strongly urging the immediate return of an advance guard of twelve men.

The Tristan Islanders may have been unsophisticated in their lack of circumspection and ignorant about bureaucratic procedures. But they are not stupid. They knew that they had presented the Colonial Office with an ultimatum that might entail considerable embarrassment if rejected. And this was confirmed by an almost unanimously sympathetic press. An editorial comment in a prominent London newspaper suggested that it was the duty of the Colonial Office to help:

Mr. Willie Repetto is organizing the return of Tristan da Cunhans to their island. Tristan—bleak, remote, shattered by a volcano—is still home in the minds of 270 refugees. They have appealed to the Colonial Office to help them go back. They must not look in vain. The island may be an outpost, its former inhabitants few, but their welfare and their happiness are as much a charge upon Britain as the fate of more imposing lands.

Time was running short if the Islanders were to return that year. The *Tristania* was scheduled to sail from Cape Town on August 27 or 28, and to catch her, the twelve men would have to be in the mail ship scheduled to leave Southampton on August 9. When the 21st of July came around without a positive reply from the Colonial Office, Chief called a meeting of all the men.

It was Saturday, a cool summer evening. The men were drifting slowly through the streets of the Tristan Close toward an open square, where the meeting was going to be held. There they gathered in small groups, talking to each other in low voices, or just standing around in tense expectation. The situation was not entirely unfamiliar to them. Even on Tristan the men used to have their informal gatherings. In former days they used to assemble at the east gable end of the church every Sunday after service, light up their pipes, and have a chat while the women went home to prepare the dinner. This assembly had acted as a kind of town meeting, but there was nothing formal about it. It was just a habit that had been kept up for many years, until an Administrator, who wanted to get on a friendly and familiar foot with the Islanders, started to join them. Then the men drifted away, and the custom died.

This time in Calshot, however, it was a solemn occasion. Not only was it probably the first time in the history of this anarchistic community that a meeting of this kind had been formally called by the Islanders themselves without the benefit of the leadership and presence of an official authority from outside; this particular meeting was even called in open defiance of authority. And while in the past, individual Islanders had occasionally rebelled when they felt that an administrator was not "dealing fair," never before in the memory of its living members had this community of fiercely independent individualists risen to united action for any cause. Now they were assembled in an attempt to preserve their simple communal way of life in defiance of the glamour and affluence of modern civilization. It was indeed a rebellion, but this time orderly, deliberate, and well planned. The men felt strong in their new sense of unity, yet insecure, as if they were about to lose something very dear to them—the cherished freedom and equality within the community.

The little square was crowded with men when Chief arrived with his brother Joe, and Chief immediately took position in front of the crowd and started to speak. He spoke with a force and authority which contrasted sharply with his usual mild manners, and his booming voice reached far beyond the confines of the square and the limits of his audience. He spoke of the seriousness of the situation, of the lack of response from the Colonial Office and its apparent unwillingness to assist, and said: "This is our last chance to get back to our homes!"

It was possible, he said, that some of the younger ones did not want to leave England, he did not know. But if some did not wish to return to Tristan, he wanted them to come and tell him right away. Then he added: "I won't say what I think of those who don't want to go back —I'll keep that to myself."

The climax of his short speech was reached when he asked for twelve "volunteers" to return to Tristan at once and prepare the island for resettlement. He spoke as a commander: "I want twelve volunteers to go back now, six men to go in the fishing ships, and six men to work on the island."

Then he named them, one by one. And one by one, the selected men stepped forward and stood before the crowd.

Discussion followed, mainly concerning the best way to provide for the families of the six men of the landing party, who would not earn any wages of their own. The men talked from where they were standing, or moved a few steps forward, each raising his voice only according to the courage of his conviction and in keeping with his social standing in the community. A few talked loud enough to be heard by most. Others raised their voices only slightly, or not at all, as if they were trying out their suggestions on those standing close by, hoping, perhaps, that someone with more weight and guts might pick up their ideas and relay them to the group. One man was nervously kicking at the pebbles on the ground, as if pondering whether he should open his mouth or not.

As the debate grew livelier, more and more people grew more interested in expressing their own opinions than in listening to those of others. At one time several discussions were going on simultaneously, and for a moment it looked as if the meeting were falling into disorder. Chief hurriedly left his place in front of the group and had a conference with his brother Joe, who was standing in the rear. Then he returned and restored order, and Joe Repetto stepped forward and declared that those who did not want to contribute to the support of the families of the six men would not have their houses on Tristan taken care of, to which many shouted approval. That seemed to settle everything, and the meeting gradually dissolved as the men drifted away in small groups.

The meeting lasted only forty-five minutes. There appeared to be almost unanimous agreement about the general course of action. Only one young man, who liked to look upon himself as a little different, more cosmopolitan than the rest of the Islanders, and who on several occasions had struck a note of caution concerning the growing defiance of official authority, muttered something about not wanting to "kick against the Colonial Office," who had helped him all his life. "The Colonial Office," he said, "has done more for me than I will ever do for them." The lame opposition never got off the ground. The remark was heard by few and ignored by all except one, who nodded his approval. And the young man certainly knew that had he raised his voice to be heard (which he was quite capable of doing), he would have stirred a storm of indignant protest.

After the meeting there was an elated atmosphere in the houses around the Tristan Close, especially in those where young men had been picked for the avant-garde. Visitors came to congratulate them, and the teapots were in action into the late hours. At last the protracted tension had been released by a quickening feeling of unity and action, a feeling which was indeed just as new and unusual to these independent, peace-loving people, but far more happy.

Even Chief was relieved. He commented on how difficult it had been to pick the twelve "volunteers" to everybody's satisfaction. He did not want to send away men who had small children at home. "And I couldn't pick all Repettos, for then they would say I's for the Repettos." He was also fully aware of the risk he had taken of exposing himself to severe criticism for having assumed authority in a community so strongly devoted to the principle of internal anarchy. Indeed, during the following days there were comments about Chief "getting a little big-headed," although the remarks probably never came to Chief's attention. Everybody realized, however, that someone had to initiate action, and since external authority had failed, there was actually no choice but to accept a temporary compromise of their much cherished freedom from internal authority and control. And Chief being the kind of man he was, there was little danger he would become permanently entrenched in his new position of self-assumed authority.

The hardest part of Chief's job was, in fact, done. The decision had been made to go back to Tristan without the aid or consent of the Colonial Office, and the twelve men had been selected. All that remained now was to carry out the decision that everybody seemed to agree with. That seemed easy enough.

More frustrations, however, were in store for the Tristan Islanders. It was as if the whole establishment of the civilized world were plotting against them. When they appeared the following Monday at the office of the Union Castle Line in Southampton, money in hand, to buy their twelve tickets to Cape Town in the *Stirling Castle,* scheduled to sail August 9, they could not obtain a passage. They were told that the ship was fully booked.

Then, suddenly, there was a change in the attitude of the authorities. What caused it is uncertain. A heavy blanket of deep secrecy was pulled over the events of the next few days. The Islanders who were taking part in the deliberations were instructed not to give out any information, not even to their own people. There were speculations among the uninformed Islanders that the change in attitude had something to do with the cabinet crisis that had just occurred in the British Government. They accused Wheeler of having misinformed the old administration about conditions on the island; now there was a new minister in charge of colonial affairs, and he had listened to "people who know the island," while Wheeler was being sent to Kenya "and will be sorry." However, as late as Tuesday, July 24, the new Colonial and Commonwealth Secretary, Duncan Sandys, declared in answer to a question in the House of Commons that it was still "unsafe" for the Tristan Islanders to return to the island, and that "in the opinion of the Government, the best course is for them to remain in this country."

There were indications that a powerful press might be behind the change in policy that became apparent during the next few days. A young journalist from an important London newspaper had been covering the Tristan Close and was, in fact, the only reporter present (with a photographer) at the dramatic meeting the preceding Saturday. This young journalist had even indicated to Chief that his newspaper would be able and willing to help get a passage for the twelve men. On Tuesday, July 24 (the same day that Mr. Sandys had made his negative statement about resettlement in the House of Commons), there had been a special high-level meeting of the administration of the paper. And now, during the crucial days that followed, the same newspaper, as well as the Argus papers of South Africa, had senior reporters stationed at Calshot, which seemed to suggest that they had information not generally available to the press of important events about to take place.

Whether it was because of internal changes or external pressure, or maybe just because the Colonial Office finally realized that the Islanders meant business and thought the prospect of having them go home on their own a little too embarrassing, a few days after the meeting in which the Tristan Islanders publicly took their stand, and only the day after the Colonial Secretary had made his statement in the House of Commons, there appeared to be an about-face in official attitude and policy. True to what seemed to be the established practice of not communicating in writing directly with the Islanders—"diplomatic relations" had apparently been broken in April—the Colonial Office wrote to the vicar of Fawley, the Reverend Noel Brewster, who had generously accepted the responsibility for the spiritual welfare of the Islanders after the Reverend Mr. Jewell had been removed, and who took a keen interest in their problems, praying warmly and earnestly for their return to Tristan. The Colonial Office asked Mr. Brewster to bring Chief the message that the officials wished to meet with the twelve selected men. And this time the authorities came to Calshot instead of calling the Islanders to London. The meeting took place in an empty mess hall in the Tristan Close the following Thursday (July 26) and, in addition to representatives of the Colonial Office, was attended by a man from the fishing company on Tristan, which had now been reorganized as the South Atlantic Islands Development Corporation. At this meeting Chief and the twelve Islanders were told confidentially that the Colonial Office would provide passage for the twelve men in one way or another, and the Islanders were invited to send four representatives to the Colonial Office the following Wednesday, August 1, presumably to receive further instructions. Finally, on Saturday July 28, it was announced in the press that the Colonial Office "will do everything it can to help them get back to their island."

That weekend there was universal celebration in the Tristan Close, and the beer flowed freely.

It was a solemn but happy foursome who traveled by bus to Southampton before dawn the following Wednesday morning to catch an early train to London. The group included Chief and the two trusted men whom he had appointed as joint leaders of the six-man landing party, Johnny Repetto and Thomas Glass. The fourth member was a young man, Joe Repetto's son Lars, who was also one of the six soon to leave for Tristan, and whose appointment to this important mission was an indication that he might be on his way into the core elite of the Tristan community. In this respect, it did not hurt him a bit that he was not only a Repetto but also, on his mother's side, a nephew of Thomas Glass, a man of influence and high esteem in the community, who was married to a granddaughter of Frances Repetto and had been a long-time member of the Island Council back on Tristan.

At the Colonial Office, the four men were introduced to Mr. Nigel Fisher, the Colonial Under-Secretary, and presented with twelve tickets for the *Stirling Castle,* which the Colonial Office had obtained, apparently with no difficulty, and paid for with money from Sir Irving Gane's Tristan da Cunha Fund. The men were also informed, however, that they would be accompanied by a Government official, who would submit an "independent report," and that a decision whether a permanent resettlement of the island were feasible could not be taken until the Secretary of State for the Colonies had studied that report.

So it appeared, after all, that the Colonial Office had not really changed its mind concerning the Islanders' return to Tristan. The strategy obviously was to reduce the significance of the vanguard of pioneer resettlers to an "exploratory visit," which was to take the place of the planned but now abandoned scientific expedition. And the officials were still determined to rely exclusively on the judgment of outsiders concerning the ultimate fate of the Islanders.

At this stage of the game, however, the Islanders could not have cared less. They were on their way back to Tristan, and once they were there, the Colonial Office would have a hard time getting them off the island again.

The following week was a busy time in the Tristan Close with packing and preparations for the big send-off. On the eve of the departure relatives and friends walked quietly around in the village from house to house to bid farewell to each of the twelve men with a silent kiss. The following day half the community was on the pier to wave good-bye. Tears were flowing freely on cheeks of demure women and husky men, not from sorrow but from deep emotion as their hearts went out to each other.

14　　　Back to Tristan

The Tristan community came back to life on the 9th of August, 1962. With the twelve men on their way to reclaim their island homes, it was as if the whole community were already on the move, and the return of the rest was now only a question of time. No more were the streets of the Tristan Close empty like those of a ghost town; no more were the people sitting behind drawn curtains and locked doors. The community was alive, with visits from house to house, with joking and ribbing and happy laughter, and rollicking children playing between the houses, swarming around the ice cream van every time the jolly tinkle of its bell was heard moving down the street. Boys were again behaving like boys, gathering in small groups on the corners or in the square, engaging in mock scuffles, having races or practicing fancy riding on their smart bicycles, or roaming the roads into Fawley if for no other reason than to show off their gadgety mounts. Accordions, mouth organs, and guitars were again heard from the houses on Sunday afternoons, as they had been on Tristan. And on Saturdays, busloads of Islanders would go on all-day shopping tours of Totton and Southampton, returning in the evening exhausted but happy, excitedly displaying their spoils of clothing, curtains, and carpets, radios and phonographs and all sorts of tools, which they had bought to take home to Tristan. Packing boxes of all shapes and sizes were in great demand and were triumphantly carried home by their procurers. Everywhere the slogan was heard: "Home for Christmas!"

All were anxiously awaiting news from Tristan—news they trusted would confirm their impatient hopes for an early return of the whole community. It was known from reports and letters from Cape Town that the two fishing vessels, the *Tristania* and the *Frances Repetto*, had sailed for Tristan on the 30th of August with the exploratory party of Islanders on board. With them was also Mr. Gerry Stableford, who had been selected as the official representative of the Colonial Office to make a special report on the condition of the island. He was an old acquaintance of the Islanders, as he had spent four years as the agricultural officer on Tristan, from 1953 to 1957, and the Islanders were happy about his choice. A short radio message had reported that the party had been landed on Tristan on the 8th of September. It was also known that the frigate H.M.S. *Puma* would be sent out to the island to bring Mr. Stableford back.

Excitement and expectations rose to a pitch in the Tristan Close when BBC news reported that the *Puma* had returned to Cape Town on October 8 with Mr. Stableford on board. And finally the eagerly awaited letters arrived. Happy shouts of joy and laughter rose from each house as the mailman proceeded from door to door with fistfuls of the familiar blue air-letters. Women were running in and out, and the exuberant Mary Swain came out in the street singing and dancing —"cavorting like a nimble elephant," as one observer described her— holding a bunch of letters high over her head while she was performing a mixture of a Highland fling and a rather obscene imitation of the twist. She had always expressed the deepest contempt for the twist and said, "the day you see me dance a twis' is when I go back to Trisst'n."

The letters did indeed give grounds for joyful optimism, although some minor problems were reported. The fact that the new volcano was still smoking and the lava field still warm was not even considered a problem. The eruption had definitely stopped. By this time, however, the rest of the sheep and all the fowl were gone. The Islanders never quite believed the story about the dogs having turned killers— besides, they had twice been reported destroyed. And since no remnants of the kills were found anywhere, they concluded that the sheep as well as the geese and the fowl had been taken by "two-legged dogs." Of course, the Islanders realized that whoever had done it could not properly be described as thieves since the island had been abandoned. It was like a derelict ship; it is anybody's take. And the blame for the losses fell heavily on the Administrator, who had not allowed a party of six Islanders and a longboat to remain on Nightingale to maintain occupation as originally planned. The Islanders were particularly upset over the loss of a number of rifles which had been left in the houses.

Most of the news, however, was good news. Dennis Green's house was the only one that had been severely damaged. The cattle were thriving, with many new calves; and the men did not have much trouble rounding up the bullocks, although they had not been under the yoke for eleven months. Lars Repetto had got the island's tractor—its only motorized vehicle—in working condition. Birds and fish were plentiful and easy to catch. And best of all, the new Garden Gate Beach was very usable; the six men had landed five tons of stores from the *Puma* in two and one-half hours, although they had only used dinghies. The problem of access to the beach down the steep embankment from the Settlement had been solved with the help of the crew from the *Puma,* who had blasted out a roadbed with dynamite and even paved the steepest part of it with a washboard cover of cement to give foothold for oxen as well as for wheeled vehicles. On the whole the six men saw no reason why the rest of the community should not be home for Christmas.

The Islanders' optimism appeared to be shared by Mr. Stableford— at least, this is the impression he conveyed to the Cape Town newspapers at a press conference on his return to that city. Although he was "noncommittal as to whether he thought the 280 islanders would be able to return to their home or not," his statements about the condition of the island were positive. In particular, both he and Captain Mellis, the commander of the *Puma,* agreed that the new beach "would provide an efficient landing-place for the islanders in the future." One of the newspapers concluded in an editorial comment:

It is plain from the interview with Mr. H. G. Stableford in the *Cape Times* yesterday that there is no physical reason why the former inhabitants of Tristan da Cunha should not return . . . .

The Islanders knew that time was essential. The weather on Tristan is unpredictable; a storm may whip the sea into a fury any time, making a landing impossible. But this much they knew, that the chances of effecting a mass landing with old people, women, and children without delays and mishaps was much greater between Christmas and

Lent than at any other time of the year. And time was running short
if they were to get home that season. The faith in the absolute goodwill of the colonial officials had been fully restored after the authorities turned around and helped the twelve men get back to Tristan, so
everything was happily and confidently left in the hands of the Colonial Office. The credulous Islanders never doubted for a moment that
the officials would live up to their promise to "do everything in their
power to help them get back to their island" as soon as it could possibly be arranged.

But the ordeal of the Tristan community was not over yet. The Colonial Office remained silent. Mr. Stableford submitted his official report; but it was never made available to the Islanders or to the public.
One month passed, and nothing happened. From Cape Town, Allan
Crawford cabled the Secretary of State for the Colonies, urging a quick
decision on the question of allowing the Islanders to return. The Secretary, in proper bureaucratic fashion, replied that the question was
under consideration and that he "expected the British Government's
decision to be announced shortly." To a question in the House of
Commons he answered in the same vein, saying that a meeting was
being held "to discuss the Islanders' possible return in the light of recent reports on conditions on the island."

The Islanders were certainly discovering—as *Time* had put it on an
earlier occasion (July 20, 1962)—"that there is a force more powerful
than Atlantic gales and flaming volcanoes—bureaucracy." It was becoming more and more evident that the Colonial Office was stalling,
playing for time. The officials were again in control of the situation,
having recaptured the confidence of the Islanders, and it appeared as
though they could not resist the temptation to make another attempt
at preventing the resettlement of Tristan da Cunha. Well aware as
they must have been of the importance of the weather and the seasons,
they appeared to be dragging their feet in fulfilling their promise to
do "everything in their power" to help the Islanders get home, hoping,
perhaps, that it would soon be too late to send the Islanders back that
year.

In the meantime, a new idea had been gaining acceptance in the
press. It was as though the unanimous desire of the Tristan Islanders
to turn their backs on our advanced civilization was just too
incredible—and too insulting—to be accepted as a fact. How could

these people want to exchange a life of security and affluence, with almost endless opportunities, for one that as far as most of us knew
would at best be drab, obviously strenuous, often maybe wanting, and
above all with such a limited range of opportunities for their young
people? Life in the twentieth century could not be all that bad. That
the old people, already set in their ways, were bewildered and con-
fused by the hustle and bustle of modern civilization was understandable enough, and that they would be pining for the tranquility of their
lonely island was only to be expected. But what about the young?
Wouldn't any normal youth be attracted by the glamour, the lights,
the excitement of our cities? Would he not reach out eagerly for the
many opportunities offered by a modern democratic society? Why
should the Tristan youth be any different from the young people flock-
ing to the cities from depopulated rural areas? Surely there had to be
an explanation for the "apparent unanimity" of the Tristan Islanders.
Could it be that the young people of Tristan were just too subdued by
their elders to express openly what their deepest desires really were,
and that the Islanders' wish to return to a bleak island in the ocean
was not so unanimous after all?

All this was, of course, a great support for the Government's delay-
ing tactics. Obviously, the longer the Islanders could be kept in England, the greater, supposedly, were the chances that the young people
would put down roots, break away from the control of their elders,
and possibly make the whole project of resettlement impossible by
leaving behind a community consisting only of the old and infirm. On
the other hand, the Government did not want to provoke criticism
from the opposite quarter by slamming the door in the Islanders'
faces. The decision had to be a voluntary one on the part of the Islanders. A downright veto from the Government was out of the question. So the Colonial Office continued to walk the tightrope between
support and discouragement.

November drawing to an end with no decisive move on the part of
the authorities, Allan Crawford sent another telegram to the Secretary
of State for the Colonies. This time he also sent a message to a member of Parliament, who gladly again raised the question of the Islanders' return in the House of Commons. Thus pressed, Mr. Nigel
Fisher, Colonial Under-Secretary, released a written statement declaring that the Islanders would have to wait another year before they

could be sent home. In the meantime another "advance party," including an administrator and a technical aid, would be sent out to investigate the situation further and prepare the island for the return of the rest.

The Under-Secretary's statement was based entirely on the confidential Stableford Report, which was quoted as saying that much needed to be done to make the island fit for resettlement. In particular, extensive repair work was claimed to be necessary to make the landing beach safe and usable, which was in sharp contrast to Mr. Stableford's own statement to the Cape Town press at the time of his return from Tristan.

The main obstacle to an immediate return of the Islanders, however, was the notion, now adopted by the authorities, that the community itself was split on the issue. As reported in an editorial comment in the *Daily Telegraph:*

Meanwhile, the Colonial Under-Secretary, Mr. Fisher, who indicated the Government's views yesterday, is faced with a difficulty. Not all the islanders wish to return. Most of them are only too anxious to do so— indeed, their experience of life in an over-populated, highly industrialised, noisy and complicated society has induced them to look back with yearning to their quiet pastoral existence. But such is the spirit of community loyalty prevailing among them that the dissidents are unwilling to reveal themselves. It may be necessary for the Colonial Office to take a secret ballot in order to detect those who prefer to remain here.

In response to the notion that only the older people wanted to return to Tristan, Chief Willie Repetto canvassed the community in Calshot for opinions. "They are roaring to go," he announced. Indeed, the Islanders were incensed at the slowness of the Colonial Office; "they are like crabs looking into this matter," wrote Thomas Glass from Tristan. And they were insulted by the authorities' continued refusal to consult with them in matters so vitally concerned with their own lives, or even to believe their words when they said they wanted to go back. Again there was talk about going home on their own initiative, and if the Union Castle Line refused to accommodate them as a group, they would book their passage by families. Several of the young men had had jobs as deckhands on Union Castle liners, and they were thinking of working their way to Cape Town, from where they hoped to get a passage in one of the fishing ships. Tension rose in the Tristan Close, and again the depression was accompanied by colds and illness, especially among the women. There was hardly a day when not someone of their number was in the hospital in Southampton.

Sunday morning, December 2, representatives of the Colonial Office suddenly appeared in the Tristan Close to arrange a secret ballot. All Islanders over twenty-one years of age were asked to cast their votes whether or not they wanted to return to Tristan da Cunha. It came as a complete surprise to the Islanders. As late as the preceding afternoon they knew nothing about it. Even Chief assured a *Times* correspondent that he had been told nothing. Only a couple of days before had the Colonial Office announced that fifty passages had been booked for an advance party to sail in February—the Islanders learned about that only from a news broadcast on television. The ballot, obviously, was arranged in the hope that a sizable number of Islanders would express a preference for staying in England; if that should turn out to be the case, the Colonial Office might even have a good reason to cancel the whole resettlement project. In this connection the *Times* remarked:

That the Tristan community does not want to remain is made clear by young and old, men and women. A young seaman remarked firmly: "There's no need for them to vote. They's nearly all done packed now, ready to go."

Indeed, the voting on that Sunday morning in the Tristan Close took place among crates and boxes, some of them already nailed and labeled, with TRISTAN DA CUNHA, SOUTH ATLANTIC OCEAN painted in large letters across the top. And if the whole arrangement of a vote came as a surprise to the Tristan Islanders, the result must have been a complete shock to the authorities. Chief had always claimed that at least 90 per cent of the Islanders wanted to return to their homes. No one seemed to believe him. As it turned out, however, Chief's estimate was a conservative one. The votes were 148 to 5, almost 97 per cent, in favor of returning.

Something had indeed happened to the Tristan community in exile. There can be no doubt that to the Tristan Islanders in Calshot, the question of returning to their homes was not merely a nostalgic wish or a fairly indifferent preference that they could be persuaded to give up. It was a matter of life and death. The wavering policy of the authorities, befogged by a secretiveness which only increased the anxiety and insecurity of the Islanders, became a threat not only to their way of life but to their very existence. What happened in Calshot during that critical year of 1962 was that this atomistic aggregate of rugged individualists, under the threat of obliteration, developed a distinct collective identity, a solidarity and feeling of obligation to the community as a collective unit. Perhaps for the first time in its entire history, the community of Tristan da Cunha was a real *community*, with a common cause and a common goal.

One would think, as did Allan Crawford, that after the overwhelming vote in favor of going home to Tristan, there would be "no reason now why the British Government should delay the return of these frustrated and unhappy people." A return before Christmas, which the Islanders had hoped for, was now out of the question. But toward the end of January 1963 Crawford made another appeal to the Colonial Office, urging the resettlement of *all* the Islanders before the end of March. He based his appeal on a radio message received from Johnny Repetto on Tristan transmitted by the *Tristania,* reporting that the beach was safe, the roads repaired, and the water reconnected to all the houses. Impatiently, Johnny added: "The people must come out in the summer!"

But for unknown reasons, unless there was still hope that a further delay might cause a number of Islanders to change their minds, the authorities ignored all requests to speed up the procedures. Early in February news was released by Reuters from Copenhagen that the Danish M.V. *Bornholm* had been chartered by the British Government for late October to bring the main party of Islanders back to Tristan. Three weeks later, the announcement was confirmed by the Colonial Office.

Meanwhile, plans went ahead for the return of an advance party, which was selected by the Colonial Office to include about fifty Islanders, mostly the families of the twelve men who were already on Tristan, and a new administrative staff. The latter included an administrator, a medical officer, and an agricultural officer, all of whom were old acquaintances of the Islanders as all three of them had served in the same capacities before.

The party, however, did not arrive at Tristan during the summer. There were new delays. And again the Islanders were irritated and incensed because the authorities continued to treat them as immature children, consistently ignoring their advice. Thomas Glass, impatiently waiting to be rejoined by his family, complained: "They are spending them out in April, which is our worst month, instead of sending them out in January or February, which are our best months." It was March 17 before the party finally sailed from Tilbury in the R.M.S. *Amazon* bound for Rio de Janeiro, where they were to be transferred to the Dutch M.V. *Boissevain,* of the Royal Interocean Lines, which, like the *Tjisadane* before, would be diverted to Tristan da Cunha on her way to Cape Town.

The *Boissevain* was expected to reach Tristan around April 10. The *Tristania*, fishing off the shores of Tristan, had been in radio contact with her, and Captain Scott had confirmed the Islanders' warnings about foul weather to be expected in those waters at the beginning of winter, adding that he himself was planning to get out of there and head for South Africa before April. Later came the welcome news that both the *Tristania* and the *Frances Repetto* would wait for the arrival of the *Boissevain* to give the Islanders a hand in the landing operations.

It was a lucky day when the *Boissevain* arrived on April 9, a day ahead of schedule, "dressed overall," flag-decked from rail to mast-top for the occasion. The wind was east-southeast, the best possible as it put the Settlement and the landing beach in dead lee. The heavy swell, however, made the lowering of a gangway too dangerous for the frail canvas boats, so the passengers, including women in their bulky skirts and several small children, had to negotiate a swaying rope ladder to get into the boats that would bring them on to the still rather rocky beach. Everything went well, however. The Islanders had brought back with them three of the four longboats that had been used in the rescue operations at the time of the evacuation—the fourth one had been presented to the Queen, and, as an Islander knowingly explained, "when you make a present to somebody of something, you can't look for it back again, you see"—and with two more longboats from the shore, in little over an hour the sixty-seven passengers were safely landed on the beach.

There was still the cargo, fifty-nine tons of stores, hardboard, nails, musical instruments, and spring matresses, that had to be off-loaded into the boats and brought ashore. But with the help of the crews from the two fishing vessels, and with the *Tristania*'s motorboat towing loaded longboats and dinghies, nearly all of it was landed before dark, and the rest was taken off by the *Tristania* to be landed the following day. After exactly twelve hours anchorage the *Boissevain* steamed off for Cape Town.

How lucky they were to get such calm weather was demonstrated less than three weeks later when the *Straat Mosambique,* of the same company, called at Tristan to pick up three reporters who had gone with the Islanders to cover the resettlement for their respective magazines and newspapers. The weather was so bad that no contact could be made with the island, and the ship went on its way. Five days later the U.S.S. *Spiegel Grove* arrived off the island. Again heavy surf and treacherous currents made it impossible to get the boats off the beach to board the ship, and the three reporters had to be taken off by the ship's helicopter, with panic-stricken cattle stampeding in all directions as the chopper settled on the grassy slope below the village.

Seven months later, on November 10, 1963, the *Bornholm* finally arrived at Tristan with the main party of Islanders, homesick and happy to be back after twenty-five long months of exile. Again, although it was early spring on Tristan, the day was calm and beautiful, and by early afternoon the two hundred Islanders were safely ashore, greeted with tears and a kiss of welcome by those who had gone out before them. Mrs. Doreen Gooch, the doctor's wife, witnessed the scene as one boatload after another was brought in on the rocky beach:

As the old and young were brought ashore, I cried freely with all the Islanders as I greeted old Granny Jane Lavarello, aged 84, and Blind William, who died just a few weeks later, and Aunty Martha, Head Woman, whose husband had died rather tragically just before he left for Tristan. The old ones just sat on the rocks and wept and said, "Thank God, now we are back. The Lord brought us a good day to return to our homes.". . .

It took twelve days for the *Bornholm* to discharge her three hundred tons of cargo. But only five of them were working days. The rest of the time was spent searching for shelter in the lee of the island, wherever it might shift, or cruising back and forth off the Settlement, with the little stone huts in full view but completely isolated from them by a frothing belt of forbidding surf on the beach. The contract with the ship's owners had calculated six days at Tristan. When eight days had passed with almost half the cargo, including beds and bedding, still on board, the situation became critical. The question was whether the ship would have to depart for Cape Town to unload the rest of the cargo for later transport to Tristan by the fishing ships when they returned to the fishing grounds after New Year. Or, if she waited any longer, she might have to return directly to England and have the cargo sent back to Tristan by some other vessel, which would delay the goods a whole year. It was decided to wait for better weather, but Thursday, November 21, at 1400, was set as the absolute deadline. At that hour, the *Bornholm* would have to leave, with or without the cargo.

That deadline was only four days off. Two more days passed before the wind finally "haul' out," shifting to the southwest, where Hottentot Point gave shelter to the exposed beach. Then, finally, there was a smooth day, and from dawn till dusk every man and boy was working in the boats and on the beach, where goods were again piling up in a disorderly heap of everything imaginable, while women were moving around slowly, looking for their possessions and picking up parcels and pieces of manageable size and weight for them to carry up to the houses. The following day, precisely at 2 P.M. the last boatload left the ship, and minutes later, the *Bornholm* weighed anchor, gave three blasts on her siren, dipped her flag in salute, and steamed off.

15   Return to Utopia

So much had happened to the community of Tristan da Cunha since my first visit to the island in 1938 that I could hardly expect anything to be unchanged when I approached the lonely rock the second time in October 1964, this time in the South African survey ship, the *R.S.A.*, which had been chartered by the British Government to bring out the semiannual supply of stores. Already the fact that there *was* such a thing as a semiannual supply of stores, not for charity but for official and commercial use, was in itself an important and significant change. And as I embarked in Cape Town and watched several tons of dynamite being gingerly loaded and stowed in the ship's hold while she was lying at her berth with a red flag of warning fluttering from her masterhead, I realized that Tristan had indeed entered a new era since I had seen her last.

My co-passengers were from different walks of life, which also reflected a mixture of new and old in the life of the Tristan community. There was Mr. John Hawtrey, the Chief Civil Engineer of the Crown Agents, a man with a wry sense of humor, who was going out to select and survey a site for a harbor, the first ever to be built on Tristan. It was for his use that we carried the dynamite and also a compressor for pneumatic tools and several other "toys," as he fondly described them. A young South African radio mechanic was being sent out to help install new equipment in the Tristan radio station, which would enable us to talk on the radio telephone not only with Cape Town but even with London; and I recalled with nostalgia the first little radio sender ever to be brought to Tristan by the Norwegian expedition twenty-seven years ago, whose eager and insistent call signal, ZOE, was completely absorbed by the land mass of the island, too weak to reach any ship on the ocean until it was practically under our noses. We also had on board two representatives of the South African Broadcasting Corporation, a reporter with a tape recorder and a film photographer with his elaborate camera outfit, who were on their way to get a story on the new Tristan.

But traveling in the ship on this voyage was also the Bishop of Damaraland, the Right Reverend R. H. Mize, representing the oldest institution of Tristan da Cunha, the Church. And—as a reminder that the Tristan community was still predominantly an agrarian community—on the "heli-deck," the ship's helicopter port, which carried no aircraft on this trip but served as our promenade deck, were two creatures so placid and affectionate that we almost adopted them as part of the group: two large Hereford bulls, a gift to the Islanders from a benevolent women's organization in Britain.

Having been for a detour to Gough Island to pick up an injured member of the meteorological team stationed there, we were approaching Tristan da Cunha from the southeast. There it was, the familiar conical shape rising from the horizon in a light bluish haze, at first hardly distinguishable from the characteristic white cloud hanging over its peak. In the bright sunshine it seemed less awesome, more friendly than the first time I had seen it emerging from a dense fog. I had a peculiar feeling of coming home after a long, long absence.

As we drew nearer, I soon recognized the familiar landmarks. There was the rugged jumble of lava blocks so appropriately named Stony Hill, and beyond it Stony Beach, where twenty-seven years ago I had accompanied the Islanders on many a trip for meat and for apples, on foot and by boat, and my memory, too, went with fondness to that big apple trip in 1938, with Henry Green and Frances Repetto and the other old-timers now gone. There was the famous Ridge-where-the-goat-jump-off, where a hundred years ago a wild goat had been cornered by dogs and had jumped into the sea to save its life; then Try-pot and Noisy Beach under the steep cliffs where molly and peeyoo had a sanctuary because man had never been able to find a foothold to reach their nests. There was Sandy Point with its shady orchards, the Streams with its lush vegetation from the moisture of several small but very high waterfalls, which from a distance looked like mere trickles, Blacksand Beach, where for the moment a young sea elephant was lying like a big bloat of blubber taking a nap; and further on, Jews Point with its dramatic landscape of cavelike gulches and sharp ridges, the Rookery (abandoned long ago by the penguins that gave the place its name), and Farmost Point.

But as we rounded the mighty Big Point, where I would expect to get the first view of the Settlement and the familiar low, sloping profile of Hottentot Point, there was the first evidence that not all was as before. Where Big Beach and Little Beach had been, the new volcano was reaching its ugly tongue of rugged black lava into the sea, where it ended in a crumbling cliff at the water's edge, partly undercut by the surf of the mighty Atlantic waves, which had already put their mark on it as if in a vain attempt to push it back where it came from. We had to round another escarpment, as yet unnamed, before we suddenly found ourselves directly off the Settlement, which was now hemmed in to the east by a black wall of lava sloping down from a new cinder cone at the foot of the towering cliffs. And directly behind the village was a long, wide scar of gray rock on the face of the cliff, from top to bottom, where the big landslide had gone the day before the eruption.

The village itself looked familiar enough. There were the characteristic stone cottages with their thatched roofs, only more of them, spread out in picturesque disorder over the grassy slope, almost merging with the landscape as if they had grown out of its very soil. But wedged between the village and the sea, more prominent to the view, was a straight row of tin-roofed bungalows flanked by two or three even more eye-catching cement brick buildings that stuck out like so many sore thumbs in the landscape. This was the Station, containing the residences of the members of the British administration besides a canteen, a power station with workshops, and a radio shack between tall, white-painted masts, which more than anything else symbolized the fact that the modern era had caught up even with this remote outpost in the South Atlantic.

I was soon to discover other significant changes in the life of this remote island, which I had last seen as a peaceful relic of the days of the sailing ships. The famous Tristan longboats were still there. But they were lying idle on shore. Keels up, their slender, white-painted hulls could be seen lashed down on the beach and at Garden Gate, the new boat place on top of the bank. And there was no sign that they were going to be launched to meet the ship. Instead, a twenty-eight-foot barge, square-ended fore and aft, with an outboard motor, came splashing out to meet us, followed by a wooden fishing dinghy, also with an outboard motor, towing an inflated rubber pontoon. And the first man to come on board was not Chief Willie Repetto, who was not even in the barge, but the British Administrator. I had a feeling that something had indeed been wedged between the village and the sea, and I was reminded of Chief's words to a reporter in England: "When the Administrators come to the island, you see, they took over."

There was one creature seemingly unaffected by official rank and noisy motors. This was springtime on Tristan, the time for the enormous right whales to come close under land for their mating games. This was a sight I had never seen before, for the last time I went to Tristan we arrived too late in the year. Most of the time the huge shapes were hidden to our view under the surface of the water. But their presence was evident from ripples and big whirls that rose from the deep and sometimes even seemed to stop the wind-driven waves. They were all around us, even between the ship and the shore, and every now and then an enormous black pair of flukes would rise several feet out of the water and slowly submerge as the magnificent animal lazily rolled over and dived to deeper water.

The next morning the passengers were taken ashore in the motorized barge, the helmsman carefully keeping a distance from the cavorting whales. As we approached the beach, the craft was run full speed up on a wooden ramp, hooked onto a wire, and pulled out of the surf by a noisy, smoke-spewing motor winch that looked as if it had seen better days.

Indeed, as I stepped ashore from the barge that October morning of 1964, it was evident in more than one way that I had come to a modern Tristan. The outboard motors were whining and roaring as two rubber pontoons were shuttled back and forth, bringing in heavy loads of oil drums and all sorts of equipment and supplies. Two tractors were competing with the motorboats and with the winch on the beach in emitting modern noise and smell as they ascended the steep road to the top of the bank, pulling trailers loaded with goods for the canteen. And the chorus of motors and engines was soon joined by the slightly more sophisticated noise of a Land-Rover, the British equivalent of a jeep, as it was brought ashore from the ship to become the third motorized vehicle on the island, making the oxcarts and donkeys of the Islanders look like so many anachronisms. Up at the Station the

roar from the electric power plant told the story of yet another blessing of civilization as the thin walls of a wooden shack built around it
were shaking to the rhythm of the motor and black exhaust was
ejected from a pipe near the ground, forcing people and cattle to keep
their distance.

In the village, which so far did not have the benefit of electric
power, and where engines had not yet replaced the old-fashioned
means of transportation, things were a little more quiet. But even here
a battery-driven radio or phonograph might be heard blaring out the
rhythm of a rock 'n' roll favorite from a house. Gone were the idyllic
—and disease-carrying—little brooks that used to flow between the
houses with flocks of geese waddling through and women gathering at
the washing places for a little gossip. Instead, in the morning there
was a stream of women, now in modern dress and many of them in nylons, going to the store for shopping.

Gone also were the not so idyllic little privies at the back of each
house—they used to be hard to distinguish from a chicken coop. But
at the front corner of every house was a square little wooden structure with no windows and a lean-to roof, looking almost like a hidden
sentry box whose unseen occupant might command a full view of the
approaches to the house and keep a watchful eye on all comings and
goings through a slit above the door. Most of them were nicely painted
in an attractive light blue or green, and one man had given his a
bright happy red color. I was soon to learn that these were the new
"flash toilets" (as the Islanders called them) which had been installed by Government decree and expense shortly before the volcanic
eruption. They were often mentioned to reporters in England as a
proof of how advanced and modern Tristan really was. Their somewhat unusual location right in front of the house, often next to the
main entrance, seems to have been dictated by technical considerations. The Crown Agent engineer, who designed the layout of the sew-
ers at his desk in London, had apparently wanted to avoid cutting
through heavy foundation walls for the sewer pipes; having never been
to Tristan, he had no way of knowing, of course, that the Tristan
houses have no foundation walls at all since they are built directly on
the ground. And the Tristan Islanders, thinking that this was the way
things ought to be, accepted the design as the normal pattern so that
even some of the newly erected houses have been furnished with that
little sentry box in front.

There were other signs of civilization as well. As I took a walk out to Hottentot Gulch, there was the inevitable eyesore of a modern town: the bottom of the gulch had been turned into a dump, with old rusty oil drums and all kinds of scrap and garbage, providing a haven for scavenging rats and skua gulls.

There were important changes in the Islanders' minds and attitudes, too. Having accepted and acquired the symbols of modern living, the Islanders' submissive deference to all outsiders had disappeared, much of their shyness as well. With their free adoption of modern styles of dress, furnishings, food habits, and forms of entertainment, the awesome social distance to outsiders had been sharply reduced. At the same time, from a closer acquaintance with the ethos of the competitive world outside, the open confidence of an isolated community had been replaced by an apparent, almost blasé indifference to visitors, as if they were none of the Islanders' concern, which was often merely a cover for a cautious circumspection nurtured by the suspicion that every visitor was out to make a fast buck at somebody's expense.

I had noticed this new reserved, almost suspicious attitude of the Islanders the very first day I stepped ashore. Here we were—the Bishop, the Chief Civil Engineer, the young radio mechanic, the two reporters, and myself. On the beach the visitors were received in a friendly enough way by a group of Station people who were making polite conversation while our baggage was being unloaded from the barge, and eventually they led the way up the steep Puma Road to one or another of the Station houses, where tea and other refreshments were served and arrangements were made for accommodations in some vacant Station barracks. During all this the Islanders went about their work under the direction of a British public works officer, or they stood about as passive onlookers, as if the whole affair did not concern them in the least except to give them a job to do or something to look at from a distance, like the crowd of a little coastal town gathering at the quayside to watch the local steamship dock and depart. Although I knew all of them by name from my visit to Calshot two years earlier and considered many of them my friends, few ventured to step up and wish me welcome to Tristan, and then only to withdraw immediately, as if they did not want to break into a party where they did not fully belong—or did not want to belong. Surely, I was greeted with friendly smiles and handshakes whenever I broke away from the Station group to say hello to a friend. But it made me feel like a dignitary condescending to step out of an arranged ceremony to shake hands with the common people. At the same time, I had a peculiar feeling of being looked upon as an intruder along with the rest of the visiting gentlemen. What a difference from December 1937, when we came as complete strangers, and every one of the Islanders, men, women, and children, came up to us and wished us welcome to Tristan with a handshake and a smile. And I realized to what extent, and in more than a literal sense, the Station had indeed come between the village and the sea.

The impression was sadly confirmed on several occasions during my six months' stay on the island. One day a Russian research ship (obviously a converted whale catcher) came in to the Settlement for water. Just then a thatching gang was at work on Fred Swain's house, and one man, catching sight of the ship, said: "Grab your trade bag, there's a ship."

Another, realizing the irony in the remark, did not even look up from his work and said: "That don't bother me."

Nobody interrupted the work or showed any excitement or even interest in the ship, although after a while they all climbed to the top of the roof to have a look. Again there was a sharp contrast to what I had observed on my first visit to Tristan, when the whole community would get into a frenzied excitement at the sight of a mast on the horizon. Now all contacts with approaching ships were made by the Administrator, who even decided whether a contact should be made at all. The Islanders had nothing to do with it except as they were hired by the Administrator to man a boat or otherwise assist.

In the case of the Russian ship, no one came ashore. An attempt was made, but the sea was rough, and a dinghy was overturned, dropping the "Admin," a Russian biologist, and a couple of oarsmen in the "drink." But even if visitors came ashore, as in the case of H.M.S. *London* and the French cruiser *Jeanne d'Arc,* there was little contact with the Islanders, and I could not help but think how sad it was that these visitors should return home thinking that the Station was "Tristan," and without having seen the real Tristan except as a group of low stone cottages back there under the hillside.

It was obvious that the establishment of an administration from outside had drastically changed the situation on Tristan da Cunha, especially in the relations of the Islanders to the Outside World. But it was also evident that much of the change was in the attitude of the Islanders themselves. Ten years of extended contact with the Outside World, topped by two years as captives in England, could not fail to have an impact upon the Tristan community and its whole style of life. Already my visit to Calshot in the summer of 1962 had revealed, for one thing, a definitely more cosmopolitan outlook. These Islanders are not any more the conservative, tradition-directed lot that we knew in 1938.

But even more importantly, the Tristan community was not any more an open community where strangers were indiscriminately received as welcome guests and friends. As the Outside World moved closer and even established a beachhead on the island itself, the Islanders learned to regard it as a threat to their own way of life and to meet it with suspicion, even hostility, constantly on guard against being exploited materially or otherwise. And now, with the breakdown of their naïve faith in the benevolence of Colonial Administration, they had finally acquired what Mr. Hammond Tooke had found lacking sixty years earlier, "the instincts of suspicion and circumspection, which ultimately, in less favoured countries, are necessary in order to carry on successfully the struggle for existence."

A closer acquaintance with the "new" Tristan, however, soon revealed that the changes that had taken place in the village and in the homes, in dress and food habits, and in the Islanders' whole style of life, however conspicuous, did not penetrate very far below the surface of the Islanders' external appearance. Two years of complete submersion in an industrial society, with affluence and waste and a total cash economy, with tough competition for jobs and material earnings, had indeed changed the Islanders' attitude to outsiders but had apparently not had the effect of damaging or replacing the internal social structure of the community with its ethical principles of basic equality, mutual aid, and voluntary cooperation along well-established personal relationships in a web of selective reciprocity. If anything, the Islanders had developed a greater awareness of their own identity as "Tristans," and a deeper appreciation of their own way of life as a value to be cherished and preserved, as something that set them apart and made them unique but far from inferior to the man from outside.

In the first place, the Islanders were fully aware of the fact that the foundation of the island's economy still lay in the traditional farming, fishing, hunting, and gathering, no matter what the Administrator and the people in the Colonial Office were saying. In this respect, the Islanders held a more realistic view, recognizing that the fishing industry could not support the whole community alone, and that the cash wages they had earned from the factory "before the volcano" were only a supplement to the traditional subsistence economy. In the present situation, of course, with the factory destroyed and no shore-based fisheries in operation, the fundamental importance of the subsistence economy with its agricultural base was even more evident. Certainly, the Islanders recognized that in the long run, since barter with passing ships was completely out of the picture, some cash would be needed for clothing, lumber, canvas, nails, and tools, and there was indeed a hope among the Islanders that the fishing industry would get started again. But to them, it was not such a vital condition for survival as the outsiders, especially the administration of Tristan da Cunha, seemed to think it was. It was still the general attitude of most of the Islanders that "we can make a living without money." Money was good for "luxuries" but was not considered essential to their livelihood.

Besides, when the Tristan Islanders decided to return to their homes, their main concern was indeed to get away from the constant money worries of the civilized world and to re-establish their own way of life with its freedom and independence and its ethos of selective reciprocity based on personal relations. The moment they stepped ashore on familiar ground, without any fanfare, they just picked up where they had left off two years before, resuming their old familiar activities. As if by throwing a switch, their intricate system of interlocking reciprocal relationships, which had been dormant for lack of expression during their two years of exile, was turned on again.

Economically, it was a drastically reduced community that finally returned to Tristan da Cunha in November 1963. The direct damage from the volcano was not extreme as volcanoes usually go. But the factory was completely destroyed and buried under some sixty feet of lava, and so were the two beaches that used to be the only moderately sheltered landing places on that side of the island. This had put an end, at least for the time being, to the only industry on the island and the main source of cash income for the Islanders. Also, some twenty acres of grassland had been covered by lava, and landslides and rock falls in two or three other places had apparently altered the course of water drainage from the mountain in heavy rainstorms, causing another four or five acres of precious grassland to be washed away or covered with rocks and cinders.

But the most serious damage to the still predominantly agrarian subsistence economy of the Tristan community came not directly from the volcano but from the fact that the island was perhaps too hastily abandoned and left unguarded for almost a year before the first exploration party of twelve Islanders returned to take possession in September 1962. Particularly, the loss of the sheep was a most serious blow to the Islanders. In addition, the island's stock of potatoes had been reduced to practically nothing from having been left unharvested and exposed to cattle and to pests ordinarily kept under control. The situation could well be summed up in the words of Mary Swain: "When we came back to Tristan, we had nothing; all our sheep gone, no potatoes, no nothing—all I found in my house was a candle and a box of matches."

After resettlement the Saint Helena and Falkland Islands Governments joined with the Colonial Office and the administration of Tristan da Cunha to compensate for some of the losses. The island was restocked with sheep and chickens, and the Islanders were generously given the opportunity to buy new seed potatoes from stores presented to the island by the Tristan da Cunha Fund but appropriated by the Administrator for restocking the canteen.

However, the 150 sheep, amounting to only two per family, and about as many chickens sent out to the island replaced only a fraction of the Islanders' losses, and the new seed potatoes were apparently not of a kind hardy enough to withstand the rather windy climate of Tristan; besides, they were infected with root worms, adding another serious potato pest to the ones already existing on the island.

So the first year back turned out to be a hard one. The potato crop failed. Some of the patches hardly returned the seed. This had happened on Tristan many times before, but there had always been the sheep to fall back on. Now there was also a shortage of mutton. But the Tristan Islanders are fatalists, and as often happens, with fatalism goes optimism. In October 1964, when I arrived on Tristan, they told me: "We have seen our bad year, now we are coming into our good one. We've got potatoes planted, and vegetables and flowers. Now we are only waiting for our crop of potatoes, and that will be in January."

As it turned out, that crop was not much better than the first one—
root worms again. Unfortunately, no proper advice and supervision
was available to deal with the situation because the agricultural officer, who went out with the advance party in April 1963, was sent
home in the *Bornholm* in November and replaced by a public works
officer as part of the new Administrator's rather unrealistic attempt to
supplant the old subsistence economy with a total cash economy.

What saved the Tristan Islanders from downright starvation during
these first two years of resettlement was indeed hard cash. The money
earned on road building and other public works, although a good
help, was far from sufficient, however, to keep the community going,
for only about half the men were gainfully employed, and only a few
of them had permanent or even fairly steady employment. Besides, a
shilling an hour certainly did not give much purchasing power in a
store that now kept prices as high as those in London or Cape Town,
if not higher. Had this been all the cash available to the Islanders,
they would have starved. The few lucky men who had jobs on the fishing vessels were a little better off. What really saved the Islanders,
however, as it had so many times before during "hard times," was their
own incredible frugality and their habit of saving "for a rainy day,"
which not even the comparative affluence of two years in England was
capable of breaking. One Islander told me, with considerable pride,
that while in England, with four adults and a baby in the house, his
household expenses (including rent and utilities) amounted to no
more than two pounds and ten shillings a week. And there is reason to
believe that this was fairly typical of the Tristan families in Calshot.

So it was that when the seventy families of Tristan Islanders returned to their homes, they had saved so much from their unskilled
labor wages that they could afford to buy and take with them all sorts
of clothing, tools, and equipment and still have money left. It is estimated that between them they brought back to Tristan some eighteen
thousand pounds in savings, of which eleven thousand pounds was in
Postal Bank deposits, the rest in cash. This is what carried them over
the difficult first two years of resettlement.

Hardest hit by the eruption was the fishing industry, whose shore facilities were completely destroyed, and for some time it was a question
whether resuming operations on Tristan would be feasible at all.
Shortly after the disaster the euption was described as a "calamity" as

far as the Company was concerned "because it obliterated the factory and eliminated the manpower on which it had depended." This was at the time it was believed that the evacuation of Tristan would be permanent. Although the degree of dependency on Tristan labor was a matter of dispute, a special meeting of shareholders decided in December 1961 to place the Tristan da Cunha Development Company in voluntary liquidation.

Soon, however, it became evident that the Tristan Islanders had not abandoned their homes and were determined to return to their island; and like the Phoenix rising from the ashes, the Company reemerged as Tristan Investments, Ltd. (Pty.), with the South Atlantic Islands Development Corporation as its main (and only) operation. The two fishing vessels, the *Tristania* and the *Frances Repetto,* continued their activities around the islands without interruption, completely unaware that in the meantime they had been liquidated and reinstated under new company auspices.

When it became apparent that the authorities might have to yield to pressures and let the Islanders return to Tristan, one of their chief concerns, naturally, was the reestablishment of a factory on shore, especially since the belief was widely held that the whole economy of the island depended entirely and exclusively on the fishing industry. Since the same authorities had argued that the island was unfit for resettlement because of a lack of adequate landing beaches, they were now caught in their own argument, and the fishing company apparently had no great difficulty persuading them that if a shore base were to be established again, improved landing facilities had to be provided.

The thought of constructing a boat harbor on Tristan had been discussed enthusiastically among the Islanders after the return of the Royal Society expedition of February and March 1962, when it was reported that debris from the lava flow washed up by the surf had formed a gravel bar with a well-protected lagoon behind it. It was stipulated that by cutting a narrow opening in the bar, a natural harbor would be provided. This hope was shattered shortly after the resettlement when an extremely heavy swell broke over the bar and filled the lagoon with stones and gravel. Nevertheless, in order to induce the fishing company to continue operations and build a new factory on Tristan, it was decided in the Colonial Office to investigate the possibility of building a small boat harbor or protected beach somewhere along the northwestern plain, where small craft could land safely even under weather conditions when the beaches would otherwise be unworkable.

The harbor project was strongly promoted by the new Administrator of Tristan da Cunha, who had indeed initiated the whole plan and who had a double interest in the project since he was scheduled to become to the Personnel Director of the South Atlantic Islands Development Corporation as soon as his tour of duty as Administrator was over. Already in September 1963, before the return of the main party of Islanders, he brought out to Tristan a South African engineer, a Mr. van der Merwe, to investigate the prospects and review several possible harbor sites. A loan of £22,000 was extended from Colonial Development and Welfare funds as a temporary measure to meet the "development needs" of the island, including "plans for improving landing facilities." During Christmas 1963, the Administrator met in Cape Town with representatives of the Colonial Office and the Development Corporation to discuss the plans, and a formal proposal was submitted to the proper British authorities. It was on the basis of this proposal that the Chief Civil Engineer of the Crown Agents went out to Tristan in October 1964 to survey the situation. And in November of that year it was decided to go ahead with the plans at a possible cost of £100,000, although formal approval of the exact amount was not obtained until January 1965.

This was a Government project, and the work was carried on, of course, under the direction of the Administrator, who took a businesslike approach to this as to any other project he was supervising, in full accordance with the ethos of the Economic Man. In fact, the harbor project became the focal point of the Administrator's general policy of pushing the transition to a pure cash economy as much as possible, which he considered to be in the best interest of the community as well as of the Company. Although he recognized that for the time being, until the fishing industry could be re-established, the agriculturally based subsistence economy was of some importance, he had little regard for the farming efforts of the Islanders, and their excursions to Sandy Point, Stony Beach, and particularly to Nightingale he considered a "waste of time." He had no patience with what he regarded as the unpredictable and irrational whims and wishes of the Islanders, who "quite arbitrarily decide to take a holiday to suit their own convenience," and he adopted as his favorite slogan that "these people must be *kicked* into the second half of the twentieth century."

Obviously, for the Company (as well as for the administration, of course), a total cash economy would mean that a "reliable" and "committed" labor force would be available at all times since all the Islanders would constantly be dependent on wages. And for the Islanders— well, part of being "kicked into the second half of the twentieth century" was to acquire some industrial discipline (by compulsion if necessary) and learn to sacrifice their precious freedom and independence for the beckoning rewards of fairly steady employment, relative affluence, and a measure of prestige. Candidly, the Administrator once remarked that "when the Islanders adopted a cash economy, they lost their independence."

In accordance with this view, several measures were taken with the apparent purpose of encouraging, persuading, or even forcing the Islanders to rely more exclusively on cash income and supplies from the Island Store, which was now run by the Administrator. Whether by design or not, some of these measures had the effect of discouraging and even hampering the reconstruction of the island's subsistence economy and its agricultural base. An important step in that direction was the dismissal of the Agricultural Officer only a few months after the arrival of the advance party of returning Islanders on the grounds that the employment of an Agricultural Officer was a "waste of public funds."

A labor policy was adopted which was arbitrarily selective on the basis of compliance with contract and tolerated no interference from activities connected with the subsistence economy except potato digging. Whoever refused to take a job in the construction works when called did not receive another call to work for several months. Temporary leaves from the contracted work were seldom granted except in emergencies, and whoever took a day off without leave for any reason except illness was fired and stood a slim chance of ever being rehired.

Policies of wages and prices were adopted which seem to have had the purpose of increasing the Islanders' dependency on a cash income, forcing them to seek and to hold a job, but in many instances had the opposite effect, as it reduced the Islanders' purchasing power, forcing them to put more effort in their subsistence economy. It was demanded that all imports should go through the Island Store, thus in fact establishing a Government monopoly with complete control of prices in the hands of the Administrator. And prices were high— higher, in fact, than retail prices in Cape Town on most items— presumably because of high transportation costs. Supplies were brought out in chartered ships at a fee of £140 per day, although they probably could have been taken in the fishing ships at a much lower cost. And they were regularly, whether by ignorance or design, brought out in October and April, when the chances of expensive delays in the off-loading operations because of weather were high. Private orders from individual Islanders to firms in Cape Town, which the officers of the fishing vessels were perfectly willing to mediate with no charge for commission and transportation, were forbidden, and competition from this source was effectively ruled out by levying what amounted to a landing fee (corresponding to what transportation costs would have been in a Government chartered ship) on anything brought ashore from the fishing ships for private use. Several intended gifts to the community from the Tristan da Cunha Fund and other sources, such as potato and vegetable seeds, oars and canvas for the longboats, were claimed for the Island Store and subsequently sold to the Islanders at the usual high prices.

At the same time, as long as the fishing company was not operating a shore base, the Administrator had effective control of the wages, and they were kept at the usual low level of one shilling per hour, with an occasional bonus given for piecework. If it was indeed the intention of this policy to maintain a low level of cash income, forcing the Islanders to put in longer hours for a livelihood, it backfired when the Islanders figured out that they could procure an equivalent amount of certain foods from their traditional subsistence economy with far less effort.

To say that the Tristan Islanders did not appreciate the new arrangements and policies is putting it mildly. On Tristan an Administrator is usually rated in an inverse ratio to the degree to which he "interferes" in the lives of the Islanders, and this one was soon rated the worst they had ever had. Obviously, many of his policies were on a direct collision course with some of the basic traditional values of the community.

In the first place, the arbitrary selectivity in the employment policy of the Administrator was considered extremely unfair and remained a source of tension throughout his two years' term of office. Since practically all the work that was available at the time was Government work, it was felt that it should have been distributed evenly among all, and the Administrator's policy of employing the same men all the time to the complete exclusion of others was a practice that in the Islanders' opinion smacked of favoritism.

Besides, in January 1964, immediately after his return from the Christmas meeting in Cape Town, the Administrator had announced the harbor project to the assembled men, and on that occasion it had been held out as a promise as well as a demand that *all* men between fifteen and sixty-five would work on the harbor. Although the project had not yet been approved by the proper authorities, preliminary work was started almost immediately and went on through the year of 1964. Roads were staked out to various possible harbor sites, such as The Hardies, Boat Harbour, and even across the new lava field to Pigbite. All this was indeed considered "harbor work" by the Islanders, and when full employment, or at least an even distribution of the available work, failed to come about, it appeared to them as a breach of promise on the part of the Administrator.

The most important issue, however, was the Administrator's demand that a labor contract take precedence over all other activities and obligations. This was a revival of the old issue from the early days of the fishing company concerning the relative importance of contractual and personal obligations. The very concept of a contract in this sense had, in fact, been solidly rejected by the Islanders as alien to their sense of fairness and justice. That was why the Company had had to revise their labor policies before the volcanic eruption, and it was one of the main reasons why the Islanders had abandoned the modern industrial society in England and returned to Tristan. After resettlement there were many incidents to demonstrate that this was still an important issue.

A man employed in some menial job was asked one day to join a thatching gang for a relative. As he might have done in any situation where he had a conflict of obligations, he asked his father to take his place at the job while he himself went to the thatching. This was undoubtedly done out of consideration for the employer; he did not want to let the Administrator down. At the same time it was a service to his unemployed father, who got a chance to earn a day's pay. It was a surprise to him as well as to his father that this arrangement was not acceptable to the Administrator, who sent the father home and fired the son.

Equally surprised were the two men who took their wives on a week's holiday to Seal Bay and found on their return that they had been fired from their jobs. These two men were cousins and friends from childhood, and their wives were sisters. For many years these two couples had been in the habit of taking a holiday together, usually in the fall after the return from the fatting trip to Nightingale had marked the end of the busy summer season, and this was the first time they had had a chance to renew the habit and the relationship after the evacuation. Obviously, to these two men and their wives the renewed expression of their old relationship was not only a pleasure but a mutual obligation, and its conflict with the job obligation was not even felt as a problem because here was a personal relationship which, in the Islanders' view, clearly took precedence over an impersonal contract relationship. It was considered extremely unfair by everybody that these two men were kept out of a job for almost a year after the incident.

Since the sojourn in England, there were indeed a few Islanders who had developed a more commercial attitude and liked to figure out, for example, the "cost" of a service given to someone in terms of lost wages (conveniently forgetting about the return service he might receive in the future). One Islander apparently felt quite sophisticated calculating the "cost" of a thatching, not in terms of actual cash expenditures, which are usually quite negligible, but in terms of the potential sales value of the sheep he has to kill to feed the gang. This kind of calculation is, of course, completely alien to a subsistence economy, where the considered value of a sheep would be relative to the wealth and status of the owner. It is also contrary to the meaning and significance of the thatching gang or any other form of voluntary service as an expression and confirmation of mutual personal relationships.

There were also some who would occasionally sell meat to other Islanders, and there were some who would buy it. Existing personal relations, however, put a definite limit on such sales. The Islanders know well the difference between a business deal and a personal relationship and are careful not to mix them—"there are no friends in business," I have heard them quote. One cannot, therefore, properly offer meat or anything else for sale to a person with whom he stands in a relationship of personal reciprocity with gratuitous exchange of gifts and services. This, of course, drastically reduces the number of potential buyers available in the community. In any case, a substantial discount is expected in any sale from one Islander to another—the meat sold in the Village is offered at a lower price (one shilling per pound) than at the Station or on the ships.

The great majority of Islanders still refused to engage in such sales or in any kind of money transaction with other Islanders, and resentment of the practice was often expressed. One Islander stated with emphasis: "I will never buy meat from an Islander, because when I kill a bullock, I won't expect him or anyone to pay me for the meat I give him!"

In this social atmosphere, where personal relations played such a prominent part both socially and economically, it was quite evident that contract labor had to take second place in the hierarchy of obligations. It was not only a question of learning the meaning and implications of a contract. The Islanders knew that already, and as far as the Administrator and his labor policies were concerned, the Islanders quickly got the message. This Administrator meant business, and if one wanted to hold a job, one stayed with it, no matter what might come up. To the Islanders, however, it was immediately clear—and it was confirmed in the relatively few cases in which Islanders had submitted themselves to a permanent labor contract—that this would not only cut a person off from the fun and excitement of a Nightingale trip and other activities in the community and tie him to a life that most of the Islanders regarded as drudgery and toil or worse. It would, in fact, isolate him from any effective participation in the established network of mutual aid and reciprocal relationships that make up the community. Obviously, if a man was to hold on to his job under this Administrator, he would not be able to ask people for assistance when he needed a new thatch on his roof because he would not be free to take a day off from his job whenever another needed his service in return. He would not have the opportunity to own cattle at Stony Beach in partnership with others because he would not be able to fulfill his obligations to the group in terms of doing his part tending the herd. Even a share in a longboat would be close to meaningless to him, not only because he could not get much use or enjoyment out of the boat himself, but particularly because he could never meet his obligations to the rest of the crew. And excluding oneself from the longboat trips with all their social implications was tantamount to resigning from the whole web of personal relations that make up the community. We know what that would mean: a complete loss of identity and status within the community.

The resistance put up by the Islanders to the explicit or implicit demands of the Administrator was at first verbal and weak. A community of convinced individualists is not easily stirred into concerted action. The Tristan Islanders had indeed demonstrated that they could act in concert when they demanded to return to their island after the evacuation. That, however, was a rare case of emergency bordering on desperation. As soon as the crisis was over and they were safely back on Tristan, they immediately reverted to their old peaceful and independent way of life, and no one, least of all Chief, was inclined to start another struggle or to put himself forward trying to tell the other fellow what to do. The deeply ingrained island code of dignity, kindness, and inoffensive behavior has created a predominant personality type which does not easily give expression to hostility or engage in open conflict.

Furthermore, in spite of the newly won self-image and the dramatic experience of having to defy the Colonial Office in their struggle to return to Tristan, the Islanders' traditional deference to official authority was unabated. In their conception, as well as by ordinance, the power of the Administrator was absolute. His decrees were the "laws" of Tristan, and his real or imagined wishes had the force of injunctions. After their experience in England, the Islanders' faith in the intrinsic benevolence of the Colonial Administration was lost, but this only made the power of the Administrator more fearsome and dangerous to oppose. It was even believed to be fully within his power to have the Government order another evacuation, this time for good, and there was no lack of hints on the part of the Administrator that this would indeed be done if the harbor were not built soon.

There were surely many who boasted readiness to fight again if necessary. Their thoughts were well expressed by Mary Swain, who openly declared: "I'm jolly well satisfied now, and I don't think no one will get me off to England again, not even the Queen!" Few really seemed to have the confidence, however, that they would once more be

able to muster the courage they had shown in Calshot and put up another fight for survival. Chief said with tragic resignation: "I don't
think that I will ever leave Tristan again unless the Government takes
everybody—then I will have to go."

So it was fully believed to be within the rightful power of the Administrator to determine his own labor policy, however unfair it might
appear to the Islanders, and to impose a labor conscription upon the
community if he should wish to do so, even at the expense of the Islanders' much cherished freedom and independence. Besides, it was
generally assumed that anyone who "spoke up to the Administrator"
stood a fair chance of remaining unemployed, and several individual
cases were pointed out as confirming the assumption.

The reward of employment and the explicit or implicit threat of unemployment were indeed the most important instruments of power for
the Administrator in this situation and a formidable deterrent to the
Islanders. Money had become important enough in the Tristan household to make the absence of it felt as a hardship, especially at this
time, with the setbacks that the subsistence economy had suffered from
the temporary abandonment of the island. And since the fishing industry was momentarily idle except for the two fishing ships, where only a
few Islanders could be employed, the only source of cash income for
most of them was the public work under the supervision of the Administrator. In this situation the Administrator could, and did, use
employment and the threat of permanent unemployment as a whip to
keep the Islanders in line. And the selective employment policy actually practiced only served to emphasize the threat.

What finally brought the issue of the Administrator's labor policy to
a crisis was its conflict with the Nightingale trips. These trips had always caused annoying interruptions in the fishing industry, and it appeared to be the Administrator's serious intention to do away with
them, at least as long as the harbor was under construction. To the Islanders, on the other hand, the Nightingale trips were, as we have
seen, the most important social events in the life of the community
and the prime instrument of self-expression within the framework of
selective personal relationships, quite apart from their economic significance.

The issue had come to a point once before, only four months after
resettlement. In early April 1964 a Falkland Islands ship, the *A.E.S.*,

was expected to arrive with 150 sheep; since the sheep were a gift to the Islanders, it was agreed that they should be off-loaded free of charge, and the Administrator prevailed on the Islanders not to go to Nightingale for bird fat until the ship had arrived since their absence might jeopardize the landing operations. Besides, he argued, with cooking oil available in the Island Store, a fatting trip would not be necessary for the supply of food and would be a "waste of time."

The *A.E.S.* arrived on April 7 and was off-loaded as arranged. Rightly or wrongly, the Islanders had understood the request to stand by to apply also to the *R.S.A.*, which arrived nine days later with supplies for the Island Store, and that the Administrator meant business with his request was concluded from the fact that he had punished five young men with a fine of two pounds each for not being available for the off-loading of the *A.E.S.* So the Islanders stood by for the *R.S.A.* as well. As it turned out, this meant that there was no fatting trip at all that year. Abolishing a fatting trip the first year after resettlement was indeed a substantial sacrifice on the part of the Islanders, and tension rose to a pitch when the *R.S.A.* arrived on April 16 and the Administrator employed only forty men in the off-loading, which was about half the available labor force.

Persuading the Islanders not to go to Nightingale for fat in March 1964 was undoubtedly part of the Administrator's program to teach the Islanders that they could live better under a cash economy, relying on the Island Store for food. His selective employment policy, however, did not strengthen his hand on this point because only a few Islanders, contemptuously referred to as "friends of the Admin," had steady jobs and could afford the luxury of buying food from the store, while others depended entirely on an impoverished subsistence economy or had to resort to savings brought along from England. Neither did the Administrator take into account that, with the wages kept at one shilling an hour, and with current prices in the canteen, it would take a full month's wages at steady employment to buy a quantity of cooking oil corresponding to the amount of bird fat that an Islander could collect in two or three days on Nightingale. The point was further weakened when, as a result of the cancellation of the fatting trip and the absence of bird fat, the store ran out of cooking oil in mid-December, just as Christmas preparations imposed a great demand.

So, when Christmas holidays came around again, the Islanders quietly picked up their usual routine of preparing the longboats for the busy season with Nightingale trips for guano in January and February and for fat in March. There was indeed some apprehension about the reaction of the Administrator, but the Islanders seemed to be determined that this year nothing would stop them from going.

By New Year the longboats were ready, crews had been set up, and all that remained was to wait for a favorable wind to go on the first guano trip of the season.

Exactly at this time, as if by design, the Administrator decided to step up the work on the access road to the harbor, and a large number of men were called to work, including most of the crews that had been set up for the longboats. The timing may have been accidental; but if the Administrator had wanted to thwart the plans for a Nightingale trip, it could not have been more aptly chosen. On January 10 it looked as if the morrow would bring a favorable wind for the trip, and last preparations were made, assembling oars and sails, guano bags, blankets, and cooking gear. Exactly on that day the Administrator received word by radio telegram that eighty thousand pounds had finally been approved for the harbor, and he immediately called in the labor force for the following day. It turned out to be a good sailing day as predicted, but no longboats were launched.

There were still enough men left unemployed to man a couple of longboats, and by shifting around men and equipment from one boat to another, two longboat crews were set up to go the next fine day. On the eve of that day, however, even this arrangement was upset when the Administrator again called in an additional number of men for the harbor work, again including the larger part of the crews that had been set up for the longboats. Again a good sailing day passed with no longboats being launched.

At no time during this had the Administrator explicitly stated that he was opposed to a Nightingale trip at this time. The Islanders, however, knew his negative attitude to these trips in general, and he had often enough declared in no uncertain terms that he would not tolerate any interference in the harbor work from such activities. They also knew from bitter experience that continued unemployment could be the lot for anyone who refused to obey the call. They had not forgotten the Administrator's promise of a year ago that everybody would be employed in the harbor construction work, and they saw the irony in having this promise belatedly fulfilled exactly at a time when it caused maximum interference with their own activities, which did not indicate a favorable attitude on the part of the Administrator. So they yielded to his implicit pressures and threats, and for a while it looked as if there would be no guano trips that year, perhaps not even a fatting trip in March.

At the harbor site, however, with sixty or seventy men on the job, the work came practically to a standstill. This was not a deliberate sit-down strike. But tension was high, and much of the time the Islanders would simply forget their work in their heated arguments and vehement outbursts against the Administrator. It was quite obvious that morale was very low, and it was only their deeply ingrained abhorrence for open conflict and their deferent respect for official authority that prevented the excited Islanders from breaking into action.

In the face of this highly charged situation, the Public Works Officer decided to take matters a little more in his own hands and try to establish a more flexible labor policy. To restore the vanishing morale at the work site, he decided on a forty-hour week, with Saturdays off to give the Islanders a chance to tend to their potatoes and cattle; and when the *Frances Repetto* arrived with the mail on a Saturday (January 16), confining the Islanders to work on the beach the whole of that day, he allowed each of them an extra day off during the following week to go digging potatoes. He even promised the Islanders that if anyone wanted to go to Nightingale for guano, he could go and would have his job back when he returned. He had apparently obtained the Administrator's reluctant consent in this, although the Administrator never came out with a public statement to that effect.

The absence of a public announcement from the Administrator was probably the reason for the Islanders' continued apprehension about employment. Undoubtedly, they trusted the sincerity of the Public Works Officer, but they did not feel reassured that the Administrator would not overrule him should it come to a test. Besides, the whole issue was not only a question of employment or unemployment. It was also a question whether to abandon an activity of the greatest economic and social significance to the Islanders or to defy the assumed wishes of an official authority. It was indeed a conflict of values in which the guano trip—usually an event of minor importance as compared to the fatting trip—was given a new symbolic significance.

On the 29th of January 1965, it came to a dramatic showdown in this struggle between two conflicting value systems. After a spell of unfavorable weather it looked as if this might turn out to be a good day for going to Nightingale. Although practically all the men were employed at the harbor work, the longboat crews were set up as before, the boats were ready, and as daylight broke that morning, instead of going to their jobs, the men started to drift toward the Hump, a place in the middle of the village, which is a favorite vantage point for watching the weather. Choosing a day for going to Nightingale must be done with care. The important thing, of course, is the wind direction at sea. Because of the great land mass of the island, however, the wind on land or offshore gives no clue at all. It takes a prolonged watch of clouds and other signs to determine whether it is "a day."

On this particular morning, practically all the men were there, whether they were planning to go on the trip or not. As usual in crowds like that, not much was said. But this time there was a tension in the air that made even the silence more poignant. The wind was very light, with almost a dead calm at the Settlement, which only made it more difficult to judge, and the men were intently watching the sky for clues. Now and then the silence was broken by one or the other of the older men, remarking that it looked like "a day"—the wind was from the northwest. But they failed to get the approving consensus from the group. Intense silence settled again, and no one moved.

Some of the younger men argued that it was not "a day," pointing to white-capped waves whipped up by a southwest wind off the Hillpiece, or drawing attention to the calm at the Settlement indicating a lee. In vain did the older men point out that the wind off the Hillpiece was only a "land breeze," and that the calm at the Settlement was a "false lee," such as often occurs on the windward side of the island when the wind is light.

It was obvious that most of the men were not keen on going. They were caught on the horns of a dilemma, and they were looking for an excuse to go back to work. One man, who was not planning to go on the trip in any case, summed the situation up well by saying, as he walked away from the group: "Is y'all is *want* to go, it's a day."

Suddenly, two or three men broke away and started to walk vigorously toward the harbor site to report for work. Immediately the whole crowd followed suit. Only four men remained, all unemployed, not enough even for one boat's crew. There was no doubt that it was indeed "a day," and the four had bitter words about the others who had backed out: "If that crowd wasn't workin', they'd be going to Nightingale like mad; they won't let go of their jobs down there, that's the trouble." Another commented: "Them fellas has money on their brains!"

Down at the harbor site the men grabbed their shovels and pickaxes and went to work. The Public Works Officer was there to give the orders for the day, but no one uttered a word to him about wanting to go to Nightingale.

In the meantime the four diehards were trying to drum up a crew for at least one longboat to go alone if necessary, and about an hour after having reported for work, two young men were persuaded to leave their jobs and join them. This became a signal for a general walkout. One by one or in small groups the men put down their tools and walked away, and before long all the men had left their jobs to join their respective boat crews. Only one or two went by the office of the Public Works Officer to tell him they were going, asking for a confirmation of his promise that they could have their jobs back when they returned. By ten o'clock that morning the whole community was geared to the big sendoff, with the usual hustle and bustle, everybody pitching in. By noon the longboats were on their way to Nightingale on a belated first guano trip.

It was a short trip. Two days later there was a fair wind to go home, and the boats returned. As it happened on a weekend, only one working day was lost. Nevertheless, it was a turning point. The following day all the men went back to their jobs and were accepted. There was, in fact, no choice if the harbor work were to progress at all. Two weeks later the second guano trip went off, with all the longboats, without any tension or protest. This time the boats stayed away for nine days before there was "a day" to go home. In the meantime the harbor work was idled for lack of workers, and again there was no choice but to accept the men as they returned to their jobs.

These longboat excursions of January and February 1965 had a far-reaching symbolic significance. Not only did they set a precedent so that, from now on, Islanders could take a leave to go fishing, dig potatoes, or take part in any activity that their subsistence economy and so-

cial obligations demanded, and return to their jobs; more important
was the fact that these Nightingale trips reinforced the traditional
value system of the Tristan community over the new values of monetary affluence and contract relations. When the Administrator made a
last attempt to force a contract in conflict with the fatting trip in
March that year, he met a firmer stand than before on the part of the
Islanders. A young woman, who was working as a part-time clerk in
the Island Store, asked the Administrator for a leave to go to Nightingale with her husband, and when this was quite unreasonably denied,
she then and there resigned and joined her husband on the trip.

The whole affair of these Nightingale trips probably came as close
to an open "labor conflict" as one could expect to get in a community
that puts such a high premium on dignity and inoffensive behavior,
and where an effective leadership is practically ruled out by the code
of equality and individual integrity. But the issue was more than a
problem of a fair distribution of material assets within a single, predominantly materialistic value system, which is what most labor conflicts in our society are about. Seen in their social and historical context, it is evident that the Nightingale trips of 1965 became a matter of
principle to the Islanders, another test case for the strength and
durability of a way of life in a struggle between two conflicting value
systems. The whole ethos and spirit of the Tristan community was indeed on trial, challenged by the value system of the Economic Man
with its emphasis on progress, affluence, and contract relations. So far
the Tristan Islanders had, in their own quiet way, met the challenge,
not by rejecting the values of affluence and progress but by putting
them in second place to independence, individual integrity, and selective reciprocity based on personal relations.

16 The Aftermath

Not more than two years after the return of the main party and only eight to ten months after the dramatic showdown about the Nightingale trips, in November 1965, a young Tristan Islander returned with fanfare to England. He was Gerald Repetto, Joe Repetto's son, a rebel who claimed that he had been pressed by his parents to go back to Tristan and had announced loudly and clearly that once he reached the legal age of maturity he would be back in England. He was not yet quite twenty-one. But he had worked and saved, receiving much encouragement and assistance from the British radio operator on Tristan, who gave him work and even took him in as a guest in his bungalow so that the young renegade should not have to surrender part of his earnings for the maintenance of his father's large family. Now he had managed to buy his one-way ticket back to Britain.

When he arrived in Cape Town, and again later when he came to Southampton in the mail ship, young Repetto had some rather sensational news to tell reporters. The Tristan Islanders, he said, were tired of living on a lonely island—75 per cent of them would like to return to England, and no less than twenty-five men, women, and children were preparing to leave the island for good in March the following year. "All you can do on a Saturday night on Tristan," he said, "is go to the bar and play snooker;" but in England "Saturday night meant dancing, brown ale, and lots of fun."

The press grabbed the news with enthusiasm and triumph on behalf of our glorious civilization so eloquently restored from the crushing blow it had received three years earlier, when the Islanders decided almost unanimously to return to Tristan. And again the name of Tristan da Cunha appeared in glaring headlines on front pages all over the world:

TRISTAN TWISTS TO ELVIS PRESLEY, BUT THE PLACE IS DEAD
BRIGHT LIGHTS CALL TO LONELY ISLANDERS
GIVE US BRITAIN, RAT-RACE AND ALL

Gerald Repetto was not, in fact, the first casualty of two years of close contact with modern civilization. When the Islanders returned to Tristan in 1963, thirteen of those who had been evacuated from the island remained in Britain. Among them were a family of five and a hydrocephalic little boy who was left at an institution for handicapped children. The rest were young men and women who had got married, or more or less engaged, to English girls and boys.

The first one actually to return from Tristan after the resettlement in November 1963 was Dennis Green. He was the one whose house had burned, apparently ignited by red-hot cinders falling on the thatched roof. Dennis Green knew before he left England that his house had burned, and a special grant of £300 had been made available from the Tristan da Cunha Fund to enable him to buy lumber to rebuild it. But the sight of the charred ruins of his former home almost at the foot of that menacing dark cinder cone was more than he could take.

He had been quite ambivalent about going back to Tristan in the first place. He had a good job in England, and he liked it. He had saved about £560 from his wages; he did not really mind working under a boss as long as he was given a feeling of doing a good job, and Dennis Green was good at practically anything he put his hand to. But he was not one to break away from the community at a time when everybody knew that it was important to stand together. And he had strong ties to hold him. The death of his father, Johnny Green, shortly after they had arrived in England had if anything tied the family even closer together, and throughout the two years' exile in England they had kept up their habit of gathering for a cup of tea on Sunday afternoons at the house of their mother, Old Sophie Green, another one of these kind and warm persons of whom Tristan has fostered so many.

It could not have been an easy decision to make. But after three days of soul searching and solemn deliberations with the family, Dennis Green and his wife Ada decided to return to England with their little daughter in the same ship that brought them to Tristan. And so it was that when the *Bornholm* weighed anchor on that clear, cold

November day in 1963, a family of three Islanders was standing at the rail, waving their last good-bye to Tristan.

The next to leave were Ada Green's parents, Big Gordon Glass and his wife, Susan. They were in their late sixties, and Big Gordon, his right arm lost in a factory accident, did not feel that he could be of much use supporting a household on Tristan. He figured he would be better off in England, where he would have a pension. Besides, they had now two daughters in England, and several grandchildren, for Lily Rogers, Victor's wife, who had stayed in Calshot with her family when the others returned to Tristan, was also their daughter. To be sure, they had three sons and a daughter on Tristan, too, and even more grandchildren, so this was now a split family. The youngest son, Eric, was still unmarried and living at home, and this was in fact given as the main reason Susan Glass had insisted on returning to the island. Tristan women have a strong sense of responsibility to their menfolk, and as long as a young man remains unmarried, it is a mother's duty to "look after" him.

Within a year or so, however, young Eric got married to his Martha with all the pomp and circumstance that goes with such an occasion, and with Eric well "looked after," comfortably settled in one of the best houses on the island, with all the cattle, sheep, and other property that went with it, including a share in the *British Trader,* there was apparently nothing to keep Gordon and Susan on Tristan any more, especially since the third daughter, Violet Swain, who was a widow with a large family, was also talking seriously about going back to England. But Gordon ran into unforeseen difficulties, which again stemmed in part from the Islanders' deeply ingrained deference to authority.

Although there was no doubt that the great majority of the Islanders were very happy to be back on Tristan in spite of the hardships of that first year, there were others besides Gordon and Susan who were talking about returning to England. And they were not only young people. Most of them, in fact, were old like Gordon and Susan themselves, and it appears that the pension they could expect to receive in England was a very attractive bait as it would give them an independence they would not enjoy on Tristan. There, they feared, they might become a burden to a son or a son-in-law or whoever took over the house as the last remaining child in the household.

But the Administrator, who had been one of the strongest advocates for keeping the Islanders in England, now took a dim view at having any of them leave the island. He repeatedly reminded the Islanders that it had been their own choice to return to Tristan, and now they would have to take the hardships with the pleasures. Besides, very shortly all hands would be employed, and would in fact be needed, in the harbor work. This was enough to discourage some of the prospective emigrants. And when the Administrator demanded that all applications for passport, obtainable at the British Consulate in Cape Town, should go through him, many of them decided that it was no use even trying. There was also the question of passage, which was completely under the Administrator's control.

Big Gordon Glass, however, was determined to leave, and after some bickering with a reluctant Administrator, who even claimed he had to have "permission from the Colonial Office" to let him go, he obtained a passage in the *R.S.A.*, which had brought the heavy equipment for the harbor work, and sailed from Tristan in May 1965.

This was just the beginning. Within a year Tristan was to have another emigration wave, in numbers comparable to the great emigrations of the 1850's and again of the 1880's and 1890's, although, because of the increased size of the community, this one did not have the same impact.

A new Administrator came to Tristan in April 1965. He had had close contact with the Islanders while they were in England as a representative of the Colonial Office and had now been "seconded" as an interim Administrator for a year. He, too, had been of the opinion that the Islanders should have stayed in England, and even now he was convinced that "had the Tristanians spent another year in Britain, many of them would never have gone back to their island . . . . Many went back with mixed feelings, particularly the younger ones."

The new Administrator took a much more liberal attitude to the question of returning to England, and when he learned that there were indeed a number of Islanders who had second thoughts about life on Tristan, he obligingly took steps to invoke Government assistance to those who wanted to return. Through the Colonial Office, inquiries were made concerning housing and jobs, and soon the Administrator could hold out the prospect that these problems would somehow be taken care of. Former employers of Tristan Islanders in England were approached and asked about their willingness to rehire, and some of them said they would. The New Forest Rural Council, who had taken over the management of the Tristan Close at Calshot when it was evacuated by the Tristan Islanders (except for Victor Rogers and his family, who stayed behind), had in the meantime rented out all the houses but agreed to put the names of prospective returners from Tristan on their waiting list, refusing, however, to give them any priority. Until vacancies occurred, the Colonial Office would endeavor to provide temporary living quarters. Concerning transportation, the Administrator suggested that if a large enough number of Islanders signed up for a return trip, a ship might be chartered or diverted from its course at Government expense to take them at least as far as Cape Town. And those who had difficulties paying their fares from there to England—of course, all of them had—were encouraged to apply to the Colonial Office for assistance.

Although the Administrator strongly denied that he had persuaded anybody to leave the island, it is quite clear that his generous offer of assistance had stirred the already troubled waters of Tristan da Cunha. The first two years after resettlement had indeed been hard times, with crop failures and dried-out pastures, low wages and unemployment. Many Islanders were now scraping the bottom of their savings— savings which the higher union wages in England had made it possible for them to acquire and which now seemed to have gone down the drain. It is obvious that this situation fostered a feeling of insecurity about the future of Tristan with many Islanders, and maybe the ugly cinder cone behind the village and the black, rugged lava mass reaching out into the sea and shutting them in to the east seemed even more depressing to mind and soul in this dim light.

So it is not to be wondered at that to some the grass on Tristan just did not seem quite as green as they had imagined in their nostalgic longing for home. And with the possibly unintended encouragement stemming from the attitude of the new Administrator, it seemed that the discontentment became contagious and soon took on almost epidemic dimensions. Suddenly it became proper and fashionable, at least in some circles among the Islanders, to say that "if I ever get enough money to buy my ticket, this place will not hold me," most of them probably feeling pretty safe that they would never really have to face the awesome decision as the likelihood that they would ever have enough money was very slim indeed.

The contrast to the situation in Calshot, now three years in the past, is striking. At that time, the community stood together with one voice, with one goal, even with one leader in an almost fanatical determination to return to Tristan da Cunha as one body. Those who in their hearts might have had different feelings and opinions did not even express them publicly out of loyalty to "the People," and Chief Willie Repetto's menacing warning on that destiny-packed Saturday night in July 1962 did only state openly what everybody felt when he declared that he would not even reveal what he thought of the possible dissenters—"I'll keep that to myself."

Now, three years later, there was an entirely different situation. The Tristan community was safely back on its island. There was nothing any more to threaten its existence and identity, and the people could relax from the intense solidarity, which circumstances had forced upon them in England. They were again free—free to honor their personal obligations in a community where each does "as seemeth right in his own eyes," to quote Mr. Hammond Tooke's observation from 1904. And it is clear that it did not take them long to revert to their traditional patterns even in this respect. Tristan was again an "atomistic" community, an aggregate of incorrigible individualists. And a handful of renegades bothered nobody. If they wanted to leave, so much the better. In November 1965, Chief was again expressing the general sentiment of the Islanders when he wrote to me in a letter that "there are a lot of people thinking about going back to England," and then added, "everybody can please their self and do what they like."

In this light it is even possible to understand Gerald Repetto's sensational remarks to the press when he arrived in England. Although his statement that 75 per cent of the people wanted to return to Britain obviously was a self-assuring exaggeration, there were indeed "a lot of people" talking about it. Nobody really knew how many were serious—"there was a certain mum-ness about it all," observed the Reverend Keith Flint, the chaplain serving Tristan at the time. Perhaps there was a lingering feeling of disloyalty on the part of some of the prospective emigrants. There certainly was ambivalence with most. It was a situation wrought with rumors and exaggerations, which could easily give somebody the impression that half the people or more were ready to leave, especially if this would bolster his own irresolute position.

It certainly appeared to be a most fertile ground for the Administrator to solicit a large enough contingent of prospective emigrants to persuade the Colonial Office to charter a ship. Inquiring around the village, holding out golden promises of possible Government assistance in transportation, housing, and job hunting, he must have received many a long, drawn-out "ya-as" in apparent confirmation of a desire to return to England. The trouble is that on Tristan a long, drawn-out "ya-as" may mean many different things. It certainly may signify approval and consent, but as often as not it has a connotation of non-commitment and uncertainty. It may in fact mean as much as "maybe" or "I don't care" and is often used with outsiders to avoid giving a straight answer or getting into an unpleasant argument. The Administrator, apparently unaware of this peculiarity of Tristan speech, quite understandably came under the impression, by his own statement, that a very large number of Islanders—his estimate, too, was 75 percent— would like to return to England if it were possible.

In actual fact, when it came to making positive commitments by having one's name put down on a list, the Administrator came up with no more than twenty-five names, less than 10 percent of the island's population. The list was submitted to the Colonial Office in October 1965. By February, however, the list had increased to include some forty-five persons—men, women, and children—who were applying for Government assistance to leave Tristan da Cunha and settle down in England.

And assistance was given. Those who were unable to raise the money for the ticket from Cape Town to Southampton were given long-term, interest-free loans, and in some cases the Colonial Office may even have paid part of the fare. Arrangements were made to divert a ship from its course to pick up the group of emigrants at Tristan and bring them to Cape Town. As it happened, it was again the *Boissevain*, which had brought the advance party of Islanders out to Tristan in April 1963. Now, exactly three years later, she was about to take some of them off the island. She was due to arrive at Easter time.

As the date of departure drew closer, the ambivalence of most of the prospective travelers became more and more evident. Mr. Flint witnessed the situation and described it in a letter:

The last few weeks, perhaps months, prior to the Exodus were naturally ones of unsettlement and of some tension in the village, and as the time went on some of those forecast as going began to get "cold feet." It was not very easy to learn who were actually anticipating leaving: there was a certain mum-ness about it all . . . .

In one or two cases the expected funds promised, or forecast from [relatives in] England did not materialise . . . and so their passages had to be cancelled. There could have been other personal or domestic reasons as well . . . . During the last week or so a number of those whose names were down to go showed strong signs of not wanting to go, and in several cases husband and wife were not of the same mind . . . .

If the weather had made embarkation impossible when the *Boissevain* arrived, I think very few of them would have wanted to avail themselves of the offer of another ship being called in in June.

Ambivalence was indicated also by the way in which the emigrants disposed of their property, particularly their houses. Only one of the returners sold his house (for eighty pounds), another gave his to a houseless brother-in-law. The rest put their houses and other property in charge of a relative to "take care of" or even to use, but with the reservation, mostly confirmed and recorded in an official agreement (with one copy deposited in the Administrator's Office), that should the owner return to Tristan, he would repossess his house. No one, obviously, wanted a repetition of the struggle that took place about Peter Green's house when the "newcomers" returned to Tristan in 1908, which was still live in island tradition after almost sixty years. Most important, the majority of them expected that they might come back to Tristan some day.

Lars Repetto, Gerald's older brother, was quite open about it. He did not want to leave the island, but his wife did. Lars, being a tractable man, said: "All right, let's go back to England to try it once more, and if we don't like it we can go back to Tristan after a year or so." He put the price of his house at two hundred pounds, probably well aware that no one would be able to buy it at that price. To raise the travel money, however, he sold all his cattle. But before he left, he took a nail and scrawled on the side of the dumper truck he was driving for the harbor work: "Book me back in another year."

The *Boissevain* arrived on schedule, and those who had hoped for a "swelly" day were disappointed. On Easter Day, April 10, 1966, ten families, comprising thirty-five men, women, and children, sailed from Tristan da Cunha for the second time. On May 3 they arrived in Southhampton in the *Capetown Castle*.

The newspapers, of course, were on hand, and a correspondent for *The Times* described with disgust the "prowling packs of the press" as the *Capetown Castle* docked. In a more sober tone, as usual, than most newspapers, *The Times* tried to analyze what had gone wrong with Tristan to bring so many disillusioned Islanders back to modern civilization:

This return to what they pronounce "the Houtside Warld" shatters the potent, sentimental myth about happy isles beyond the sunset, frugal life and the golden age, Calypso and Crusoe. Having tasted the fruit of the tree of affluence, have they been corrupted so that they can never again enter into the simple life? This would be ironic at a time when urbanized Britons in droves try to escape from it all, back to nature in tents and boats.

In fact the Tristans do not seem particularly driven by lust for affluence. Television sets, washing machines, and wage packets do not feature high, or at all, on their list of reasons. Only one made the point that he was earning 8s. a day in Tristan compared with £20 a week in Britain.

In fact, the Islanders were rather vague, even in their own minds, as to why they had left Tristan. They seemed to have been carried away on a wave of imagination, only half wittingly. Now the wave had crested and died, and they found themselves washed up on the shores of England, somewhat bewildered, trying to face the question "Why?" A year later I visited most of them in England. I was talking to one of them, who was then preparing to return to Tristan again. I asked him why he had left Tristan. "I don't know," was the answer, and he seemed as amazed and puzzled as I was.

One thing was certain. This was not a movement staged by a rebellious youth with a lingering taste of glamour and excitement in their mouths rising against a stubborn and domineering older generation. Among the 55 Islanders who up until now had remained in England or returned there after the resettlement, only eight were young single

persons who had separated themselves from the community independently of their parents; and this in a community where in October
1961 almost half of the 263 people were unmarried youths under twenty-five. The remaining 47 migrants stayed or came to England in family groups and included 17 dependent children and only one young,
still childless, couple in their twenties. And their ages ran the whole
spectrum from infancy to old age. Of the 38 independent migrants
almost half were over forty, ten were over fifty, and no less than six
of them were over sixty years of age. No, it could hardly be called
a youth movement by any stretch of the imagination.

Once the emigration had started, severed kinship ties may certainly
have played a role in continuing the movement as if by some sort of
chain reaction. All of the thirty-five migrants of April 1966 had close
relatives in England from earlier migrations—brothers, sisters, sons,
and daughters. But kinship ties pulled both ways. In the end the migrations left more rather than fewer kinship ties severed, with more instead of fewer families split between Tristan and the Outside World.

My good friend Roland Svensson, the Swedish artist and writer who
has taken such a warm interest in islands and island people (including
Tristan), made a keen observation, and it is only fitting that I should
give him the credit he deserves. Viewing the list of recent emigrants
from Tristan, he remarked that "it looks like the Glasses are pulling
foot for the Repettos." Indeed, the name Glass was quite prominent
on that list. Besides Gordon Glass and his two daughters Lily Rogers
and Ada Green, there were two of his brothers, Sidney and Godfrey,
and his son Eric, who decided in the end that the grass was greener in
England after all; Godfrey Glass already had two daughters in England and was now taking his son along, and Sidney Glass was planning to bring his whole family, including his two daughters and their
husbands and children. As it turned out, only one of them came
along; but the other one was planning to follow in October. A sister of
the Glasses was also on the list with her husband, Ned Green. And if
we take a look at the actual kinship structure of the Tristan community, the preponderance of "Glasses" among the emigrants is even
more striking.

With a bilateral kinship system, recognizing "relations" both
through mother and father, there are no clearly circumscribed patro-
nymic clans on Tristan following exactly the lines of the seven surnames

Glass, Swain, Green, Rogers, Hagan, Repetto, and Lavarello. But the Islanders do indeed talk about the Glasses, the Greens, the Swains, and the Repettos, referring to vaguely defined groupings within the community consisting of those who are identified (and identify them-selves) with certain lineages, whether they happen to belong through their mothers or fathers. And since kinship ties through the mother may be just as strong or, in some cases, even stronger than the paternal ones, a well-integrated family may indeed hold the loyalty of most of its offspring, both cognate and agnate, through several generations, re-sulting in a more or less well-defined group, including persons of var-ious surnames. This, in fact, is in no way different from the usual kin-ship patterns in Western society.

One such strongly integrated kinship group was Frances Repetto's family. Frances Repetto, we recall, was a daughter of William Green, Peter Green's oldest son, and her mother was a Cotton; and we have already noted that she and her family came to stand in the eyes of the Islanders as an incarnation of the Cotton-Green tradition of equality and independence for all in an orderly anarchy. Even now, starting the fifth generation, a large number of her descendants remain tied to-gether by established personal relationships to form a fairly closely knit group, which is still referred to by the Islanders as "the Repet-tos," although it now embraces a number of Swains, Greens, Lavarel-los, and even one or two Glasses. And this group is still regarded as the main carrier of the old Tristan traditions and has a great influence in the community. In fact, some of the recent discontents, eager to put the blame on somebody for their present dilemma about returning to England, reproached not only Chief but all of "the Repettos" for hav-ing pressed for the return of the whole community to Tristan, imply-ing that without this pressure many people (including presumably the critics themselves) would have stayed in England.

"The Glasses" comprise another well-recognized and fairly well-inte-grated group. Traditionally they are the opponents and most outspo-ken critics of "the Repettos," a tradition that obviously has its roots in the tension that used to exist between the Glasses and the Greens dur-ing the latter half of the nineteenth century when the Glasses were twice practically driven off the island. The rift was never entirely closed and was reopened widely by the "newcomer" struggle in 1908 and by Bob Glass's bid for power and leadership up through the 1920's. In fact, when the Islanders talk about "the Glasses" they are particularly thinking of the agnate and cognate progeny of Bob Glass. The group does not include all persons of the name Glass, notably not Thomas Glass and his brother Joe, nor is it confined to persons wearing that name, as it includes husbands of Glass girls who have chosen to identify themselves with the Glasses, and their children. Explicitly excluded are the descendants of Bob Glass's oldest brother, John—as one of the Glasses explained, "they took more after their mother," who was a Swain.

This group did indeed contribute heavily to the recent migrations from Tristan back to England. Of the 55 persons who had abandoned the community of Tristan da Cunha since the evacuation, well over half—32 to be exact—were descendants of Bob Glass and their spouses. If we include six young people who had left Tristan before the evacuation as well as ten persons whose names had been entered on the Administrator's list in 1966 but whose trip was delayed for the time being, we have 71 actual and prospective emigrants from Tristan since 1930, of whom almost two-thirds belonged to "the Glasses" in this sense. It really looked as if the Glasses were again quitting the island. It was the third time it happened. Whether they were really "pulling foot for the Repettos" is an open question. It looked more like a vessel breaking apart along an old crack that had been covered up but never properly mended.

None of Bob Glass's seven sons had taken up the old man's dream of bringing Tristan under the Law of Progress to affluence and prosperity through his own leadership; and no one could shake the position of the Repettos had he wanted to, or penetrate the wall of inaction and passive resistance that he would probably meet had he tried. But in some of them I seemed to notice much of the same resigned aloofness I had found in old Bob Glass himself, as if they were still watching the community from outside, reluctantly adapting to it, but not really a part of it, and sometimes quite critical of its unchanging traditions. It was like hearing the old man's voice rising from the grave when one of his sons exclaimed: "That's why the Island is so far behind—nobody wants to listen to the other fellow!" And I recalled that in 1938 the only one who had even whispered a desire to quit the island was one of Bob Glass's boys. Another one had in fact left in 1930, the only person to move from Tristan during the whole period from 1910 until the Second World War.

At the same time the Glasses were proud of being Glasses and the direct descendants of Corporal Glass, the founder of the community. While in England during the evacuation, one of them made what amounted to a pilgrimage to the little town of Kelso in Scotland, William Glass's birthplace. In fact, they were a little *too* proud in the eyes of many and won a reputation for regarding themselves as a little better, a little more progressive, perhaps even a little more intelligent than the rest of the Tristan people. Since they were generally dignified, independent, and good managers of their own affairs, they enjoyed high prestige in the community. But they were not generally well liked.

So it seems that "the Glasses" continued to stand slightly apart from the rest of the community. Among these peaceful and gentle people, nothing was obvious on the surface. There was no expressed animosity or open avoidance. But it was evident that "the Glasses" were not great joiners. They mostly went their own ways, and generally they seemed to be engaged in fewer reciprocal relationships than most. Some of them stayed pretty much within the circle of their closest relatives, and some were regular loners. Love, of course, always seems to find a way across social barriers, and marriages did occur even between a Glass and a Repetto; but in such cases the loyalty of the budding family tended to go definitely one way or the other, and mostly in favor of the Glasses. One former "Repetto" woman who was married to a Glass claimed that she hardly ever saw her brothers and sisters or even her parents, whom she referred to by their names rather than as Mom and Dad. In another case, where it looked as if the loyalty of the young couple might go the other way, the marriage was vigorously opposed by the Glass parents.

When industry moved in on Tristan, it found its most reliable supporters among the progressive Glasses. They were the ones who first learned to give full priority to a labor contract over whatever personal obligations they might have, and since the Company would naturally hire selectively on the basis of compliance with contract, we soon find that more than half of the "permanent staff" consisted of "Glasses." They were also the ones who most readily adopted the principles of a cash economy, who would engage in monetary transactions even with other Islanders, and on the whole developed a more commercial attitude toward their fellow man. After resettlement they naturally became the pillars and anchor men in the Administrator's modernization efforts. They were again the reliable ones, who were willing and ready to jeopardize and even abandon their personal relationships to other Islanders with their mutual obligations in order to hold a job or comply with a contract, which tended to emphasize even more their estrangement from the rest of the community. And soon "the Glasses" were again in possession of most of the trusted and responsible permanent positions, such as beach foreman, caretaker of the power plant, manager of water supplies to ships, and drivers of tractors, dumpers, and other heavy equipment for the harbor work.

It might seem ironic that precisely these people were leaving at this time. Just as a new, industrialized Tristan appeared to be rising more vigorously than ever from the rubble left by the eruption and evacuation, those who were best equipped both in skills and in attitudes to play a leading role in this development were pulling up stakes to seek their fortune elsewhere. The British plant manager for the harbor work was complaining bitterly that exactly the people whom he had painstakingly trained to run the heavy equipment were now moving away.

This, however, is what regularly happens when modern industrial society reaches its beckoning arm into a small rural community. Those who are ready to accept its value system and acquire the skills and, particularly, the attitudes that go with it, often become strangers in their own home and wander away to ever larger cities, where the promise of a reward for their skills and attitudes always seems greater. This is the essence of the urbanization process in Western society that has depleted and depopulated so many rural towns and communities.

The Tristan community had now lost one-fifth of its people to the industrial society, with an additional number ready to pull up stakes at the first opportunity, threatening to make it a fourth of the population. This was the aftermath of the evacuation. But it did not constitute another crisis, on the contrary. Throughout the history of this utopian, individualistic community, an important factor in preserving its homogeneity, concord, and relative harmony (so amazing to visiting outsiders) was perhaps the fact that the dissenters, the discontents, could pick up and leave and be absorbed by the Outside World. This is what seemed to be happening now. Perhaps the recent triumph of the traditional values of the Tristan community in connection with the Nightingale trips had convinced the discontents and the waverers that Tristan would never turn commercial and would never amount to much as a cog in the industrial world community. And all it took was the sympathetic attitude of a new Administrator (and some assistance from the Colonial Office) to create what amounted to a landslide of emigration. To the remaining Tristan community it was in fact not a "shattering of a myth" but another triumph and a reinforcement of the traditional values and way of life. But it was a sad day for many when the people left, severing still more family ties, perhaps forever.

This, however, was not the end of the story. Just as the thirty-five emigrants were leaving Tristan, yet another Administrator took over the reign of the tiny colony. He had been in the Colonial Service before but had not had any connection with the Tristan Islanders. He immediately declared that he had "plans for the island" and is reported to have said that he was "not going to preside over a mass exodus." It seemed to be this Administrator's idea that since the bright lights of Southampton and Totton appeared to be pulling people away from the island, the tide could be stopped by bringing the bright lights to Tristan. Electric wires were strung from the Station through the Village to furnish streetlights, and the old cart tracks were paved with blacktop or tarmacadam. They were even given names, and the houses were numbered like in a real town. I was already imagining myself returning to Tristan some day and really feeling the history of this remarkable community run through my veins as I would walk up Corporal Glass's Road, cross Peter Green's Street, and turn down Frances Repetto's Lane—all named for people who had really made an impact on the community. It was a disappointment to find that the streets had been named after the Administrators who had served on the island since 1950, including the incumbent.

There were also plans to bring electricity into the houses free of charge except for an initial installation fee of ten pounds. But the modernization of Tristan da Cunha really got underway when the island got its police force, consisting of one uniformed constable and four assistants. A young man was selected and, with his wife, was sent to England to receive training at the Metropolitan Police College at Hendon. Crime, of course, is still unknown on Tristan, and a policeman seemed to be what the Islanders least of all needed. In British newspapers it had been announced that his function would be to patrol the coastline against poaching by foreign fishing vessels, and he was provided with a police launch for the purpose. But the Islanders were not at all convinced that this would be his only function, and there was great apprehension in the community because one Islander appeared to be given power over the others. Albert Glass, who was selected for the job, however, is a level-headed young man, and soon it could be reported, as one letter put it, that "Albert is all right, he don't cause any trouble."

There was one more thing that had to be taken care of to make Tristan look, smell, and sound like a modern town. Something had to be done about the noise level. True, there were the tractors and bulldozers and dumpers and cranes, but they were largely confined to the harbor area, and their sounds could hardly cut through the rush of the wind and penetrate the solid stone walls of the cottages up in the Village. What was needed was a broadcasting station. Nearly every house on the island had a transistor radio brought along from England, and the Islanders could easily pick up the BBC overseas programs as well as any broadcast from South Africa. But they seldom did. They were only interested in listening to the fishing ships, and every day at a given time, as well known to every Islander as is the Saturday TV schedule to any youngster in America, when the ships had their daily "sched" and the familiar voices of the fishing masters of the two ships were exchanging news about fishing luck and weather, occasionally about their wives and sweethearts and domestic problems in Cape Town, the whole island was listening in and was greatly entertained. But now they were getting their very own broadcasting station, courtesy of the Administrator. According to Hugh Mulligan, of the *Associated Press,* who visited the island in the Norwegian cruise ship *Sagafjord* in February 1968, "Herman's Hermits have taken up permanent residence on the loneliest island in the world. Three hours a day, three days a week, their raucous rhythms, and that of other rock 'n' roll favorites, issue forth from the community radio station and find grudging acceptance in the 60 thatched roof cottages."

All this, however, was hardly what actually stemmed the tide of emigration from Tristan da Cunha. Far more important was the fact that the economy of the island was finally getting on its feet. The harbor was nearing completion and was soon proven very effective not only in making landing easier but, most importantly, in making the beach

workable under conditions of weather and sea that would otherwise
have been forbidding. A new freezing plant had been completed, and
the shore base was in full production, providing jobs and fishing facilities for those who wished to partake. The *Frances Repetto* had been
replaced by a new and ultramodern fishing ship, the *Gillian Gaggins*,
named after a daughter of Mr. Gaggins, the able manager of the fishing company. The two ships, the *Gillian Gaggins* and the *Tristania*,
continued their seasonal operations in the surrounding waters, still
mostly with South African fishermen but with the opportunity for several Islanders to hire out for a season with good earnings. Even the agriculture had improved, in spite of continued neglect on the part of the
authorities. The potato crop was back to normal, the Falkland Islands
sheep, which had not been doing so well, were replaced with new
stock from South Africa and were gradually building up. By the end
of 1966, three years after the resettlement, the economy of Tristan was
almost back to its pre-eruption level and offered a much rosier picture
of the future of the island than had been apparent only nine months
earlier.

But what really not only stemmed the tide of emigration from Tristan but *turned* it was the experience of the recent emigrants in England. It appeared that since the last mass emigration from Tristan da
Cunha at the turn of the century the industrialized, urbanized, and
rapidly changing Outside World had grown so far apart from this still
rather rustic island community that it could no longer readily absorb
her renegade sons and daughters, not even the progressive "Glasses."
Within five months from their arrival in Britain, telegrams were sent
to relatives and friends on Tristan telling them not to follow as
planned, and by Christmas a large number of the emigrants had decided to return to Tristan.

There were many disappointments, as hard to pin down as the reasons why they had left Tristan in the first place. For one thing the
problems of housing and jobs were not at all solved on their arrival in
England. Before they left Tristan they had been warned by Mr. Flint
and other outsiders who knew the housing situation in Britain that
this would probably be the case, "but their pathetic confidence in the
British Government as represented by the Administrator and his Colonial Office was too strong." Now this confidence, which seemed to
bounce back unscathed after each setback—and there had been many

of them lately—received another jolt when they discovered that the Colonial Office was not quite as powerful as they had imagined. To some it was inconceivable that the Colonial Office would be *unable* to solve the housing problem, so they even doubted the goodwill of the Government, which in this case was decidedly unfair. For the Colonial Office had gone out of its way and done everything in its power to provide for the stranded emigrants until they could be settled down in the New Forest area of Calshot, Fawley, Holbury, and Hythe, which was the area they were acquainted with and seemed to prefer. But the temporary housing that could be provided was less than adequate: cramped quarters in leaky old house trailers with inadequate heating, "tin houses" where the snow would drift in with the draft and water pipes would freeze and burst in the winter, sparsely furnished with old, discarded, rickety chairs and a table if they were lucky. One family had to eat their Christmas dinner from their laps. It was a hard winter.

These, however, were problems that would be resolved in time. In fact, when I visited these Tristan Islanders in England during the summer of 1967, only one family remained in a house trailer camp at Andover; the rest were fairly comfortably housed in the familiar Tristan Close at Calshot, or in Fawley, Blackfield, and Hythe. And all who were able to work had well paid jobs.

Still they were unhappy and determined to return to Tristan, although this time they would have to go entirely on their own with no assistance from the Colonial Office. It appeared that the housing situation had only been an excuse, a defensive rationalization of a course of action whose real motivations lay buried deep in the unconscious attitudes and feelings of the Tristan Islanders.

Few clues came to the surface. One very close associate of the Islanders in England offered the comment that "they just don't want to mix with others." Although this obviously was a rather superficial explanation of the willingness to spend hundreds of pounds to get back to a bleak island in the middle of the ocean, it might contain an element of truth. Talking about entertainment on Tristan and in England, one of the emigrants remarked that on Tristan you had the dances and a movie once or twice a week, and he and his wife wouldn't miss one of them; but since they had returned to England more than a year ago, they had not gone to a movie once, not because they didn't like them but because they were not interested. He seemed amazed that this should be the case. With equal amazement, one or two others remarked that even their teen-age children, who had "always been on the go" back on Tristan, now preferred to stay at home after school; they were not interested in going anywhere. It was not that they were shy or afraid; two years in England had once and for all removed that characteristic from the young people of Tristan. They were just not interested. And they were pining for Tristan as much as their parents, or even more.

One very intelligent housewife among the emigrants remarked not once but several times that "here in England there is no one to talk to." Oh, yes, she talked to her neighbors, and some of them were very nice; they even went for walks together, visited in each other's homes, with an occasional game of bridge, or the men would go to the pub together. "But it isn't the same."

From my conversations with this young woman I gathered that most of the Tristan Islanders in England were lonely in the midst of the constant stream of humanity that surrounded them. And the more sensitive among them felt sorry for the English because they realized that they, too, were lonely, perhaps without even knowing it. There was no lack of friendly relationships and conversations across the garden gate; but they were hollow, empty, superficial. They were not *personal* relationships comparable to the ones that permeate the Tristan community, expressed and reinforced by a constant exchange of gifts and services. They lacked the warmth, the involvement, commitment, and concern that can only be found in a small community where everybody has grown up together, where all know each other from childhood. This is something that the congested urban community, with all its togetherness and all its freedom of voluntary association, may have lost forever, to the extent that some of us will never partake of it and do not even know that it could exist.

The recent emigrants from Tristan da Cunha had never before experienced anything like it. The last time they were in England, they had been together among themselves. Now they were strangers, extremely lonesome, in a lonely crowd.

On July 21, 1967, three Tristan families, comprising eleven individuals, sailed from Southampton in the *Windsor Castle* to start the first lap of their long journey back to Tristan da Cunha. By April 1970, four years after the great exodus, most of the thirty-five emigrants of 1966 save one family had returned to the island.

This time the press was silent. There was not a word in the papers, and with a big boyish grin of delight mixed with scorn, Lars Repetto remarked that this was the first time the Tristans had gone anywhere without the newspapers having something to say about it.

17 *Epilogue*

Western Man has never lacked excuses and justifications for his expansive conquest and exploitation of the world at home and abroad. To the men of the eighteenth century it was simply part of inevitable Progress regarded as Providential Plan or Law of Nature or both. The more "positive" minds of the nineteenth century abandoned such metaphysical ideas but were no less impressed by the spectacular achievements in science and mechanical techniques and discoveries than their predecessors had been. They, too, believed firmly in Progress as an irreversible "natural" process, and combining this belief with idealistic thoughts about the unity of mankind and the pursuit of happiness as the right of all, they developed the notion of "the White Man's Burden." Since there could be no doubt in the minds of these men that Western civilization was the most advanced culture that mankind had ever seen, and since they fully shared Adam Smith's idea of opulence as the surest if not only road to human happiness, it became the moral obligation of Western Man to bring the gospel of modern technology and industrialism to the ends of the earth. For according to this view, neither was it the "right" of "primitive" peoples to sit on rich natural resources and keep them from being exploited for the good of mankind, nor did the illiterate and superstitious peasants and natives always understand "their own best interest."

It was in this atmosphere that the concept of the Economic Man flourished and became popular. The assumption was that man will always and everywhere be in pursuit of "happiness" in terms of wealth, profit, and economic advancement unless prevented or frustrated by ignorance, habit, or poverty. It was regarded as part of Human Nature.

The men of the twentieth century are a little more sophisticated. At least we think we are. For we recognize that man has many different needs and desires besides the economic ones, and we believe in the right of peoples to choose their own destiny, just as long as they don't turn Communist. Even we are convinced, however, that our way of life is the best that man has ever created, and that the surest (if not the only) road to the good life goes through technical advancements and economic development. And since this, to us, is the only "rational" way of life, we find it inconceivable that anyone in his right mind should think otherwise.

So Progress (in a very material sense) continues to be the supreme value in life to most Westerners of the twentieth century. The Economic Man—with his drive for material wealth and technical achievement, with his calculating rationality—is still with us, not any more as an "explanation" of human nature, but as a rational ideal rewarded by prestige and high power. And the assumption is still that this is a universal human ideal that all would share—unless prevented and misled by ignorance, habit, or poverty. So we continue to spread the gospel of modern technology and industrialism at home and abroad, not so much any more as a moral obligation but as a generous gesture of goodwill—and with generous profits for a burgeoning business world.

In 1887, a young German provincial wrote and published a small pamphlet, which has received little attention in the general and popular social debate but has had a profound influence on sociological theory and is now regarded as a "classic" in sociological literature. His name was Ferdinand Tönnies. The title of his little book, *Gemeinschaft und Gesellschaft,* is not easily translated into English. The usual rendition, *Community and Society,* is misleading, but no one has been able to produce a better one. The book was a gauntlet to Western civilization with its scientific technology and rational commercialism, for it challenged the notion of Progress.

Tönnies' basic observation is that in all human social life there are two opposing types of human relations. The first type, *Gemeinschaft,* is an association of the hearts and is typified by the relationship between mother and child, between husband and wife, and between brothers and sisters. It is the kind of relationship that has no ulterior motive or purpose and is, in this sense, irrational. Its value to the individual lies in the relationship itself because it is a mutual affirmation, a reinforcement of the self. It is expressed in cooperation and mutual aid for its own sake. Tönnies looks upon human action as an expression of human will, and *Gemeinschaft* is characterized by the kind of human will that he describes as *Wesenwille,* or "spontaneous will." The relationship as well as the interaction by which it is expressed is spontaneous and affectional and involves the whole person. It could be described as a *personal relationship,* whether it is an association of two individuals or a relationship of an individual person to an integral group regarded as a "social person." Its typical attitude is loyalty, and in its fulfillment it leads to complete mutual identification.

The other type of human relations, *Gesellschaft,* is typified by the business relationship. This is a relationship with extraneous purpose. It is a means to an end and, in that sense, rational, calculating. It is based on the kind of will that Tönnies describes as *Kürwille,* or "arbitrary will." It is basically selfish, and since the end is individual gain at the expense of the other person, it is not a mutual affirmation but a mutual exploitation, a match of strength rather than a reinforcement. In this kind of relationship, the individual is on his own and will seek a balance of give and take according to his strength. Essentially, it is a *contract relationship.* It is always a bargain. It is in this kind of relationship, and only here, that money belongs as an objective measure of value, and only here can the idea of profit find a place.

Even though the two types of human relations coexist in every human society, they are mutually exclusive, even contradictory—as even the Tristan Islanders know, "there are no friends in business." In fact, *Gemeinschaft* and *Gesellschaft* spell the difference between "friend" and "stranger." Like Sir Henry Maine before him, however, Tönnies saw a prevalence of personal relationships (Maine called them "status relationships") in the rural village community with its neighborhoods and strong kinship ties, its cooperation and mutual aid. In the towns and cities, with their complex division of functions, their commercialism and competition, contract relationships become increasingly dominant, until the *people* (that is, the nation or the community) is transformed into an aggregate of separate and dispersed strangers:

When the people has become subservient to commerce or to capitalism in its work, . . . it ceases to be a people; it is adapted to external forces and conditions which are alien to it. . . . Thus . . . the people, transformed into a "proletariat," learns to think about, and to become conscious of, the conditions to which it is chained in the labor market. From this knowledge originate decisions and strivings to break such chains, the proletariat unites for societal and political action into trade unions and parties, and these organizations, too, . . . become active participants in *Gesellschaft*. . . .

While *Gemeinschaft* develops and shapes the spontaneous will and binds and limits the arbitrary will, *Gesellschaft* not only unchains the arbitrary will but requires and promotes it, even makes its unscrupulous use in the competition a condition for the survival of the individual, thereby causing the blossoms and fruits of the natural human will to wither away, break, and die.

Indeed, as Tönnies himself said in the preface to the eighth edition of the book, published in 1935 shortly before the author's death, this was not a view that could expect a sympathetic reception at the time of its first publication. For our present purpose, however, it does not matter whether we share Tönnies' dismal view of modern industrial civilization. His great contribution to the understanding of human society is the insight that social life is a product of human thinking and feeling rather than of mechanical laws of nature, that the transition from an agrarian peasant culture to a commercial-industrial civilization was not the result of an inevitable development (for better or worse) but of a change in the thinking of people, and that this transition from one way of thinking to another involved a conflict of irreconcilable values rooted in man's double nature as a sensitive as well as rational being.

What happened in the community of Tristan da Cunha is a fair illustration of Tönnies' view. From its very inception, the community set up a norm pattern which, in spite of its "contractual" form of a signed agreement, emphasized personal relations between its members by explicitly rejecting any form of institutional or contractual government, and by establishing a communal organization that practically excluded any bargain relationship within the community. At the same time, a commercial relationship was visualized between the community as a whole and the outside world, thus establishing a clear distinction in principle between "peer" and "stranger."

As time went on, the increasingly materialistic and commercial values and attitudes of the Western World repeatedly encroached upon the community from within and without, occasionally threatening its very survival out of sheer benevolence. And as the community went through and survived one crisis after another, most of the established patterns of personal relations only grew stronger by the opposition and were augmented and reinforced by certain concepts, such as kinship and selective cooperation, adopted from the cultural heritage of the settlers. Out of it grew a community, atomistic in structure and individualistic in attitude, yet firmly integrated by a network of personal relationships in selective reciprocity, a community where no one is inherently superior to the other, yet where each has a position and status according to his personal ability.

The factors that made it possible for such a community to develop and survive may have been many and complex. Of obvious importance was the isolation of the community, which only became more extreme as Western technology developed and replaced the sailing ships with machine-driven vessels. Also the small size of the community must be taken into account, as well as the fact that sufficient contact was kept up with the Outside World to allow dissenters and otherwise estranged members to leave the island, which helped to keep it a homogeneous community with a high degree of consensus in attitudes and values. But the most important factor seems to have been an extraordinary awareness among the Tristan Isanders of the value of their own unique way of life. Coupled with the conviction which Frances Repetto never grew tired of asserting and reasserting, that "every man on Tristan da Cunha can make his own living," it made them less vulnerable to the lures and enticements of modern technology than their extreme poverty during the period of isolation would seem to indicate.

The crucial test in this conflict of values came, however, when modern industry finally invaded the Tristan island itself after the Second World War. The grandiose plan developed by the Reverend Mr. Lawrence and a team of scientists on the *Pequena* expedition of 1948 would, if implemented, have turned the whole community into a diversified industrial enterprise with fisheries, commercial farming, and various subsidiary smaller industries. It would have been an almost complete transformation from *Gemeinschaft* to *Gesellschaft,* with affluence and prosperity for all.

But here is where developments took a different course from Tönnies' dismal prediction. The Tristan Islanders refused to become "chained to the labor market." They refused to give up their subsis-

tence economy with its network of reciprocal personal relationships
and its independence. These were values that they would not sacrifice
for all the affluence and prosperity that the fishing industry could
offer. And they soon got an opportunity to give explicit emphasis to
their rejection of modern industrial civilization when the British authorities used the occasion of a volcanic eruption to try to get rid of
this anarchistic anomaly on the imperial crown by evacuating the island and transferring the whole population to England. The Islanders'
almost unanimous decision to return to Tristan was indeed, as William Connor of the *Daily Mirror* expressed it, "the most eloquent and
contemptuous rebuff that our smug and deviously contrived society
could have received."

The Islanders, however, did not entirely reject all the values of modern industrial society. Indeed, there was "good money in fishing." Although they refused to get into any kind of bargain or contract relationship to each other "for to buy and sell off one 'nother," which they
knew could only result in estrangement, they were not entirely averse
to entering into such relationships with outsiders, who were already
"strangers" anyway, in order to make a little money, just as long as it
did not interfere with their independence and personal obligations.
And in these relationships, the Tristan Islanders eventually learned to
bargain from strength, as demonstrated by a recent strike against the
fishing company.

There had been occasional pay disputes between the Islanders and
their employers before. But there were seldom any positive results for
the Islanders because they did not stick together. As in the case of the
imperious ministers of the 1930's, the strict island code of minding
one's own business prevented the Islanders from giving more than a
moral support to a griper, and divided they fell. Only once had the Islanders struck the Company successfully to prevent a proposed reduc-
tion in the fishermen's pay, and even then there were some who did
not go along. That was before the volcano. The first Administrator
after the resettlement—the otherwise so "progressive" promoter of the
harbor project, who had ideas about transforming the economy of the
island into a total cash economy—had no difficulty turning the clock
backward in the question of wages, reducing them again to the usual
one shilling an hour, although the Islanders had made up to ten times
as much in England.

This time, however, the Islanders had organized. Some of the patterns, such as shop committee and picket line, were obviously picked up in England. In July 1968, the Islanders approached the factory manager through their Fishermen's Committee and demanded £1 per "basket" (100 pounds) of crayfish caught and delivered to the factory, more than twice the then current rate. The factory manager referred the case to the Company's managing director, who was expected for a visit to the island the following month. The Islanders knew *him* well enough. He was the same man who had pushed the harbor project so hard during his service as Administrator on the island and had reduced their pay to a shilling an hour.

As expected, the managing director refused the Islanders' demand outright. He also refused to have the matter referred for arbitration, in spite of the Islanders' threat of strike action if their demands were not met. He left the island to return to Cape Town, and the strike was called.

The strength of the Islanders in any dispute with the management lay in the fact that, economically, they were not entirely dependent on the Company. The traditional subsistence economy was still intact and had by this time been restored to its pre-volcano level. The striking fishermen continued as before to tend to their cattle and potato patches, their private fishing and hunting, selling a little meat and vegetables at the Station for a cash supplement. When it was not a "fishing day," they could even earn some money by working for the Government. There is a long standing agreement between the administration of Tristan and the Company that on a "fishing day," that is, when the weather is suitable for fishing from the land base and the gong has called the fishermen to the beach, the Government will not compete for the available labor force by employing any casual labor. On such days, all casual wage labor stops, and this was kept up even during the strike. But when it was not a "fishing day," the fishermen could take jobs with the Government, and some of them would even work for the struck Company along with the permanent staff, who were not affected by the strike.

The story of the strike was told almost a year later to Tony Hocking, staff reporter for *The Star,* Johannesburg. It appears that a climax in the dispute was reached when it came to the fishermen's attention that the Company would try to break the strike by sending the eight men of the permanent staff out to fish in motorboats. The striking fishermen responded by seeking the Administrator's support, declaring that they would post a picket line around the crane that was used to lower the motorboats into the harbor, and that they would throw any man into the water who tried to mount the crane. The Administrator, however, replied that he was the Queen's representative on the island and asked what would happen if he were the first man to enter the crane. "Then you," was the reply, "would be the first man to be thrown into the harbor."

This was the story told to the reporter. It was indeed a story to the Islanders' liking. They loved to tell similar stories, daydreaming about putting the mighty Administrator in his place. This time, however, the story was apparently true—if so, it certainly indicates an important change in the Islanders' attitude and thinking. Defiance of established authority seems to come easier to them. They were again ready to fight for what they considered their right, even in opposition to the representatives of the Crown. This time, however, the value involved was a material one—money.

It appears that the Administrator regarded the unaccustomed aggressive attitude of the Islanders as a threat to his personal safety. Rumors were soon afoot that he had flashed a coded telegram to London asking for protection, and that a warship had been sent to the island to maintain peace and order. In actual fact, H.M.S. *Naiad* was already on her way to Tristan for an official visit. According to Mr. Hocking, however, she was indeed alerted for possible trouble.

The strike went on for three months throughout the better part of the "big season" before a compromise was reached. The fishermen obtained a graded pay scale of 13, 14, and 15 shillings per basket, depending on the size of the catch, and a promise that the rates would be adjusted each year in August. It was not all they had asked for, but enough to call it a victory.

The Tristan Islanders, it seems, have learned quite well to bargain a contract relationship. The question now is whether this type of relationship, with its commercialism and material concerns, will dominate their lives as it dominates the lives of most people in modern Western civilization. Will it "cause the blossoms and fruits of the natural human will to wither away, break, and die"? That would mean the end of the traditional way of life, for the sake of which the Tristan Islanders had defied the authorities, suffered and fought, in order to return to their lonely island.

Only time will tell. So far the Tristan Islanders seem to have succeeded where so many peasant and folk communities in a similar situation have failed: to get the best of two worlds. They have obtained a relative affluence in a greatly increased economic level of living by "learning the ropes" of an industrial society with its contract relationships and cash economy. At the same time, they have—so far, at least—retained the internal social structure of their community, based on personal relationships in a network of selective reciprocity.

How was it possible? Again, it was of great importance that the Islanders were able to retreat to a lonely spot which has little attraction for industrial tycoons. But again, the most important factors lie in the attitudes and thoughtways of the Islanders themselves. In the first place, they retained their traditional subsistence economy as the basis for their livelihood, reducing the cash economy of the fishing industry to a welcome but partly suspensible supplement. Secondly, they continued in all their behavior to maintain a sharp distinction between "peer" and "stranger," effectively excluding contractual relationships and the spirit of commercialism from their internal social life. Thirdly, and most importantly, they subordinated the value of affluence and material gain to independence and personal reciprocity.

How vulnerable they are—when their whole way of life depends on frail human thoughts and desires! Will another generation grow up which will brutally reject what their parents and grandparents fought for and choose a road that they can only hope will lead to more and ever more affluence and monetary gain? Maybe Arthur Repetto had the answer: "No—we never come to *that* stage . . . for to buy and sell off one 'nother. Maybe generation after generation, in 'nother hunnert years, I can't say what'll happen then. But not yet of all."

It is ironic that the man who said this has now decided to abandon island life and has settled for good in the highly industrial area of Southampton.

Bibliography

MANUSCRIPTS

"A private Journal of the Proceedings of a party of men employed on the Island of Tristan d'Acunha, Commencing 14th of August 1816 and ending 27th of November 1816," (by) W. B. Greene, Midshipman, H.M.S. Falmouth. Roland Svensson, Stockholm.

British Museum, Manuscript Collection, Add. 43864 and 44085T, containing various documents from the period 1816–1884.

Last Will and Testament of William Glass, witnessed by A. Earle, August 30, 1824. Bob Glass, Tristan da Cunha (1938).

Journal kept by the Reverend William F. Taylor, September 1851–March 1858. United Society for the Propagation of the Gospel, London.

Birth, Death, and Marriage Registers, Tristan da Cunha, 1880 to present. Administrator's Office, Tristan da Cunha.

Boarding Book, Tristan da Cunha, 1904–1930. Administrator's Office, Tristan da Cunha.

BOOKS AND ARTICLES

BARROW, K. M. *Three Years in Tristan da Cunha*. London: Skeffington & Son, Ltd., 1910.

BLAIR, JAMES P. "Home to Lonely Tristan da Cunha," *The National Geographic Magazine*, 125 (January 1964): 60–81.

BRANDER, JAN. *Tristan da Cunha, 1506–1902*. London: George Allen and Unwin, Ltd., 1940.

BULL, HENRIK J. *Sydover: Expeditionen til Sydishavet i 1893–1895*. Kristiania, 1898.

CHRISTOPHERSEN, ERLING (ed.). *Results of the Norwegian Scientific Expedition to Tristan da Cunha, 1937–1938*, 5 volumes. Oslo: Det Norske Videnskaps-Akademi, 1946–1968.

———. *Tristan da Cunha, the Lonely Island*. London, 1940.

Correspondence Relating to the Island of Tristan d'Acunha. London: Printed for Her Majesty's Stationery Office, 1876, 1887.

CRAWFORD, ALLAN B. *I Went to Tristan.* London: Hodder and Stoughton, 1941.

DEHÉRAIN, HENRI. "L'occupation de Tristan da Cunha par la Grande-Bretagne," *La Géographie,* 25 (1912): 105–116.

DICK-HENRIKSEN, SVERRE, and PER OEDING. *Medical Survey of Tristan da Cunha.* Results of the Norwegian Scientific Expedition to Tristan da Cunha, 1937–1938, No. 5. Oslo: Det Norske Videnskaps-Akademi, 1940.

DU PETIT-THOUARS, AUBERT. *Mélanges de botanique et voyage.* Paris, 1811.

EARLE, AUGUSTUS. *A Narrative of a Nine Months' Residence in New Zealand in 1827; Together with a Journal of a Residence in Tristan d'Acunha, an Island between South America and the Cape of Good Hope.* London: Longman, etc., 1832.

Further Correspondence Relating to the Island of Tristan da Cunha. London: Printed for His Majesty's Stationery Office, 1897, 1903, 1906, 1907.

GANE, DOUGLAS M. "Early Records of Tristan da Cunha: The Discovery in New London," *United Empire,* 1933: 589–598, 651–658, 709–713.

―――. "Tristan da Cunha: A Lonely Island and its Place in the Empire," *The Empire Review,* 1922: 1–16.

―――. *Tristan da Cunha: An Empire Outpost and Its Keepers, with Glimpses of Its Past and Consideration of the Future.* London: George Allen and Unwin, Ltd., 1932.

GANE, IRVING. "Tristan da Cunha Wins Through," *Commonwealth Journal,* 4 (September–October 1961): 228–233.

HAMMOND TOOKE, WILLIAM. "Report on Tristan da Cunha," *Further Correspondence Relating to the Island of Tristan da Cunha,* 1906: 12–55.

HONIGMANN JOHN J. "Interpersonal Relations in Atomistic Communities," *Human Organization,* 27 (Fall 1968): 220–229.

KRISTENSEN, L. *Antarctics Reise til Sydishavet.* Tonsberg, 1895.

LOUDON, J. B. "Teasing and Socialization on Tristan da Cunha," stencil privately distributed.

MAINE, HENRY J. S. *Ancient Law.* London, 1861.

MARX, KARL. *Early Writings,* translated and edited by T. B. Bottomore. New York, Toronto, London: McGraw-Hill, 1963.

MUNCH, PETER A. "Cultural Contacts in an Isolated Community:

Tristan da Cunha," *American Journal of Sociology,* 53 (July 1947): 1–8.

————. "Culture and Superculture in a Displaced Community: Tristan da Cunha," *Ethnology,* 3 (October 1964): 369–376.

————. "Economic Development and Conflicting Values: A Social Experiment in Tristan da Cunha," *American Anthropologist,* 72 (December 1970).

————. *Sociology of Tristan da Cunha.* Results of the Norwegian Scientific Expedition to Tristan da Cunha 1937–1938, No. 13. Oslo: Det Norske Videnskaps-Akademi, 1945.

————. *The Song Tradition of Tristan da Cunha.* Folklore Institute Monograph Series, 22. Bloomington: Indiana University Publications, 1970.

————. "Traditional Songs of Tristan da Cunha," *Journal of American Folklore,* 74 (July–September 1961): 216–229.

MYDANS, CARL. "The 20th Century vs. The 19th, in Microcosm: The Natives' Return to Tristan da Cunha," *Life International,* 34, No. 10 (June 3, 1963): 16–29.

PAINE, RALPH D. *Lost Ships and Lonely Seas.* New York: The Century Company, 1920.

PUAUX, RENÉ. "Tristan da Cunha," *La Grande Revue,* 13 (June 1909): 511–532.

REDFIELD, ROBERT. *Peasant Society and Culture: An Anthropological Approach to Culture.* Chicago: University of Chicago Press, 1956.

ROGERS, ROSE ANNIE. *The Lonely Island.* London: George Allen and Unwin, Ltd., 1926.

The South African Shipping News and Fishing Industry Review: Exclusive Report on the Tristan da Cunha Fishing Industry Expedition. April 1948.

TAYLOR, WILLIAM F. *Some Account of the Settlement of Tristan d' Acunha, in the South Atlantic Ocean.* London: Society for the Propagation of the Gospel, 1856.

THEAL, GEORGE MCCALL. *History of South Africa since September 1795.* London, 1908.

————. *Records of the Cape Colony.* Cape Town, 1901–1902.

TÖNNIES, FERDINAND. *Gemeinschaft und Gesellschaft: Grundriss der reinen Soziologie,* 3. ed. Berlin: Karl Curtius, 1920. (*Fundamental Concepts of Sociology,* translated and supplemented by Charles P. Loomis. New York: American Book Company, 1940. *Community and Society,* translated and edited by CHARLES P. LOOMIS. New York: Harper Torchbooks, 1963.)

WALTON, ALEXR. "Tristan d' Acunha, etc.: Jonathan Lambert, late Sovereign thereof," *Blackwood's Magazine,* 4 (1818): 280–285.

WHEELER, PETER J. F. "Death of an Island," *The National Geographic Magazine,* 121 (May 1962): 678–695.

WHITESIDE, THOMAS. "Annals of Migration: Something Wrong with the Island," *The New Yorker,* November 9, 1963: 154–207.

———. *Alone Through the Dark Sea.* New York: George Braziller, 1964.

WILD, FRANK. *Shackleton's Last Voyage: The Story of the Quest.* From the Official Journal and Private Diary kept by Dr. A. H. Macklin. London, New York, Toronto, Melbourne: Cassel & Co., 1923.

Index